Y0-BBW-711

# THE MIRROR
## AND THE
# KILLER-QUEEN

*The Mirror and the Killer-Queen:*
*Otherness in Literary Language* is Volume 18 in the series

THEORIES OF CONTEMPORARY CULTURE

Center for Twentieth Century Studies

University of Wisconsin-Milwaukee


KATHLEEN WOODWARD

GENERAL EDITOR

# THE MIRROR AND THE KILLER-QUEEN

## Otherness in Literary Language

GABRIELE SCHWAB

INDIANA
UNIVERSITY
PRESS
*Bloomington • Indianapolis*

© 1996 by Gabriele Schwab
All rights reserved

No part of this book may be reproduced or utilized in any form
or by any means, electronic or mechanical, including photocopying
and recording, or by any information storage and retrieval system,
without permission in writing from the publisher. The Association
of American University Presses' Resolution on Permissions
constitutes the only exception to this prohibition.

The paper used in this publication meets the minimum
requirements of American National Standard for Information
Sciences—Permanence of Paper for Printed Library Materials,
ANSI Z39.48-1984.

Manufactured in the United States of America
**Library of Congress Cataloging-in-Publication Data**
Schwab, Gabriele.
The mirror and the killer-queen : otherness in literary language / Gabriele Schwab.
p.      cm. — (Theories of contemporary culture ; v. 18)
Includes bibliographical references (p.      ) and index.
ISBN 0-253-33037-8 (cl : alk. paper). — ISBN 0-253-21051-8 (pa : alk. paper)
1. American fiction—History and criticism—Theory, etc.
2. Difference (Psychology) in literature.   3. English fiction—
History and criticism—Theory, etc.   4. Sex differences
(Psychology) in literature.   5. Gender identity in literature.
6. Discourse analysis, Literary.   7. Feminism and literature.
8. Women and literature.   I. Title.   II. Series.
PS374.D45S39      1996
813'.009'353—dc20                                          95-31865
1   2   3   4   5   01   00   99   98   97   96

❖     FOR MY SON     ❖
MANUEL

# CONTENTS

Preface   *ix*
Acknowledgments   *xix*

## Toward an Ethnography of Reading: A Theoretical Framework

Reading, Otherness, and Cultural Contact   *1*

## Nonsense, Dream, and Chaos: The Otherness of Literary Language

**2.** Nonsense and Metacommunication: *Alice in Wonderland*   *49*

**3.** Joyce, Cage, and Chaos:
*Finnegans Wake, Roaratorio,* and French Feminism   *71*

## Witches, Mothers, and Male Fantasies: The Otherness of Woman

**4.** Seduced by Witches: *The Scarlet Letter*   *103*

**5.** Carnival and Abjection:
The Mother's Dead Body in *As I Lay Dying*   *124*

## Trauma, Transgression, and Transference: The Otherness of Gender

**6.** The Jungle and the Drawing Room: Urban Nomads in *Nightwood*   *153*

**7.** "While she lives she invites murder": *The Malady of Death*   *170*

Notes   *185*
Works Cited   *197*
Index   *207*

# PREFACE

> They stood on tiptoes to watch Snow White wake up. She
> told them about the mirror and the killer-queen and they
> asked her to stay and keep house.
>
> —Anne Sexton, "Snow White and the Seven Dwarfs"

THE MIRROR AND THE KILLER-QUEEN maps out a theoretical as well as interpretive space for exploring literature's relation to otherness. The epigraph, borrowed from Anne Sexton's *Transformations* (which also inspired the title of
this book), invokes a powerful mode of predicating otherness on the gaze of
the Other—a gaze that mirrors and gives shape, as well as desire, to human
subjects. The mirroring Other transfers emotions—love, jealousy, envy, rejection—and provides a rudimentary framework for judgments such as comparison, anticipation, self-criticism, and self-scrutiny. Yet, in a mirroring glance, we
also see ourselves from the outside, as both self and other. The essays in this
book seek to rethink and complicate the familiar trope of literature as a mirror
of the world. Instead of treating the mirror as an object of representation, the
readings collected here all conceive the mirroring function of literature in
terms of transference and contact. As in Lewis Carroll's *Through the Looking
Glass*, the mirror marks a transition to other worlds with other languages and
rules. Linking transference and contact, the trope of the mirror alludes to the
connections between rhetorical, cultural, and psychological spheres. The rhetorical and aesthetic dimension of literature is highly overdetermined, producing its so-called reality-effects at a psychological as well as cultural level. Precisely the interplay between these different spheres secures the aesthetic
practice of literature a space in our culture, its pedagogical institutions, and its
forms of self-representation for other cultures.

The theoretical as well as interpretive chapters in *The Mirror and the Killer-Queen* show how, during the act of reading, psychological and cultural effects are linked by operations of transference and cultural contact. In *Steps to an Ecology of Mind*, Gregory Bateson demonstrates that the term "cultural contact" may be productively used to include the processes by which we are socialized into our own culture. Literature, I argue, plays a crucial role in such processes because it engages language as the most basic medium of acculturation. In *The Mirror and the Killer-Queen* I approach the otherness of literary language in two ways: one deals with how language mediates cultural, historical, or psychological otherness, the other deals with how literary language generates and insists upon its own otherness in relation to other discourses.

Anne Sexton's poetic meditation on Snow White also invokes the mirror as a gendered cultural object. The gaze of the Other—even if it is a mirror of self-reflection—may enforce or question the marks of gender passed on from generation to generation. The "Killer-Queen" as a powerful legendary figure reveals how often the phantasmatic space in which we create Others as effects of our own narcissistic desires turns deadly. And the seven dwarfs, who are standing in awe before that beautiful girl from a different class and culture, nonetheless do not hesitate to make her their maid, thus affirming the patriarchal gender hierarchies through a cultural contact in which, from the very beginning, the power is on their side.

Recalling this mythological tradition in which the mirror invokes the dynamic of the gaze and its predication of otherness, I use "mirroring" as a facilitating trope that leads into a more encompassing study of the cultural function of literature. The theoretical section of this book relies on another trope, namely, cultural contact, in order to analyze reading as an experience of otherness. Borrowing Gregory Bateson's broad definition of the term, I do not restrict it to actual encounters between different cultures or members and groups of the same culture, but include also the processes through which subjects are socialized to function in a specific cultural environment as well as the processes that shape their changing relationship to this culture. Literature is only one medium through which such relationships are formed, but it is one of the most powerful ones because it engages the boundaries of language.

In this vein, my theoretical framework sketches out what it means to look at literature as a medium that facilitates transference and reading as a process of cultural contact. In particular, I am interested in the status of literary language as a discourse that distinguishes itself from other forms of discourse— whether through its very framing as literature or through rhetorical and formal

*Preface*

devices that we have traditionally perceived as aesthetic. In this specific sense I argue that literary language itself is marked by a certain otherness—a trait that may not always be obvious, but is used prolifically in the so-called experimental texts that exhibit their poetic license to transgress the boundaries of linguistic and cultural codes. One of my main arguments is that literature may intervene in other forms of cultural contact or sharpen and change our own patterns of relating to otherness. I posit literature as an institutionalized cultural space that negotiates and shapes patterns of contact that a culture establishes with other cultures. Especially in a global economy of publishing, reading functions as a medium of cultural contact with foreign or historically remote cultures.[1] In this context, *The Mirror and the Killer-Queen* is deeply concerned with those formal and aesthetic features of literary language that generate what we may perceive as an experience of otherness. Even though I am concerned with the aesthetic mediation of otherness in general, my readings deemphasize thematic issues in favor of formal aspects that determine the figuration and mediation of otherness.

The second part of *The Mirror and the Killer-Queen* contains three sections of readings of literary texts. I understand these readings as performing the type of cultural contact that I analyze in my theoretical part. Since my theory concerns literary reception rather than production, I cannot simply "apply" my framework to my readings. Rather I perform the activity I have analyzed and establish the connection between my theory and my readings by emphasizing what motivates both, namely, the concern with literature's relation to otherness. Most of the texts I analyze are highly experimental and commonly considered difficult to read—if not, as with *Finnegans Wake*, unreadable. Refusing easy access, these texts tend to withhold their "meaning" and refrain from telling coherent narratives. But, at the same time, this strategy of withholding seems to render them all the more powerful and enables them to draw readers into their artificial and artistic textual worlds. In certain respects, the experience of reading these texts is comparable to an encounter with otherness. Working with these texts, in fact, increasingly convinced me that what I call "aesthetic experience of otherness" can be seen as a basic function of reading literature in general. The experimental texts under consideration vigorously insist on a recognition of otherness—be it the materiality of their poetic language or the unconscious as the Other of language.

My goal in privileging the cultural study of literary form is to show that formal and aesthetic practices play a crucial role in shaping not only cultural figurations of otherness but also the modes of cultural contact. I claim, in short, that aesthetic practices are relevant to the "world out there"—be it the real world of words or that other one that seems to be lost in words. In *The Mirror and the Killer-Queen* I will look mainly at three aspects of literary figurations of otherness: the otherness of literary language, figurations of women as Other, and gender boundaries (or "gender trouble") and otherness.

The first section of readings, "Nonsense, Dream, and Chaos," contains two chapters, one on Lewis Carroll and one on James Joyce and John Cage. The chapter on Carroll looks at literary nonsense as a form of discursive otherness that produces several cultural interventions: it asserts and simultaneously mocks the role of logic in our culture in order to question the very conditions and boundaries of communication. Carroll is particularly interesting for my emphasis on cultural contact because *Alice in Wonderland* and *Through the Looking Glass* stage a Victorian girl's encounter with an imaginary culture in which all familiar rules and codes of language and communication (as well as some other basics of human cultures such as the law of gravity or the embedding of history in chronological time) are suspended. I show how Carroll uses the sheer impossibility of appropriating the otherness of nonsense under the familiar parameters of cultural contact as a means of stimulating a metacommunication about the ways we communicate and thereby make culture.

The chapter on *Finnegans Wake*, "Joyce, Cage, and Chaos," challenges the conventional notion of chaos as the Other of order. I use the framework of chaos theory to examine the aesthetic paradox of this "chaotic" literary text that disrupts the ways we commonly perceive the order of language and literary composition. I then analyze *Roaratorio*, John Cage's musico-textual response to the *Wake*, as an aesthetic experiment with chance operations. In his own reflections on *Roaratorio*, Cage debates the political and cultural implications of the "chaos" produced by random operations in the context of his own attempt to forgo the constraints of a preconceived aesthetic of "law and order" that, in his view, determines even the most willfully resistant act of creative production. In a further step I place my own reflections on Joyce, Cage, and chaos theory in the context of the cultural coding of "chaos" as feminine—a coding derived from the familiar metonymic chain that links woman with the unconscious, the irrational, otherness, emotion, and chaos. In particular, I explore the claim of some proponents of the concept of *écriture feminine* in French feminism that Joyce is one of its most prominent practitioners. I conclude this chapter with a brief note on the "dark side" of chaos, namely, its proximity to abjection—a link which is prominent in Joyce, but is missing in those critics who romanticize the free and anarchistic play of chaos.

The second section of readings, "Witches, Mothers, and Male Fantasies," takes up the figuration of woman as Other from a psychohistorical perspective. I have chosen two canonical texts by male authors which may be considered representative of the two most basic qualities that mark the phantasmatic space of woman's threatening otherness: seduction and abjection. "Seduced by Witches" analyzes Hawthorne's *The Scarlet Letter* in the context of the New England witchcraft narratives. I argue that, long after the actual public hysteria about witches and the actual witch hunts had died down, the phantasmatic space that organizes the cultural perceptions of women still relied on what I call a witchcraft pattern. *The Scarlet Letter* brings this displacement to the foreground in numerous allusions to the Salem witch craze that reveal how, despite the fact that the actual image of the witch has been replaced by other images such as that of the adulteress, the phantasm of the witch continues to exert its powerful grip on the public imagination of nineteenth-century Puritan New England. Faulkner's *As I Lay Dying* invokes another phantasm of the deadly power of woman. Addie Bundren is cast as the devouring primordial mother who keeps her family in bondage beyond her own death. I read the pilgrimage of the Bundrens to bury their mother as a carnivalesque enactment of fantasies about female abjection. The decaying body of the mother is the ultimate Other, an abyss of monstrosity. By exposing the grotesque and phantasmatic spectacle that stages the dead mother's abject body, Faulkner draws his readers into a ghostly literary transference in which they are compelled to replay the drama of the primordial mother and the ensuing cultural abjection of woman.

The third and last section of my readings, "Trauma, Transgression, and Transference," begins with a chapter on *Nightwood*. I analyze Barnes's fictional space, mostly set in Paris and Vienna between the two world wars, as organized by what one of her characters calls an "economy of fear." Mostly cast as an effect of marginality and exile, otherness in *Nightwood* exposes a new type of exile and nomadology in twentieth-century urban cultures, especially within the spatial economies of European cities between the two world wars. My reading of *Nightwood* argues that the "spatial form" of this novel is highly overdetermined, confronting the cosmopolitan city-space and territorial politics that determine the contact between different countries and continents with the archaic space of dreams and culturally disavowed desire. All characters in *Nightwood* are exiled from their own country and live on the margins of a culture that ostracizes them because of their racial or cultural otherness as well as their sexual preferences and politics of transgression. In this context, the urban nomadism that characterizes the economy of the characters' movements through space appears as a reflection of social conditions that many characters perceive as a form of madness. Barnes's transcoding between space, motion, and emotion reveals that exile is never merely an empirical space, but a space interiorized and inhabited as an inner space. In this way, Djuna Barnes grounds her aesthetics of exile in a cultural if not geopolitical unconscious. This "postmodern" reading attributes a new actuality to *Nightwood* by revealing how Barnes foreshadows the new waves of migration, cultural displacement, and enforced transculturation, as well as the current reorganization of sexual politics in many countries of the world.

The last chapter deals with Marguerite Duras's short piece *The Malady of Death*. I read Duras's work as a literary meditation on the power of phantasm and transference in the organization of cultural and psychological spaces in the context of her own implied aesthetics of transference. *The Malady of Death* stages the fragility and artifice of emotions in a complex transactional game between two presumably homosexual men and a woman who figures as ultimate otherness, phantasma, empty screen, and object of a man's desire to learn how to love. *The Malady of Death* occupies a special place at the end of my readings because, in her appendix, Duras reflects on literary form and its effects in transmitting one of the most crucial cultural functions of literature, namely, its opening of a space of transference that brings its readers in contact with a tacit, unformulated, yet distinct knowledge. In this context, I show how the creation of literary moods functions as a seismographic indicator of prevalent cultural moods, phantasms, desires, and fears of the time.

In the original conception of this project, I had planned to include two further sections that would focus specifically on literary figurations of cultural contact proper, one dealing with colonial and the other with postcolonial encounters. Over the years—particularly because the outline of my theory required more space than anticipated—this project developed into a separate book, tentatively entitled *Imaginary Ethnographies*. *The Mirror and the Killer-Queen* and *Imaginary Ethnographies* have now become companion books, both relying on as well as mirroring each other from different perspectives. Argentinian writer José Saer once defined literature as a "speculative anthropology." In a similar vein, I am asking what literary texts tell us about a culture if we perceive them as "imaginary ethnographies." In this context, *Imaginary Ethnographies* develops different implications of my theory of literature as cultural contact, exploring particularly the intersections between literature and anthropology from the perspective of literature's role in the continual transformation of historical models of cultural contact. While *The Mirror and the*

*Killer-Queen* focuses primarily on the otherness of experimental literary language and its use in figurations of gender, *Imaginary Ethnographies* deals with cultural otherness as it is portrayed in fictional encounters between different cultures and ethnic groups. Rather than referring to a narrowly defined new genre of literature, the term "imaginary ethnographies" thus indicates a specific perspective on literary figurations of cultural contact. In order further to scrutinize the role of literature as a medium of cultural contact, I will—in my readings on José Saer, Marianne Wiggins, Maxine Hong Kingston, Gerald Vizenor, Don DeLillo, and Leslie Silko—pay specific attention to the rhetorical strategies and aesthetic devices that mediate these fictional cultural encounters for readers.

I hope that, as companion projects, *The Mirror and the Killer-Queen* and *Imaginary Ethnographies* may highlight crucial aspects of the cultural function of literature that have not been fully explored despite the current focus of literary criticism on culture, ethnicity, multiculturalism, and cultural contact, as well as local and global knowledge. The theoretical framework that explores reading as a form of cultural contact and literature as a speculative or imaginary anthropology foregrounds the cultural function of literature by highlighting how through the specificity of the medium and its status as an aesthetic practice, literature creates a powerful cultural intervention. I thus bring aesthetics back into the discussion of culture, as I am convinced that formal, stylistic, or rhetorical devices or, in short, aesthetic practices in general cannot be separated from the cultural function of literature but form its very material basis.

Believing that the theories we are drawn to or develop emerge from the cultural spaces we have traversed, be they material or imaginary, I would like to add a more personal note. I began to work on this project shortly after moving to the United States while experiencing the turbulence of cultural contact and shock. It was in 1983, during my first year of teaching at the University of California at Irvine, that I wrote the brief article "Reader-Response as an Aesthetic Experience of Otherness," which I have now rewritten and developed into the theoretical section of *The Mirror and the Killer-Queen*. The encounter with another culture and the beginnings of a new academic and social acculturation induced a sudden sharpening of my senses, the effects of which ranged from pain to ecstasy. I vividly remember the ugliness of Orange County's nonurbanity assaulting not only my aesthetic norms but my being in the world altogether. The thought of living somewhere where I couldn't go "downtown" made the arrival in this Never-Never-Land somewhat ghostly and uprooting. Now, years later, both my sense and my senses have changed. Still craving the feeling of urban centeredness and the flair of old European coffeehouses, I have also developed a taste for Orange County postmodernism with its aesthetics of overstatement, its involuntary pastiche of Old World glamor. I even admit to a taste for Irvine, the global village which names a tiny shopping area near campus "The Town Center" and the surrounding streets after the big dream of the Ivy League brothers, Harvard, Yale, Dartmouth, Cornell. The "loss of the aura" in the age of technological reproduction has its own, perversely negative charms and now, ten years later, I can even find, in the midst of nowhere, a new hyperauratic space, "The Lab," marketed as an Anti-Mall and harboring trendy alternative stores as well as "real" atmosphere (and poetry readings) in its coffee place, the Gypsy Den.

This experience of emigration from Europe to the United States became crucial for my theoretical interests, not the least because it happened at a time when the debates in literary criticism were obsessed with the blurring of differences rather than with the experience of otherness; a time when reader-response critics asserted that literature made no difference, that a text means whatever a reader wants it to mean, and that identity recreates itself in the act of reading, simply effacing, absorbing, or violating the otherness of texts or cultural objects.[2] While in Europe, I had written a book on the boundaries and transitional spaces in modern fiction in which the question of otherness had imposed itself with increasing force. Now, I was ready to theorize it in a larger cultural context, particularly addressing the role of cultural contact.

In a sense, I am still trying to find out what literature does to the world, to a culture, and to readers who cross cultures in their readings. And this question, in turn, still draws on the energies spent and gained from childhood reading passions and from the deep belief that I have "survived on literature," in the strong sense that literature has helped me to reach beyond the narrowness of my environment and the cultural and ideological spaces into which I was born. During my childhood the world of books was an "other world," to be sure, but at the same time I positioned it, without any trace of doubt, as *my* real world, superior to the one in which I had to eat, sleep, and deal with others, especially parents and teachers. With my everyday-life world pushed into the background and devalued as a false transitory stage, reading meant both plunging into the "other world" and preparing for the "real world." This experience continues to nourish my interest in the symbolic, the imaginary, the unconscious, the aesthetic, and their role in the formation of subjects and cultures.

## Preface

Perhaps it is due to this childhood craving for other worlds that I begin my readings with *Alice in Wonderland* and *Through the Looking Glass.* The figure of this little girl reminds one that the looking glass of literature was never meant merely to replicate the world, but to bring us in contact with those other worlds—be they those of the dream or schizophrenia, utterly alien cultures or uncannily familiar ones. By keeping us in touch with other worlds, literature brings us back to ourselves, albeit changed and different. This is why, in the encounter with literature, seeing ourselves in the other may not be reduced to a mere appropriation of the other's image nor to a narcissistic self-reflection. Instead, this encounter constitutes an experience that transforms the very boundaries between self and other. Then the mirror ceases to be the deadly instrument it was for Narcissus or the Killer-Queen and transforms itself into an object that moves us by reflecting our own exotopy, our irreducible (need for) otherness.

# ACKNOWLEDGMENTS

THE IDEA FOR *The Mirror and the Killer-Queen* was conceived in 1985, while I was a Fellow at the Center for Twentieth Century Studies at the University of Wisconsin-Milwaukee. We had a most stimulating, vital, and congenial group of fellows and colleagues from different departments discussing the yearly topic, "The Reorganization of Knowledge," supplemented by a range of speakers that greatly enriched the interdisciplinary scope of our debates. When I approached Kathleen Woodward, the director, with the idea of reworking a collection of my work into a coherent book on literary language and otherness, she gave me enthusiastic support from the very beginning and commissioned my project for Theories of Contemporary Culture. Her continued enthusiasm and invaluable advice has accompanied me through all these years. My deepest gratitude goes to her. Equally invaluable was the practical support for the preparation of the manuscript provided by the Center staff. Particular thanks go to Carol Tennesson and Nigel Rothfels. Both Carol and Nigel combine extraordinary efficiency with personal warmth and, most importantly, as editors they become truly involved with the intellectual life of a book. Their enthusiasm and sense of humor helped me greatly through the final stages of editing. I also thank Eric Hayot for reading the final version before it went to press.

The people involved with my work at Indiana University Press were unrelenting in their support, and most efficient and undogmatic in handling practical details. My warmest thanks go to my editor Joan Catapano—not least for her persistence in tracking me down and faxing my contract to a hotel in Athens in order to get the book into an earlier schedule. I also thank LuAnne Holladay, the assistant editor, and Michael A. Baker, the copy editor. My friend, the Cuban-American painter Jorge Sicre, deserves very special thanks for designing the cover of *The Mirror and the Killer-Queen*.

My deepest gratitude also goes to the John Simon Guggenheim Memorial

Foundation, which has supported this project with a generous fellowship that allowed me to take a one-year leave in 1990. This fellowship was supplemented with a research fellowship from the University of California-Irvine and a stipend from the School of Humanities. I extend my special thanks both to the Guggenheim Foundation and UCI, my home university. I would not have been able to carry this project through without their generous support. Thanks also go to the Center for German and European Studies at the University of California-Berkeley for a fellowship that allowed me to participate in their interdisciplinary research group on "The Changing Concept of Experience," as well as for providing research assistance for the chapters on Barnes and Duras.

I would like to thank the many readers of my manuscript who have helped me with their patience and advice. Wolfgang Iser, my mentor and friend, and Lore Iser have supported my work with enthusiasm as well as active interest and advice for over twenty years. They are among those rare readers who fully understand and participate in its bicultural dimension. Gregg Lambert and Clara McLean have been most supportive and generous with intellectual and editorial advice. I am deeply grateful for Henry Sussman's highly perceptive and intuitive reading of my book which greatly helped to speed up its publication. My gratitude also goes to the colleagues who have supported my grant applications: Ralph Cohen, Wolfgang Iser, Murray Krieger, Hillis Miller, Jochen Schulte-Sasse, and Kathleen Woodward. As always, I owe many thanks to my colleagues and students at Irvine and elsewhere—particularly those who have lucidly commented on specific chapters: Julie Bangs, Lisa Carstens, Rey Chow, Michael Clark, Alexander Gelley, Ihab Hassan, Jim McMichael, John-Paul Riquelme, John Rowe, Martin Schwab, Mihai Spariosu, and Irene Wei.

I was also fortunate to see my work supported by colleagues who facilitated earlier publications and presentations to diverse foreign audiences: Aleida Assman, Anselm Haverkamp, Renate Lachmann, Roland Galle, Rudolf Behrens, Christoph Menke (Germany), Emily Budick, Sandor Budick, Zephyra Porat, Hana Wirth-Nesher (Israel), Iwao Iwamoto, and Kazuko Takemura (Japan).

Perhaps the most inspiring moments that carried me through the usual ups and downs that mark the development of a manuscript were the poetry readings performed by my son Manuel. His poetry, more than anything else, allows me to believe in the unbroken force of literature. Manuel and I both share the belief that we have "survived" on literature, that it has kept us from falling into madness or despair, and that it has filled us with an "uncontrollable passion."

Here is also the place to thank my companion Paul Harris who is always the first to read my work and whose untiring enthusiasm, advice, patience, and generosity keep me going. Our son Leon helps us to keep in touch with that other world of shapeshifters who turn into dinosaurs, spirits, or cats, and once in a while "grow back" to be babies again. His "literature" nourishes our whole family. "Reading, Otherness, and Cultural Contact" is written in memory of my father, Erwin Haack, and my beloved friend, Avraham Zloczower, both of whom I lost when I had just begun writing. "Seduced by Witches" is dedicated to the memory of Carlos Dominguez. Last but not least, everything I ever wrote bears the traces of remembering my sister, Stephanie Haack, whom I lost nearly 25 years ago.

Earlier versions or sections of chapters have been previously published and are reprinted here with permission. They have all been substantially modified, revised and edited for this book, but I have not considered criticism on individual authors that appeared after the first publication. The theoretical section, "Reading, Otherness, and Cultural Contact," considerably expands and modifies a framework first developed in "Reader-Response and the Aesthetic Experience of Otherness," published in Russell Berman and David Wellbery, eds., *Interpretation-Discourse-Society: Interdisciplinary Paradigms in Literary Scholarship*, special issue of *Stanford Literature Review* 3.1 (Spring 1986): 107–36. "Nonsense and Metacommunication: *Alice in Wonderland*" appeared under the title "Nonsense and Metacommunication: Reflections on Lewis Carroll," in Ronald Bogue and Mihai I. Spariosu, eds., *The Play of the Self*, Albany: SUNY Press, 1994, 157–79. A German version, "Lewis Carroll's Traumlogik und die Lesbarkeit des Unsinns," is forthcoming in Aleida Assmann, ed., *Die Lesbarkeit der Texte*, Munich: Wilhelm Fink Verlag. An early version of "Seduced by Witches: *The Scarlet Letter*" appeared under the title "Seduced by Witches: Nathaniel Hawthorne's *The Scarlet Letter in the Context of New England Witchcraft Fictions*," in Dianne Hunter, ed., *Seduction and Theory: Readings of Gender, Representation and Rhetoric*, Urbana/Chicago: University of Illinois Press, 1989. 170–91. "Carnival and Abjection: The Mother's Dead Body in *As I Lay Dying*" first appeared in a considerably different German version in Walter Haug and Rainer Warning, eds., *Das Fest in der Literatur*, Poetik und Hermeneutik XIV, Munich: Wilhelm Fink Verlag, 1989. "The Multiple Lives of Addie Bundren's Dead Body: On William Faulkner's *As I Lay Dying*," appeared in Juliet Flower MacCannell, ed., *The Other Perspective in Gender and Culture: Rewriting Women and the Symbolic*, New York: Columbia University Press, 1990, 209–41. "The Jungle and the Drawing Room: Urban Nomads in *Nightwood*" appeared in German as "Poetik der Stadtnomaden: Djuna Barnes'

*Nachtgewaechs*," in Christoph Menke and Martin Seel, eds., *Zur Verteidigung der Vernunft gegen ihre Liebhaber und Veraechter*, Frankfurt: Suhrkamp Verlag, 1993, 368–84. A German version of " 'While she lives she invites murder': *The Malady of Death*," is forthcoming under the title "Die Semiotik des weiblichen Koerpers: Marguerite Duras und die Krankheit des Todes," in Rudolf Behrens and Roland Galle, eds., *Kreatuerlichkeit im Roman des 20. Jahrhunderts*, Würzburg: Königshausen & Neumann.

# TOWARD AN ETHNOGRAPHY OF READING:
## A THEORETICAL FRAMEWORK

# READING, OTHERNESS, AND CULTURAL CONTACT[1]

## 1. The Tiv, Their Anthropologist, and Her Shakespeare

IN THE EARLY sixties, American anthropologist Laura Bohannan studied a West African tribe, the Tiv. Inspired by a previous controversy about Shakespeare with an Oxford scholar, she decided to perform a test with the Tiv that was meant to demonstrate the universality of Shakespeare's plays. The results of her exchange with the elders of the tribe, during which she was, in her own words, "taught the true meaning of *Hamlet*," were published in her widely discussed essay "Shakespeare in the Bush." Before Bohannan's departure for Africa, her Oxford friend had told her, "You Americans . . . often have difficulty with Shakespeare. He was, after all, a very English poet, and one can easily misinterpret the universal by misunderstanding the particular" (28). She protested "that human nature is pretty much the same the whole world over" (28), and that the core of the greater tragedies would always be clear everywhere. Discussing *Hamlet* with the Tiv was meant to prove this assumption.

In the Tiv's oral culture storytelling is a highly refined art whose standards are controlled by the elders. For the Tiv, every story must convey a specific, true meaning. And so the elders, who exert power over the meaning of things, events, and actions, also determine "the meaning of meaning." Unchallenged rulers of their interpretive community, they seem to share at least one concern with Bohannan's Oxford scholar friend: they use their privilege to eliminate "misreadings." Their system of signs and their practices of interpretation are thus hermetically sealed from outside perspectives that might see Tiv hermeneutics as relative, limited by the boundaries of cultural affiliation and tradition.

The Tiv's reaction to Bohannan's narration of the story of *Hamlet* provides an interesting example of interpretive power that allows one to "defamiliarize" current debates on reading, interpretation, agency, and cultural contact. I will use the example of Bohannan's exchange with the elders to introduce a more general notion of reading as a form of cultural contact.

> "Not yesterday, not yesterday, but long ago, a thing occurred. One night three men were keeping watch outside the homestead of the great chief, when suddenly they saw the former chief approach them!"
> "Why was he no longer their chief?"
> "He was dead . . . that is why they were afraid when they saw him."
> "Impossible" began one of the elders. . . . "Of course it wasn't the dead chief. It was an omen sent by a witch. . . . "(29)

The elders, who do not believe in ghosts, were bewildered: "Omens can't talk!" and "Dead men can't walk" (30). Bohannan continued her story telling how Prince Hamlet, the dead chief's son, was very upset because his uncle, Claudius, had become the great chief and also married his elder brother's widow only a month or so after the funeral. " 'He did well,' the old man beamed. . . . 'I told you that if we knew more about Europeans, we could find they really were like us. In our country also . . . the younger brother marries the elder brother's widow and becomes the father of his children' " (29–30).

And this is what the elders finally decided to be the "true meaning" of the story: Hamlet was surely a villain, for he had scolded his mother, killed Polonius, and raised his hand against his father's brother Claudius. This alone would have made *Hamlet* a bad story. And yet, not all hope was lost for its aesthetic value:

> But if his father's brother had indeed been wicked enough to bewitch Hamlet and make him mad that would be a good story indeed, for it would be his fault that Hamlet, being mad, no longer had any sense and thus was ready to kill his father's brother. (32)

One of the elders concluded, "Sometime you must tell us some more stories of your country. We, who are elders, will instruct you in their true meaning" (33). Thus, the Tiv's interpretation, more than simply assimilating Shakespeare's *Hamlet* as told by Bohannan, also assimilated, in a way, Bohannan herself. After submitting to the elders, she was granted access to the interpretive community of storytellers.

The playfully ironical tone in which Bohannan relates her encounter with the Tiv assumes a certain complicity with her Western readers, many of whom might smile at the Tiv's reaction as naive, ignorant, out of place. Many might also agree that it is a deformation of Shakespeare's play, but find it a charming one, reminiscent of children's reactions. But just how much of this effect is staged by Bohannan herself? The way in which she translates Shakespeare's plot into an oral story, for example, reminds one of Bernard Miles's tales from Shakespeare for children. Cast in the role of children, the elders appear somewhat infantilized and their response is thus used to confirm a familiar prejudice against so-called primitive cultures. Interestingly, Bohannan seems to think that the Tiv's response speaks for itself. This is why ultimately her ironical tone, at the surface directed at her own belief in the universality of art and human nature, falls back on the Tiv, exposing them for the amusement of Bohannan's own cultural peers.

Given the history of colonialism—to which Bohannan's encounter with the Tiv is already linked through the discipline of anthropology—the treatment of the Tiv as "children" recalls the problematic tropological affiliation of primitive cultures with children who must be civilized and educated. Even though Bohannan does not reveal any pedagogical zeal, her rhetorical figuration of the Tiv as childlike reproduces the colonial infantilization of the native other. This example shows that the framing of a cultural contact by a narrative is itself a crucial part of this contact.

The fact that Bohannan's rhetorical pose remains caught up in certain anthropological stereotypes reminds one that anthropology, traditionally dedicated to the study of primitive cultures, has developed not only its own methods of reading otherness and forms of cultural contact, but also its own rhetorical codes and performative enactments of the anthropologist's encounter with otherness. In this context, "Shakespeare in the Bush" is particularly interesting because it confronts us with a rare instance in which an anthropologist explicitly invites the natives to "read" her own culture, thus exposing her readers to the mirror effects of layered readings of the other: her telling of Shakespeare's plot—motivated explicitly as a translation of a written artifact into a story attuned to an oral culture of storytellers—already mirrors Bohannan's own reading of the Tiv who, in turn, mirror their reading of Bohannan in their own reaction to her story. This highly mediated exchange reveals that, instead of a straightforward cultural contact between the Tiv and Shakespeare, we witness a complex network of multiple effects of reading and translating otherness. We are thus never exposed to the mere "facts" of a cultural encounter, but to its multiple refractions in narratives that reflect relations formed by specific expectations, prejudices, desires, needs, or fears projected on the other. This is why the "aesthetics" or performativity of the exchange between Bohannan and the Tiv becomes crucial.

Looking back at this exchange from the perspective of current debates in both literary criticism and anthropology may serve to highlight interesting shifts in critical sensibility. Bohannan raises the issue of universality, both of art and of human nature. Playing with the idea of a universal human nature, she stresses the universal communicability of literature.

Less concerned with aesthetic form and experience, literature for her is a communication about human nature through stories about fictional human beings. As a consequence, the performativity of Shakespeare's play seems as negligible to her as that of her own storytelling. Yet, as we have seen, the way in which she tells her story transmits what Jameson calls the "ideology of form." What we encounter here is a certain tension between aesthetic and cultural negotiation of boundaries. Shakespeare's play seems marked by a double otherness: that of the culturally embedded aesthetic medium and performative practice—the Elizabethan drama—and that of the cultural otherness of its fictional world. Bohannan reduces the first in order to emphasize the second.

Literary criticism has tended to give priority to the aesthetic over the cultural. Aesthetic production and experience have been singled out as specific cultural practices that follow their own rules, develop their own traditions and possess a certain quasi autonomy from their various fields of reference. At the same time, however, the aesthetic has always been defined in relation to other cultural spheres—with certain traditions or periods emphasizing specific affiliations over others, giving priority, for example, to the social, the psychological, or the philosophical. Currently we witness a shift from aesthetics to culture within literary criticism and theory that profoundly affects the ways in which we read and theorize reading. While reader-response theories and reception aesthetics in the seventies and eighties still emphasized the particularity of aesthetic experience, it has now become nearly obsolete to focus primarily on aesthetics. In the following, I will try to avoid this polarization by addressing the cultural function of aesthetic practices and particularly of reading and interpretation.

"Shakespeare in the Bush," in fact, might invite us to look at reading in general in terms of cultural contact. This perspective guides my own concept of reading and the reconsideration of various theories of reading from the last decades. Isn't it true that even readers to whom Shakespeare is culturally much closer than he is to the Tiv must negotiate a certain otherness in order to relate to his embeddedness in Elizabethan culture? If we understand reading as a negotiation across cultural and historical boundaries and a form of making contact with otherness, then we perceive a double movement toward the culture of the text/play and back toward the culture of the reader. As readers of Shakespeare, for example, we usually do not try to become an Elizabethan (unless we follow a certain ideal of literary historicism), but rather to encounter in the otherness of Elizabethan culture something to which we respond and may import into our own culture or our own selves. Reading as a border operation is thus not only an activity of "leaving home" but also one of "bringing home." This example already makes it clear that reading, though different from cultural contact in the narrow sense of the phrase, may be compared to it in the sense that it constitutes a specific form of cultural contact facilitated within a culture through the institutionalization of literature as a space of aesthetic practice. Bohannan's piece reminds us that in order to understand the terms of this contact we need in each case to take into account the historical and cultural distance between a work and its recipients.

This is where the problem of the aesthetic needs to be addressed more explicitly. As I said earlier, the effects of the "story of Hamlet" cannot be reduced to the plot itself—as Bohannan seems to assume—but are determined by Shakespeare's or Bohannan's performative enactment. As we all know, this is why the very cultural function of literature largely resides in its forms and styles of figuration and cannot be reduced to semantic information or thematic consideration. This is also why cultural critics, if they take literature seriously, must address the function of aesthetics, that is, the forms and modes of literary presentation and reception. The reason why aesthetics has been relegated to the margins, if not discredited, by certain cultural critics is that it tended to establish itself in isolation from cultural critiques. But to eliminate aesthetics, in turn, from cultural criticism would mean to ignore the very material conditions of cultural practices such as literature or art and their specific conditions of reception. What we need, on the contrary, is—as Bohannan's exchange with the Tiv clearly demonstrates—a theory that allows one to differentiate between the multiple modes of aesthetic production and reception and their cultural functions. In the case of the Tiv, it is relevant, for example, that storytelling is a thoroughly integrated cultural sphere and communal practice, while the Elizabethan drama is already a theatrical practice performed within a specialized aesthetic sphere.

Seen from this larger perspective, the Tiv's response to Bohannan may not seem as far removed from familiar modes of reception as it first appears. At stake is the production of meaning for a community of readers, its universality or relativity, and the constraints on our freedom of interpretation, particularly in adaptations to a new cultural, historical, or even individual environment. Seen in this way, the elders' response is, in its basic premises, not as different

from many current theories of interpretation as it might seem when we compare the Tiv's "deformation" of *Hamlet* to the many historical and cultural "deformations" in the play's other history of reception. Contemporary rewritings
or stagings of Shakespeare, such as Giorgio Strehler's famous staging of *King
Lear* as a punk rock play, ultimately perform a similar transposition from the
Elizabethan to a new cultural environment.

The issue of constraints on interpretation has fueled heated controversies
among critics in the seventies and eighties. Constraints may emerge from both
poles in the interaction, the reader and the text. Readers may approach a text
with specific norms and expectations that operate as constraints, while a text
may deploy strategies to undermine certain expectations or delimit interpretation in other ways. Like Bohannan's Oxford friend, the elders do not believe
that meaning may vary from individual to individual or community to community; they create and negotiate meaning according to clearly delineated conventions of their own interpretive community. Similarly, many Western critics
insist that, even though any individual reader can perform the activity of making sense, meaning is still controlled by communal conventions and hence by
powers beyond the reach of the individual. The most crucial difference seems
to be that in Western cultures the elders have become replaced by the more
anonymous forces that Foucault has highlighted in his theories as "agencies of
power." Despite the fact that the latter are less centralized and hence more con-
tested than the power of the elders, they nonetheless impose social constraints
on interpretation and meaning.

Simultaneously, however, Western traditions have also developed ongoing
controversies concerning the power inherent in the production of knowledge
through interpretation. Faced with continuous challenges from within and
through contact with other cultures, the very status of reading has become a
heavily debated issue. Western traditions have for a long time operated on the
basis of various and competing centers of interpretive power, emerging from
different sources such as the nation, the church, different schools of thought,
or philosophical trends. At least since Montaigne, Diderot, and Rousseau, these
debates have addressed issues of otherness and its appropriation. On the one
hand, the secularization of meaning heralded by the Enlightenment challenged
from within the notion of truth in both text and interpretation. On the other
hand, Enlightenment values were shaped by the history of colonialism and imperialism that compelled Western civilizations to read and define themselves
in relation to cultural otherness.

The current movement in cultural criticism profoundly questions the tradi-

## Reading, Otherness, and Cultural Contact

tional values of the West, and particularly its self-definition in relation to its own either degrading or romanticizing figurations of otherness in the guises of primitivism, orientalism, racism, or sexism. Issues of interpretive power and violence have led some critics to question the very legitimacy of interpretation, especially in anthropology, where, following a new trend in postmodern ethnographies, many ethnographers try to operate as "passive" recorders of other, native voices.[2] Among literary critics, a similar attitude has challenged traditional practices of literary readings and induced numerous critics to shift their activity of interpretation from literature to theory (interestingly, to my knowledge no one so far has attempted to protect theoretical texts from the violence of interpretation). Ongoing controversies divide critics who consider all interpretation an act of violence from those who, on the contrary, believe that interpretation forms a kind of symbiosis with texts that would remain incomplete without interpretive enactment. Other debates concerning textual constraints and the boundaries of texts separate critics who stipulate that readings be limited by textual constraints from others who insist that no restriction on interpretation may ever be supported by a text.

A model of reading as cultural contact may give such debates a new turn because it highlights the cultural implications of the attitudes readers bring to a text, as well as the ways in which texts perform cultural interventions. It is interesting to observe that critics who are not willing to acknowledge boundaries and negotiations between texts and readers often end up declaring either that "anything goes" and no interpretation is more valid than any other or, on the contrary, that "nothing goes" and that interpretation or theory must stop. Even though, on the surface, they pose as opposites, these two positions are, in fact, intimately related to each other. Jonathan Culler's verdict, "one thing we do not need any more is more interpretations of literary works" (6), is symptomatic of the discussion in the early eighties, as is Stephen Knapp's and Walter Benn Michaels's laconic response to the controversy about their polemical essay "Against Theory":

> The antiformalist point of "Against Theory" is to insist that anything can be used to mean anything or, as Crewe rightly puts it, "quite radically to deny that the forms of language possess any defining power. . . . " If our arguments are true, they can have only one consequence . . . theory should stop. (799–800)

The problem with this position lies in its relativistic conclusion. Even if one would agree that language has no "defining power," or, to put it differently, that language is not the master of our readings, this would not necessarily turn us into the master of language, allowing us to make a text mean whatever we want. But only such a hasty conclusion would justify that theory should stop.

More than a century ago Lewis Carroll—to whom I return in the first interpretive chapter—mocked this linguistic relativism with his nonsense character Humpty Dumpty:

> "When I use a word," Humpty-Dumpty said in a rather scornful tone, "it means just what I choose it to mean—neither more nor less." "The question is," said Alice, "whether you *can* make words mean so many different things." "The question is," said Humpty-Dumpty, "which is to be the Master that's all." (209–10)

Masters who control language in this way, or, for that matter, critics who play the role of a Humpty Dumpty in theory, appropriate language according to their own desires, thus precluding any challenge posed by its virtual otherness. For them, interpretation and meaning will always be the same, an affirmation of their own presuppositions, expectations, or ideologies—a colonizing textual practice.

While on the surface less restrictive, critics who turn the openness of language into an "anything goes" for interpretation, are, as Norman Holland's interpretive liberalism illustrates, no less prone endlessly to reaffirm their own presuppositions. On the one hand, he invites us to an all-embracing variety of responses: "Instead of subtracting readings so as to narrow them down or cancel some . . . let us use human differences to add response to response, to multiply possibilities and to enrich the whole experience" ("Re-Covering" 370). On the other hand, he shows that this proliferation of multiple meanings notwithstanding, texts will never change us, but on the contrary affirm us as we are: "Thus the overarching principle is: identity recreates itself . . . all of us, as we read, use the literary work to symbolize and finally to replicate ourselves" ("Unity" 124).

It may look as if the Tiv confirm this assumption. They did enact their own cultural patterns and codes of reading within Shakespeare's plot. But in doing so, haven't they, as Bohannan felt, transformed *Hamlet* into a different play? And has not Bohannan herself, in her Hamlet story for the Tiv, done something similar—if in a manner less striking to Western ears? If we are willing to acknowledge boundaries between texts and readers and see interpretation as a kind of border operation or negotiation, the issue of interpretive power or violence may be focused more sharply. As the Tiv's initial reaction shows, they first tend to react to the otherness of Bohannan's story with denial: "Impossible. . . . Omens can't talk! . . . Dead men can't walk." Then they try what most people listening to a story would do, namely, to make sense of it in relation to their own world. Next, they relate their interpretation to the story's context, the cultural contact between anthropologist Bohannan and their tribe: "if we knew more about Europeans, we could find they really were like us." In its assertion of similarity rather than difference, this statement is not only a friendly negotiation across the boundaries of cultural otherness, it also mirrors Bohannan's own initial belief in the "universality" of Shakespeare—ironically, precisely when the "otherness" of the Tiv's response leads Bohannan to question it. Both the Tiv's interpretation and Bohannan's reaction to it make us aware that we *do* have internalized norms for judging interpretations and that these norms are precisely related to cultural context. Unless one is confronted either with an utterly foreign text, a radically innovative aesthetic practice or a strikingly different interpretation, one easily forgets that reading always requires a certain negotiation of otherness, a mediation between two more or less different cultural or historical contexts, the text's and the reader's.

## 2. Reading, Otherness, and Cultural Contact

If one understands the act of reading as a border operation that requires negotiations across boundaries marked by cultural, historical, or aesthetic difference, one needs to define how otherness and cultural contact operate specifically in literary production and reception as compared to actual encounters between different cultures. When asked by the Social Sciences Research Council to devise categories for the study of cultural contact, Gregory Bateson replied, "I suggest that we should consider under the head of 'culture contact' not only those cases in which the contact occurs between two communities with different cultures . . . but also cases of contact within a single community. . . . I would even extend the idea of 'contact' so widely as to include those processes whereby a child is molded and trained to fit the culture into which he was born . . . " (64). Following Bateson, we may analyze as a form of cultural contact the relationship that a literary text establishes between its readers and the culture within which the text is produced and with which it interferes. This perspective grasps not only our individual acts of reading, but also the processes by which we are socialized into our own reading habits as forms of cultural contact.

What do we gain if we thus look at reading in terms of a highly specialized form of cultural contact? And what do we presume when we speak of the otherness of a literary text? At the most general level, I use the model of cultural contact in a dynamic sense as a heuristic frame for highlighting the transactions or negotiations between readers and texts, and, by extension, texts and contexts, theories, or other texts. Among other things, this new perspective links the cultural function of literature to its power to affect and change us and to intervene in other cultural practices. In general, changes are often provoked by encounters with otherness that challenge familiar assumptions or open up new perspectives. Literature, however, requires a specific dynamic between familiarity and otherness, or closeness and distance, in order to affect readers. The old cliché that we "find ourselves" in literature refers to the fact that unless literature resonates with us we remain cold to it. On the other hand, complete familiarity would never engage our interest but leave us equally indifferent.

Literature, in other words, affects us most when it displays a resonating otherness or unfamiliar, if not uncanny, resonance. Aesthetic categories such as "innovation" or "defamiliarization" grasp the structural and aesthetic aspect of this phenomenon. In order to assess its cultural implications we need to distinguish and explore the relationship between different modalities of literary otherness. Formalist, structuralist, and poststructuralist aesthetics perceive the generation of otherness mainly as a textual operation that produces a certain tension or rupture within the symbolic order. From this perspective, poetic language and literary reception appear as practices of writing or reading "otherwise."[3] By contrast, a hermeneutic aesthetics, especially a Gadamerian one, perceives alterity mainly as an effect of changing traditions and reading accordingly as a "fusion" of different horizons. Psychoanalytic theories add the notion of an "internal otherness" as an effect of unconscious operations. Whatever is repressed from consciousness will be perceived as other, foreign, abject, or taboo. Poetic language in psychoanalytic aesthetics assumes the function of creating a space of resonance that stimulates the transference of internal otherness.

We can see that none of these theoretical movements emphasizes cultural otherness as such, even though textual, historical, and internal otherness are all effects of cultural transactions. The shift in theoretical debates toward cultural criticism has reversed this trend, placing the emphasis on literary figurations of cultural otherness, the reading of other cultures, the proliferation of hybrid texts, and the changing modes of production as well as modalities of cultural contact in increasingly globalized cultures. In this context, theories of reading shift their emphasis from aesthetic experience to cultural negotiation or appropriation. This shift affects what we perceive as the otherness of a text or in what sense we conceive reading as a border operation. In this process, the very terms of reader-response and aesthetic experience are reframed and renegotiated in terms of culture and cultural contact.

If we take the notion of reading as a border operation seriously, we may assume that, like other forms of cultural contact, reading affects boundaries, be they those of an individual reader or an interpretive community or, by extension, a culture at large. As agents of cultural contact, literary texts work across the boundaries of their own culture as well as those cultures that admit them to their canon. Moreover, they engage readers in a continual process of dissolving, reshaping, expanding, or transgressing the boundaries they have drawn at the various levels of being socialized into their own culture.[4] These alterations of boundaries are determined by the histories of reading of cultural communities as well as individual readers. By looking more closely at such histories we may detect phases of change and development that reflect the changing relationship to otherness in both the cultural histories under consideration and the psychogenesis of their subjects. Modes of relating to the otherness of a literary text vary according to its readers' stages of life, their experience and competence in reading, and the norms of their cultural communities.

Such a framework casts cultural patterns of relating to otherness also as a pedagogical issue. There is a cultural education, just as there is a cognitive and emotional one. All these spheres—including the practices and cultural politics of reading—are developed through maturational processes that intersect with and affect each other. In the early stages of individual development, the child's boundaries are particularly porous and receptive to readings, but at the same time reading is likely to be more projective and "narcissistic," since a certain experience of difference and differentiation must be acquired to alter or reduce projection. Similarly, without a thorough knowledge of another culture, reading will necessarily entail a certain "ethnocentric" translation of a foreign culture's otherness into one's own terms.

On the other hand, the most devastating ethnocentrism has historically developed—as Said has demonstrated—from within an intimate and highly invested knowledge of the other culture. The modes of translating otherness thus vary greatly and must be understood from within the larger dynamics of a specific cultural encounter. For example, when the Tiv adjusted Bohannan's *Hamlet* to their own situated knowledge in order to reduce the otherness that would otherwise have made the story incomprehensible to them, they did not use the story to emphasize difference, but to establish a link between the two cultures.

Moreover, in assuming authority over the meaning of a Western anthropologist's own stories, they cheerfully reversed the power relation constituted by her very presence. This example demonstrates that the mode of cultural contact implied in cross-cultural readings cannot be understood in isolation from the power relation between the cultures involved.

Two extreme forms of aesthetic experience—romantic identification and aesthetic distance—may serve more concretely to illustrate how during varying histories of reading the culturally privileged modes of contact with a text change drastically. A model of cultural contact assumes that the reading process affects both text and reader through negotiations across their mutual boundaries. On the most general level, the mutual transformation of text and reader unfolds between two poles. In one case, the text is assimilated by a reader who appropriates it according to familiar parameters; in the other case, the reader is assimilated by a text—a reception that Flaubert satirizes in Emma Bovary's assimilation by her literary models. In contrast to the most common appropriation of a text according to familiar parameters, writers and critics alike often expose the assimilation of an adult reader by a text as pathological. Cervantes's Don Quixote, the classical model for this type of fusion with a fictional world, becomes entirely absorbed by phantasmatic hallucinations of the fictional adventures that structure his desire. Foucault, who calls this quixotic fusion "madness by romantic identification," takes it nonetheless to be "the most important and persistent" form of literary reception.

> Its features have been fixed once and for all by Cervantes. But the theme is tirelessly repeated: direct adaptations . . . reinterpretations of a particular episode . . . or in a more indirect fashion, satire on novels of fantasy. . . . The chimeras are transmitted from author to reader, but what was fantasy on one side becomes hallucination on the other; the writer's stratagem is quite naively accepted as an image of reality. In appearance, this is nothing but the simple minded critique of novels of fantasy, but just under the surface lies an enormous anxiety concerning the relationships, in a work of art, between the real and the imaginary, and perhaps also concerning the confused communication between fantastic invention and the fascinations of delirium. (*Madness* 28–29)

A milder form of "madness by romantic identification" lives on throughout the history of fashions created by literature, art, or other media—as, for example, in the notorious *Werther* cult in Weimar Germany that created a wave of fashionable melancholic suicides. Even in the current age of mass media, we read in the daily newspaper that an adolescent, committed for orchestrating a collective murder of his schoolmate, claims that this act was inspired by Camus's novel *The Stranger* (*Lait*). All this is not to say that the Weimar youths would not have committed suicide without reading *Werther*, or that Robert Chan would not have committed the murder without reading Camus, but that literary models provide a foil for individual and collective self-fashioning.[5] Cultural objects, in other words, use their transformational energy to mold subjectivity and to provide collective images that shape the cultural unconscious. In this sense they partake in what Bateson sees as the processes of cultural contact that socialize adolescents into their own culture.

Literature has throughout history created such cultural forms of "self-fashioning." Sartre's psychohistorical portrait of Flaubert in *The Family Idiot* as well as his literary autobiography, *The Words*, for example, highlight the cultural formation of an "imaginary personality," a derivative subjectivity inspired by literary models. *The Words* shows how the forms of reading and concomitant desires acquired in early childhood remain active in structuring subjectivity and unconscious desires throughout adult life. This strong impact of literature emerges from the intense affective cathexis of fictional worlds, and particularly the moods in which they are transmitted through style and rhythm—moods which, in turn, are transferred to the reader.

Due to this cathexis, the temporary fusion with literary characters is quite generally one of the most intensely enjoyed pleasures of reading. As the medieval spectator of a miracle play testifies when he rushes on stage to save Christ from being crucified, such fusion involves a spontaneous breakdown of the boundaries between the real and the imaginary. Calvino's *If on a winter's night a traveler*, moreover, reminds us that even highly mediated, distanced, and self-reflective readings retain a nostalgia for such fusions. The harder they become to achieve, the more one might feel the loss of one of the most overwhelming powers of the imaginary. Nietzsche already saw Greek tragedy as one of the last art forms that allowed its audience to experience the loss imposed by individuation in a cathartic process of fusion with imaginary characters.

As Nietzsche's assessment of Greek tragedy suggests, the fusion between text and reader or performance and audience draws on an archaic desire for primordial undifferentiatedness from others and the world. In Foucault's "madness by romantic identification," the power of imaginary objects to break down the boundaries of recipients, to literally penetrate or occupy their subjectivity and their unconscious enables a temporary experience of undifferentiation and fusion. In such extreme forms of reception, a text's potential otherness is spontaneously absorbed. Instead of precluding aesthetic experience of otherness altogether, however, this extreme encounter with an other transforms otherness by incorporation. In contact with the literary object, the recipient temporarily becomes the object, that is, other. This is precisely why reading may become a form of madness through loss of self-boundaries comparable to what Freud describes as the temporary madness of people in love. From a perspective of cultural contact in a narrower sense, one could also see this "madness by romantic identification" as a form of "going native." Yet, in contrast to native people, literary objects from medieval plays to Goethe's *Werther* and beyond actively induce this temporary madness—be it because they resonate in us, bringing us in contact with the internal otherness of the unconscious, or because they recreate us as other, occupying our desire and turning us into imaginary characters of the type of Emma Bovary or Don Quixote.

Twentieth-century canonical literature—in particular modernist and postmodernist experimentalism—has tended to devalue this identificatory reception. In the wake of fascism and other atrocities that mark our century, many writers as well as critics share a profound suspicion toward the manipulation of emotions. This turn is most distinctly expressed in the Brechtian aesthetics of distance that inspired not only drama but aesthetic practices of the time in general. At the same time, the profound impact of psychoanalysis stimulated artists and critics to reflect upon literary figurations of the unconscious and its incorporation into aesthetic experience. Experimental aesthetic practices of the time—from surrealism to Artaud's "theater of cruelty"—try to open poetic language (including that of the body) to the effects of the unconscious. Both an aesthetics of distance and an aesthetics of cruelty equally preclude romantic identification. Artaud's somatic semiotics aims at a theater beyond words and representation in order to reach the audience's unconscious through the drama of the body.[6] Significantly, these aesthetic models have been produced for the theater, that is, the art form that is most intimately concerned with its audience's closeness and distance. Comparing the two alternative models, we see that both entail an encounter with otherness, yet in diametrically opposed ways. While Brecht exposes the otherness and artifice of his plays in order to maintain the audience's otherness, which is effaced in Foucault's "madness by romantic identification," Artaud envisions that the excessive exoticism of the body in pain or ecstasy exposes his audience to the otherness of its own unconscious.

In the current cultural scene, the identification and fusion with characters has become increasingly relegated to children's literature, popular culture, and the mass media. Due to the fleeting modes of reception in the media, however, the old "madness by romantic identification" has given way to a delirious cathexis of ever-new fetish objects, a phantasmatic identification with "heroes" of family romances and cultural icons of violence that only faintly recalls the old "madness." Yet, much of contemporary literature—even in its most experimental forms—remains nostalgic for the old madness by romantic identification. This may be one reason why we currently witness a flourishing return of narrative, epic, and even romance.

More generally, the highly technologized and media dominated environment of contemporary global cultures, with its shift from literary to visual culture, decreases the public space and attention granted to literature. Under the impact of the mass media, new technologies of writing and information, and mixed-media art forms, literature itself has developed new forms that reflect the fate of reading and the specific experience literature may provide within this new cultural formation. It is all the more important to recall that, under the pressure of this challenging cultural climate, literature has not receded but produced the proliferating experimental forms inaugurated by high modernism, which have, in turn, been appropriated and altered by the playful syncretism and pastiche of postmodernism. Doesn't Joyce already reflect and incorporate the increasing globalization and hybridization of culture and its shift to new technologies into the formal qualities of his texts, particularly the globalized transnational language of the *Wake*? This is, in fact, what Kristeva refers to as "the revolution" of poetic language. The proliferating forms of literary experimentalism open up experiences of cultural contact that are fundamentally different from those facilitated by other cultural practices or forms of discourse.

To explore such experiences will be the focus of this project. In my theoretical model as well as my readings of literary texts, I will explore the relationships and interconnections between different forms of literary otherness, instead of foregrounding one at the expense of others. My interpretive chapters deal with authors who experiment with the production of textual otherness—Carroll's literary nonsense, Hawthorne's historical dialogicity, Joyce's experimental multilingualism, Faulkner's phantasmatic voices, Barnes's experiments with paradoxical tropes and spatial form, or Duras's performative triangulation of voices. From this perspective, the otherness of poetic language appears as an experimental device aimed at soliciting specific forms of aesthetic experience. A closer look at the latter, however, reveals the connection of literary alterity with other cultural manifestations of otherness, including the cultural unconscious. Historical otherness, for example, is often established by intertextuality, pastiche, and parody, while internal otherness may appear as an effect of primary process language, phantasmatic imagery, literary moods, or the use of language as a space of transference. The link to cultural otherness proper appears not only in literary figurations of other cultures, but also—on a more formal level—as an effect of cross-cultural intertextuality, textual hybridity, and the incorporation of foreign languages or mythologies.

As my discussion of "Shakespeare in the Bush" illustrates, I consider formal, rhetorical, and aesthetic devices to be crucial for determining the modes of cultural contact facilitated by a literary text or work of art. Looking at reading as an experience of otherness, in fact, presupposes a dynamic interaction between aesthetic, cultural, political, and psychological aspects, including the effects of a cultural unconscious that we may trace in the fantasies and fetish objects of a specific culture. My theory of reading therefore explores the aesthetic in relation to other cultural spheres, thus creating the notion of a textual ecology attentive to the literary formation of and intervention in cultural practices, including the cultural unconscious.[7]

I am particularly interested in understanding texts that experiment with "othering" language and in the different ways in which we may relate, in our acts of reading, to their textual "otherness." The question of a text's "otherness" is, of course, as controversial as that of textual agency. The contact between reader and text is not "neutral," but motivated and structured by emotional investments, desires, cultural and aesthetic values, and receptive habits. If it is true—as I believe—that our culturally acquired and internalized patterns of reacting to otherness will also shape our habits of reading, then reading also affects and mobilizes our relationship to "otherness" in general. Reading might influence and change these patterns, and, at its best, widen the abilities to perceive and to acknowledge otherness. I see this relationship to a text as other as the most basic dynamic that determines the politics of reading.[8]

Apart from asserting their own alterity and thereby differentiating and changing conventional habits of reading, modern and postmodern experimental texts have also inspired new theories of reading modeled after what one could call experimentalism's practice of poetic difference. Experimental modernist literature has, in fact, had a decisive impact on many of the most influential postmodern theories and philosophies, from Adorno to Kristeva or Derrida. Regarding my own project, the insistence on otherness, heterogeneity, openness, and ambiguity in experimental literature has not only inspired my own theory but also the ways in which I read and use theories, including my evaluations of theoretical debates. Generally, I understand not only the act of reading but also the intertextuality between theories and the dynamics of theoretical interventions and critical debates according to a model of cultural contact. Theoretical debates, modes of exchange and appropriation then appear according to the ways in which they draw their boundaries and deal with other theories. They may be more incorporating or more assertive of boundaries, more ridden by an anxiety of influence or more inspired by a spirit of constructive ecclecticism, more faithful or critical toward tradition, more open or defensive, if not hostile, toward competing theories.

Within this framework, I will reconsider a set of relevant theories of reading according to their implicit models of cultural contact in order to demonstrate how they reflect or interfere with their cultures' prominent constructions of otherness. My focus, however, remains specific. I discuss theories mainly in terms of their relevance for understanding poetic language, and particularly the literary practice and aesthetic experience of texts that insist on their own alterity.

My own methodology reflects my theoretical assumptions about otherness and cultural contact. Rather than critically evaluating theoretical positions in a descriptive way, my discussion brings different theoretical and historical positions in contact with each other. I am less interested in demonstrating how theories outmode each other than in how new theories develop in tension and in contact with older theories and how they rewrite traditions in different ways, both absorbing and rejecting or simply "othering" certain elements or ways of thinking.

## 3. Hermeneutic Circles, Dialogic Spirals, and Interactive Loops

Among the theories that conceive interpretation according to a dialogical model, Hans-Georg Gadamer's hermeneutics has become the most prominent among literary critics—especially in its critical appropriation or transformation by the so-called Constance School, namely Wolfgang Iser's reader-response theory (*Wirkungsaesthetik*) and Hans Robert Jauss's reception aesthetics. In "Text and Interpretation," Gadamer reminds us that the term "interpretation" is derived from the role of the translator as mediator between the languages of different cultures (33). In a more general sense, interpretation, for Gadamer, is an anthropological modality of being that achieves a never-completed mediation between human beings and the world. Texts serve as intermediary objects (*Zwischenprodukte*) in such a mediation; their manifestation as writing operates as a temporary stasis in an ongoing dialogical process.

Gadamer grants literary texts a special status in this context since their self-presentation of language causes its referential dimension, its linkage to a represented outside, temporarily to disappear. In Gadamer's interactive and dialogical theory of interpretation, the meaning of literary texts is never fixed or enclosed in them, but created by readers who actively mediate the "horizon" of a text—its historical or linguistic alterity—with their own horizon. Drawing on this Gadamerian model, Jauss develops his theory of literary reception, arguing that readers perform a "fusion of horizons" (*Horizontverschmelzung*) in order to receive historically remote literary texts (see "Literary History"). Interestingly, according to Jauss an "aesthetic event" only occurs when a text resists such a fusion and, refusing to confirm the reader's expectations and preconceptions, asserts its own alterity. For both Gadamer and Jauss, the reception of a literary work is thus an experience of alterity. Yet this alterity is not given and may therefore not be "found" in a text, but appears only as an effect of frustrated expectations regarding the aesthetic norms, tastes, and cultural prejudices that readers derive from their own tradition and history of reading. Alterity is thus not a property of texts but is generated in the production of meaning. As works pass from one cultural or historical context to another, their meaning, as well as their alterity, changes accordingly because they will be generated within a new horizon of expectations.

Judging from this perspective, Gadamer would, for example, have to find the Tiv's interpretation of Bohannan's *Hamlet* utterly appropriate, especially since they also follow another of his main principles of understanding: instead of rejecting Bohannan's story as other, meaningless, or aesthetically inferior to their own stories, they, on the contrary, go out of their way to make it as strong as possible in order to be able to accept it within their own tradition. This is precisely what Gadamer requires from interpreters and critics, namely, that, instead of finding weakness in whatever appears as cultural or theoretical alterity, they engage another position at its highest level.

I do not know how Gadamer would really react to the Tiv's *Hamlet*, but his reaction would be a challenging testing ground for his position in relation to cross-cultural readings, especially because the weakness in Gadamer's hermeneutics lies in the fact that it considers the appropriation of otherness only within one's own tradition. Gadamer emphasizes the alterity of Greek culture in relation to German culture, for example, not as a cultural otherness but as a historical otherness of one single Western tradition. This exclusive emphasis on appropriations of historical otherness at the expense of intercultural otherness all but ignores the fundamental ambivalence and historical violence of intercultural appropriations. That cultural, sexist, or racist prejudices against otherness may determine the interpretation of literary works does not enter Gadamer's horizon, just as he does not consider the impact of historical processes of oppression, domination, exclusion, and struggle on the production and reception of literature and the arts.

Moreover, as Derrida has pointed out, Gadamer's hermeneutics lacks a concept of the unconscious and its operation in processes of reception and interpretation ("Guter Wille" 52). Accordingly, it also lacks a sense that ambivalence and violence in interpretation may result from a negative unconscious cathexis of otherness. Destructive relations to otherness are deeply engraved into the cultural unconscious, its phantasms and mythologies that vilify or romanticize the other.[9] In his tendency to ontologize his own ethics of otherness, Gadamer conceptually precludes ambivalence, conflict, denial, and oppression as crucial forces in reading and interpretation—just as his notion of dialogue ignores processes of hierarchization and marginalization, including the ensuing inequality of positions within dialogical encounters such as those between men and women.[10]

While Gadamer and Jauss base their theories of literary reception on a model of interpersonal dialogue, Wolfgang Iser's concept of the "implied reader,"[11] by contrast, emphasizes the communicative dimension inherent in texts themselves. In a sense, Iser argues that texts carry within themselves their own model according to which they attempt to shape their contact with readers. The category of the implied reader does not refer to an individual, empirical, or ideal reader of a literary text, but to the text's strategies of communication, its "guiding devices" that exert a certain control by inviting or privileging specific responses. The implicit reader is, in other words, a textual agency that actively confirms, interferes with, or disrupts a culture's familiar communicative patterns that are presumably internalized by its readers. Granting that a text cannot adapt to individual readers who, in turn, can never fully verify their responses in a face-to-face situation, Iser nonetheless insists on the interactive quality of reading. Epistemologically, the metaphor "interaction" refers to a textual agency that guides the text's reception and a reader who actively "processes" the text.

As Iser formulates it, the " 'transfer' of text to reader is often regarded as being brought about solely by the text. Any successful transfer however—though initiated by the text—depends upon the extent to which this text can activate the individual reader's faculties of perceiving and processing" (*Act* 107).

In my own model, I will expand some of Iser's assumptions, mainly by differentiating between concrete historical and psychological modes of processing, including unconscious ones. "Processing" will then appear less as a neutral "transfer" than a heavily invested "transference" between reader and text that may be understood as a process in which psychogenetic and cultural formations of otherness are brought into play. The notion of transference also allows one to perceive the literary text as an agency that invites a certain interaction, or, more precisely, a certain form of "controlled projection." While retaining the notion of two agencies involved in the reading process, the model of transference takes into account that the agency of the text performs a different role from that of the reader. Texts are thus perceived as active agencies that produce certain subject-effects in their recipients, thus enabling a form of cultural contact that transforms both agencies involved.

Working with a notion of transference requires a theory of reading with a psychological grounding. Moreover, if transference is conceived as a process that works collectively as well as individually, this grounding must draw on a cultural psychology. Among literary theorists, Mikhail Bakhtin has probed this direction most deeply. "I cannot become myself without the other. I must find myself in the other, finding the other in me" ("Toward" 311–12), writes Bakhtin, whose theory of language is inseparable from a psychology in which the psyche, the body, and language form an indivisible unit. The basic premise in Bakhtin's "philosophical anthropology" is what he calls the "absolute aesthetic need" for the other, for "the other's activity of seeing, holding, putting together and unifying, which alone can bring into being the externally finished personality; if someone else does not do it, this personality will have no existence" (qtd. in Todorov 99).[12]

Bakhtin's cultural psychology links sign to matter and meaning to the body, or—in Renate Lachmann's formulation, *soma* and *sema* are woven together into a "somatic semiotics" (242). The gaze, for Bakhtin, is not a medium of alienation but of completion. Contrary to Lacan's mirror phase, during which the subject succumbs to the ecstasy of a narcissistic illusion of unity, Bakhtin insists on the perceptual and emotional "void" of the mirror experience that bespeaks the lack of the other: "what is striking, in our external image, is a sort of strange *void*, its *ghostlike* character, and its somewhat *sinister* loneliness" (qtd. in Todorov 99).[13]

Like Sartre, Lacan sees a fatal reciprocity in the formation of the subject by the gaze of the other. In infinitely regressing spirals, two paranoid and self-conscious subjects gaze at each other, all the while trying to preserve what Sartre calls their "pseudosingularity." Bakhtin, on the contrary, stresses the "mutual gazing" of subjects who find themselves "on the boundary toward" or "outside" in the other, knowing that the attempt to preserve oneself by escaping the other means loss of self: "Cutting oneself off, isolating oneself, closing oneself off, those are the basic reasons for loss of self. . . . It turns out that every internal experience occurs on the border" ("Toward" 311).

Bakhtin coins a new word, *vnenakhodimost*, "finding oneself outside," which Todorov translates as "exotopy." Exotopy, the self-experience of an eccentric "I" on the border toward the other, is diametrically opposed to Sartre's "usurpation" by the other. The drastic difference between a Sartrean or Lacanian tradition that emphasizes mutual usurpation and a related paranoia of the other on the one hand, and a Bakhtinian notion of mutual completion and exotopy on the other, is grounded in a diametrically opposed ethics of otherness and cultural contact. If we assume that the patterns according to which a culture constructs otherness are related to its socio- and psychogenetic formation of subjects in relation to others, then these differences in perspective may be read as symptomatic indicators of a theory's implicit politics toward otherness.

Bakhtin structures not only his anthropology but also his aesthetics on the basis of his psychogenetic theory of the subject. Exotopy becomes the basic mode of artistic production: "Only the other as such can be the axiological center of the artistic vision . . . *I* is, aesthetically, unreal for itself. . . . In all aesthetic forms, the organizing force is the axiological category of the other, the relation to the other . . . " (qtd. in Todorov 99). The same holds true for Bakhtin's dialogical model of aesthetic reception. For Bakhtin, reading entails enacting one's exotopy by absorbing a text in a tension of sameness and difference in which one finds oneself on the border by transforming the other into a "self-other."

Rejecting the romantic impulse of "going native," Bakhtin also posits exotopy as the most creative mode of cultural contact.

> There is an enduring image . . . according to which to better understand a foreign culture one should live in it, and, forgetting one's own, look at the world through the eyes of this culture. . . . To be sure, to enter in some measure into an alien culture and look at the world through its eyes, is a necessary moment in the process of its understanding; but if understanding were exhausted in this moment, it would have been no more than a single duplication. . . . *Creative understanding* does not renounce its self, its place in time, its culture: it does not forget anything. The chief matter of understanding is the *exotopy* of the one who does the understanding—in time, space, and culture." (Qtd. in Todorov 109)

"To read these lines," writes Todorov, "it would seem that Bakhtin is intent in imposing to all reading, all cognition, the status of ethnology, the discipline

that defines itself by the exotopy of its researcher in relation to his object . . . "
(110). And Bakhtin indeed predicates aesthetic experience upon a model of
cultural contact. Just as, for Bakhtin, one must first approach a foreign culture
on its own terms, in order then "to use one's temporal and cultural exotopy"
(109) to mediate its otherness, aesthetic experience cannot be exhausted in
pure mimesis but must provide a transformative mediation of otherness from
the position of exotopy.

Bakhtin's theory of literary language reflects this model of aesthetic experience. In its most productive form, literary language is itself dialogical, retaining
the traces of otherness, of "alien voices." Carnivalesque texts carry within
them the memory of the cultural unconscious, and of the body's Other, the
grotesque body whose drama repeats the exotopy of the subject. They celebrate
and exalt the heterogeneous voices of those excluded from the official cultural
codes.

Despite the sinister conditions under which it was produced during the
Stalin era, Bakhtin's utopian concept of carnivalesque literature retains a re-
markable cultural optimism. Literary language and aesthetic experience fulfill
for Bakhtin a positive, subversive, and transformative cultural function. Neither cultural contact nor the psychogenetic formation of the subject appear
under their dark aspects because Bakhtin tries to emphasize structural conditions of cultural encounters rather than historical pathologies. But this choice
runs the risk of romanticizing and ontologizing positive or utopian dialogical
encounters. Bakhtinian critics remind us of the many historical phases of a
"carnival gone bad," releasing destructive rather than liberating energies, or of
the fact that the periodic contestation of power in carnivalesque rituals may
ultimately remain nothing but a stabilizing release from within (see especially
Stallybrass and White). "Indeed carnival is so vivaciously celebrated," writes
Terry Eagleton, "that the necessary political criticism is almost too obvious to
make. Carnival, after all, is a *licensed* affair in every sense, a permissible rupture
of hegemony. . . . As Shakespeare's Olivia remarks, there is no slander in an allowed fool" (148). In a similar vein, Mary Russo and Julia Kristeva show that,
throughout history, the grotesque body has been gendered. Accordingly, its
figuration in literature operates not only as a liberation from constraining conventions of the body or the threat of its mortality, but also enforces cultural
stereotypes of the feminine body and its phantasmatic abjection.[14] Cultural
and feminist critics alike insist on politicizing the carnivalesque, its dialogical
potential and its inherent ambivalence: it may work as a ritual that ultimately

reinforces institutionalized power, but it may also become a site of symbolic struggle, a catalyst that releases powerful subversive energies.

## 4. Socio- and Psychogenesis of Reading

As we have seen, Bakhtin's anthropological theory of culture draws heavily on a psychogenetic theory of the subject, placing a particular emphasis on language as a mediator of otherness. Yet, Bakhtin pays hardly any attention to individual or collective histories of reading and their cultural effects. Such histories do not evolve according to linear or set teleological patterns. While it is true that we "grow up" in our reading habits, it is equally true that parts of our early experiences of reading or listening to stories will be preserved throughout our lives as a potential source of vital pleasure. Instead of being completely abandoned, these early modes of reading are altered when fused with new modes we acquire later. Different modes of reading may compete with or supplement each other and, depending on given historical or psychological needs, we may privilege one form over the other or enjoy them alternately. The further we develop our habits of reading, the more differentiated, complex, and ambivalent they become. Just as the child increasingly perceives the outside world or other people as differentiated and other, imaginary worlds and characters become other too. Habits of ignoring or effacing otherness that appear adequate at a certain stage of development or in a certain cultural setting may appear inadequate, violent, or destructive in others. Generally, processes of socialization work toward an increasing differentiation between self and other, inside and outside, and a related capacity to negotiate otherness. This process of differentiation, however, should not be viewed merely in terms of separation, but also in terms of relatedness. The capacity to relate to otherness in nondestructive ways is as important as the ability to distinguish between self and other. In the case of aesthetic experience, relatedness is particularly crucial since—as I stated earlier—literary otherness needs to resonate in order to unfold its effects. I would even argue that literature initiates us into new modes of relatedness as well as separation. In the following I will look in more detail at the two most extreme forms of relatedness and separation, namely, introjection and rejection.

In the genesis of the subject as well as the history of cultural relations, introjection and rejection are considered to be archaic modes of relating to otherness. We take in, eat, or devour what we want to assimilate; we spit out or vomit what we want to reject. The use of oral metaphors in describing the act of reading reflects this "cannibalistic" mode of reception. We "devour" a book and sometimes we cannot "digest" it. Oral imagery also pervades the rhetoric of philosophical aesthetics and literary criticism, suggesting that reading may follow archaic modes of appropriating or rejecting otherness—as we can see, for example, in Hegel's metaphorical description of reading where the written word is "taken in" and disappears like bread and wine when we take the Holy Sacrament.[15]

Rejection as the opposite of introjection, fusion, or assimilation is a more ambiguous form of relating to otherness. At a very early phase of relating to fictional worlds, a child still integrates the two archaic modes of rejection and introjection or fusion. After all, the rejection of evil characters takes place during the fusion with an imaginary world. In itself very complex and ambivalent, this rejection is frequently accompanied by a latent fascination or imaginary identification with the oppressor. Early forms of cultural experience hardly ever reveal a complete rejection of an imaginary world. Rejecting specific cultural experiences already presupposes a function of judgment or defense mechanisms against otherness.

Winnicott describes another early relation to language: the use of sounds as a transitional object in early childhood. A child may perceive the sound of her own voice as both inside and outside, "I" and "Not-I." Constitutive of the transitional space, this paradoxical experience initiates the differentiation of self and other and helps the establishment of self-boundaries. Winnicott considers the transitional objects as forerunners of cultural objects, maintaining that even in later life our experience of cultural objects will take place in a transitional space in which conventional boundaries and distinctions between objects are temporarily altered or removed. Literature and art provide, according to Winnicott, a protected "transitional space"[16] that may temporarily reinvoke the pleasures of primordial experiences by breaking down the boundaries between the real and the imaginary. While such a breakdown would entail the threat of psychosis if experienced in everyday life, the transitional space rather induces it to reshape the boundaries of subjectivity.

Since I have elsewhere developed a theory of the transitional space of poetic language, I recall here only those aspects directly relevant for a theory that posits reading as a form of cultural contact. During a specific phase in the development of reading, children typically treat literary characters or imaginary worlds in a "transitional" way, partly assimilating, partly maintaining their otherness. Listening to a fairy tale or watching a puppet play, a child might, for example, say, "I *am* the princess," and have nonetheless a diffuse knowledge that she (or he, since literary identification works across gender boundaries) simultaneously is and is not the princess. Reality-testing is simply not at stake. When he was about three years old, my son Manuel used to enact characters from his books, while referring to himself as the "reader." While he "was" Cleopatra's tiger (inspired by *Asterix and Cleopatra*), he talked about Manuel (himself) as someone else. I once asked him, "So you do know Manuel, Tiger? Where do you know him from?" "Oh, sure I know him," he answered, "don't you remember that he used to look at me in a book?"

Such "transitional reading" may never completely disappear. Georges Poulet's phenomenological theory of reading, in fact, is particularly sensitive to this type of reception. Poulet's metaphors describe paradoxical aesthetic experiences similar to those Winnicott considers typical for the transitional space:

> The extraordinary fact in the case of a book is the falling away of the barriers between you and it. You are inside it; it is inside you; there is no longer outside nor inside. (42)

> Reading, then, is the act in which the subjective principle which I call I, is modified in such a way that I no longer have the right, strictly speaking, to consider it as my *I*. (45)

In this reading process, the experience of otherness is no longer separate from the experience of the self. Poulet's rhetoric posits the text as an agency that displaces the reader's "I": "a work of literature becomes at the expense of the reader whose own life it suspends a sort of human being, that is a mind conscious of itself and constituting itself in me as the subject of its own objects" (47). Thus perceiving reading as an "annexation of my consciousness by another" (47), Poulet relegates the reader to a peripheral onlooker: "I myself, although conscious of whatever I may be conscious of, play a much more humble role, content to record passively all that is going on in me" (47).

Curiously, the notion of "passive recording" seems to be motivated by the fear of bringing something alien to the text that violates its otherness. Yet, while it may, at first glance, appear as if Poulet empowered the text by endowing it with the capacity completely to occupy the reader's consciousness, he ultimately deemphasizes the most dramatic impact of literature, namely, its capacity to elicit the reader's active involvement. In contrast to Poulet, whose passive reader succumbs to an "annexation of consciousness," a Winnicottian model rather posits a reader who actively shapes the text that, in turn, will transform her.

Winnicott's model is crucial for my own theory of reading because he emphasizes the ways in which we transpose early patterns of relating to otherness onto later cultural encounters. Even though such patterns are further developed and adapted to new conditions, their psychogenetic formation may illustrate the permanence of certain archaic reactions to, desires for, or fears of otherness. Moreover, Winnicott develops a psychological and cultural theory in one; or, more precisely, he performs a systematic transcoding between psychological and cultural aspects of maturational processes. Used as a theory of reading, Winnicott's model then helps to perceive how psychological and cultural aspects of reading are inextricably interwoven.

The notion of a transitional space of literature emphasizes not only the affinities but also the differences between reading and other forms of cultural contact. The transitional space grants a certain license from the constraints of the social, the requirements of censorship, and other normative operations of consciousness. Therefore we may, in the transitional space, act out fantasies and fears, enact relations that would otherwise be restricted if not taboo, or temporarily dissolve boundaries that are necessary to maintain in actual cultural encounters. We may even expose ourselves to a dissolution of the boundaries between the real and the imaginary, which would otherwise induce a psychotic experience.

In this context, unconscious aesthetic experience is crucial because it brings us in contact with various forms of internal otherness. According to Winnicott, we encounter otherness not only as external otherness (the outside world, another person, a foreign culture), but also as internal otherness, constituted by repressed or unconscious thoughts, emotions, or moods. Apart from the repressed, the unconscious, according to Winnicott, also includes the most intimate aspects of the self that must be protected from intrusion and violation through direct communication. Paradoxically, however, there is also a desire to bring others in contact with or, as Winnicott says, to be "found" in this secret inner space.[17] Since such a contact must be indirect, it requires an alternative language which, similar to dream language, may communicate without violating the censorship of consciousness. Winnicott identifies literature as a privileged space of resonance that allows one through complex processes of mediation and transference indirectly to communicate about the secret inner space and the unconscious. Winnicott's spatial metaphors must be understood according to a dynamic model in which cultural and internal otherness alike are formed and transmitted through transcoding operations that continually loop back and forth across the flexible boundaries between outside and inside. In this dynamic mutual transcoding, the cultural is continually forming the psychological and vice versa. The unconscious as an inner space does not appear as an essence, but results from an ongoing reshaping of self-boundaries. Within this context, literature appears as a medium that takes part in renegotiating what is defined as otherness. We may then say, like Poulet, that in reading we become "other." Winnicott, however, would not take this as an "annexation of consciousness," but as the most creative expansion of oneself.

## 5. Symbolic Vicissitudes: Constructions of Otherness in French Theory[18]

Within the range of psychoanalytic theories, Jacques Lacan presents a very different view of the subject's relation to the other/Other. The most crucial difference results from the fact that Lacan tends to ontologize and universalize the subject's negative formation by the other, while Winnicott sees it as culturally variable. In one of Lacan's tirades against Piaget, he speaks about the child's "invasion" by myths and fairy tales in a way that recalls the "annexation of consciousness" in Poulet's reader. "This child, we see that he is prodigiously open to everything concerning the way of the world that the adult brings to him. Doesn't anyone ever reflect on what this prodigious porosity to everything in myth, legend, fairy tales, history, the ease with which he lets himself be invaded by these stories, signifies, as to his sense of the other?" ("The ego" 49). Language in general or, more precisely, speech, for Lacan functions violently to cut the subject off from itself. The function of speech, for Lacan, becomes "so firmly inclined in the direction of the other that it is no longer even mediation, but only implicit violence, a reduction of the other to a correlative function of the subject's ego" ("The ego" 51).

Here we encounter one of the most influential figures of contemporary French thought: the figuration of language and the symbolic order as Other, as a divisive force in the subject. Yet, this otherness of language is perceived as an internal one, marking the subject's ambivalent relation to the symbolic order which is always both inside and outside, self and other. By temporarily bridging the internal gap within the subject, language operates paradoxically as the only means to heal the wound it has caused.[19] A particular use of language such as the transference in the psychoanalytic talking cure or the indirection of poetic language may outwit the constraints of the symbolic and allow the subject temporarily to emerge within language.

Lacan's linguistic revision of psychoanalysis has provided the background against which other French theorists such as Foucault, Derrida, Kristeva, or Irigaray have formulated their own theories of the relationship between language and the subject. My following discussion focuses on the role specific theories attribute to poetic language as a mediator of otherness. Most French theorists, in fact, privilege literature as a form of discourse, another voice that transgresses the boundaries of the symbolic order and—under certain conditions—operates as a discourse of the Other transmitted via literary transference.

Lacan himself reads literary texts mainly to confirm his basic assumptions about the supremacy of the signifier. For Lacan, the symbolic order operates as an Other that divides the subject from its own truth. In a triadic model that distinguishes the symbolic, the imaginary, and the real, the subject is trapped by the narcissistic functions of the imaginary and therefore marked by *méconnaissance*. Interestingly, Lacan presupposes a certain "othering" of language as a basis for overcoming the narcissistic negation of the other performed in the common encounters between "imaginary intersubjectivities." While confirming the supremacy of the signifier, poetic language also serves as a model of speaking or reading against the grain—which is why literature, as Lacan suggests in his "Seminar on 'The Purloined Letter,' " affects our history and the "rootedness of our being."

Lacan's own readings of literature operate mainly as illustrations of his theory. Shakespeare's Hamlet, for example, is used to demonstrate how, scarred by "insufficient mourning" ("Desire" 39), Hamlet "has lost the way of his desire" ("Desire" 12) for the mother as the Other of every demand. Afflicted by melancholia, Hamlet acts as impersonator of the death drive: "Life is concerned solely with dying—'To die, to sleep, perchance to dream,' as a certain gentleman put it, just when what was at issue was exactly that—to be or not to be" ("Desire, Life" 233). For Lacan, Hamlet's melancholic condition, however, only radicalizes what he posits as the human condition in general: "This life we're captive of, this essentially alienated life, ex-sisting, this life in the other, is as such joined to death, it always returns to death . . . " ("Desire, Life" 233).

In this reading, otherness is literally impersonated by the mother as the addressee of every demand, an incorporation of the symbolic order, the Other. Consequently, for Lacan, this desire for the mother also generates the "life in the other" that joins the subject to death. Interestingly, in this context Lacan defines "healing" as "[t]he realization of the subject through a speech which comes from elsewhere, traversing it" ("Desire, Life" 233). Lacan does not ask how we are affected by reading *Hamlet*, but if it is true, as Lacan says, that literature affects our history and being, then it may function, like psychoanalytic transference, as a "speech which comes from elsewhere," thus connecting this "life in the other" back to the subject.

Methodologically, however, instead of using *Hamlet* as a "speech which comes from elsewhere," Lacan uses it to echo his own discourse. In this sense his procedure resembles that of the Tiv. Just as the Tiv used Hamlet to affirm their own cultural values, so Lacan, too, interpellates him as witness to confirm his most valued assumptions about the subject: its subjection to the Other and the death drive. Both the Tiv and Lacan thus treat Shakespeare's (or Bohannan's) story less as an informant about a different culture, than as a witness to their own. Interestingly, they diverge in reading the very same act, namely, Gertrude's marriage to Claudius, in opposite ways: for the Tiv, the marriage of a younger brother to the older brother's widow *is* an act of mourning, whereas, for Lacan, it indicates its scandalous omission. Lacan's reading is thus not as fundamentally different from the Tiv's as it may appear at first glance; it only remains closer to home.

In contrast to Lacan, for whom the symbolic order functions in every culture as Other, Foucault emphasizes otherness as a force generated within cultures for the sake of their self-definition. Otherness is generated by deviations from culturally determined norms or transgressions of the boundaries that cultures draw in order to mark what they want to include or exclude. Foucault thus defines the symbolic order according to its distinction from and rejection of a counterpart, an Other that will henceforth threaten the order (as if it came) from outside. This relationship between an order and its other varies historically and can, in principle, produce three types of ex- or inclusion: A culture reserves a place for otherness in the topography of the order, be it in the center or at the periphery; a culture attempts the total exclusion and excommunication of otherness; or a culture performs a kind of repressive incommunication where otherness is absorbed under the conditions of order by means of a rationalization or, as Foucault calls it, "colonizing reason" (*Madness* ix-xii).

Even though, for Foucault, otherness is always culturally determined, he is less interested in concrete encounters with other cultures than in the various forms of internal otherness encountered within one's own culture—such as madness, criminality, sexual deviancy, poverty, or even childhood. A culture has different options in dealing with internal otherness, for example, by trying through incarceration to delimit contact with criminals and the mentally insane or by effacing the otherness of childhood through the training of little adults.

Literature, for Foucault, relates directly to a culture's internal otherness. Distinguishing the literature of the last two centuries from that of earlier periods, Foucault claims that only the cultural isolation of a particular literary language led to the emergence of literature proper in its form as "nondiscursive language" (*Order* ch. 8, sect. V). Foucault treats literature as a culturally sanctioned practice of transgression, a space of discourse within the void of what remains otherwise silenced, unsayable. By voicing the other, the excluded and the unsayable, literature establishes itself as a privileged medium for bringing the internal otherness of a culture back into contact and circulation. To fulfill this transgressive function, literature needs to invent modes of breaking through official codes—for example, by using indirection, self-reference, or silence. This is why, for Foucault, the cultural function of literary language is neither determined by what it says nor by the structures that create meaning, but by the "folds" through which language doubles itself up, implies itself, and reveals the codes from which it breaks away. Speaking the voice of the Other, poetic language as a signifier radically differs from and interferes with all other signifiers ("La Folie" 573–82).

Aesthetic experience accordingly resides not in a game of interpretation and attribution of meaning, but in an opening toward the radical otherness of the literary signifier—an experience that borders on paradox and resembles an exposure to madness. After having been established until the end of the nineteenth century as two incompatible forms of speech, literature and madness, according to Foucault, have since then started to communicate with each other (see "La Folie"). Perceived as a culture's internal otherness, madness and literature thus open us to the Other of our own or different cultures.

Foucault's concept of modernist literature as mediator of its culture's internal otherness calls for a particular form of reading that retains otherness. As David Carroll writes, "Foucault's 'paraesthetic' critical strategy, to a large extent, is aimed at giving these texts their due, allowing them to speak in their own terms and act according to their own strategies, that is, without any interference from discourses that would limit their force and conceptualize and thus destroy their beauty" (109). Ultimately, this ethics of noninterference leads to a critical impasse, namely, a refutation of interpretation that would make criticism superfluous or at least epigonic to the texts it allows to stand on their own.

But, as Carroll argues, "the strategy of non-interpretation is difficult to practice" (127), and it comes therefore as no surprise that Foucault's own readings of literature "are all marked by the very theories they most strenuously attempt to avoid" (215).

Foucault's position is crucial for theories that consider reading as a form of cultural contact. In arguing that literature brings us in contact with a culture's internal otherness, he also demonstrates that the ways in which we read literature determine our own contact with that otherness. Foucault takes an extreme stance that recalls that of an anthropologist "going native." His resistance against interpretation stems from a radical identification with these transgressive literary voices, a claim "to be one with their disruptive force" (D. Carroll 128), and a related fear that any interpretation would contaminate their otherness by subjecting it to the power relations that have "othered" or marginalized them in the first place. But this politics of noninterference would in the end, as Carroll rightly points out, reduce the critic to "stand[ing] silently in reverence and terror before it" (127). Does this romantic impulse not entail that the very "gift" of literature is refused, namely, to serve as a *mediator* of internal otherness? If we attempt to leave literature standing on its own, do we not turn it into a museum piece to be looked at from the outside, without interference, but also without transference, engagement, and interaction?

Derrida shares Foucault's threat of reappropriation and his impulse to protect literature from the imposition of philosophical categories and conceptualization, but at the same time he affirms that, even though literary texts may determine our approach to them, no reading of literature can ever be completely on its own terms or purely literary. Literature is other than philosophy, has its own specificity, its own relation to writing (*écriture*), but turning it into the Other of philosophy or, more generally, a delimited space of alterity, would mean for Derrida, as Carroll argues, to isolate it from "the general context of literature's relations with the multiple forms of the 'non-literary' that it both opens onto and is closed off from" (97).

Literature, in other words, is permanently in contact with its nonliterary environment—be it philosophical, political, cultural, psychological—but, since Derrida refuses to draw boundaries between these spheres, literature may not assume a position of radical alterity. If there is an outside of literature it is already inside since, instead of boundaries, Derrida imagines a constant flux. Instead of a distinct otherness of poetic language, Derrida rather stresses poetic language as process. Texts are produced by and produce movements of *différance*, of deferring differentiation. Difference as a distinctness of defined elements emerges from the same process of *différance* in which, as the neologism suggests, nothing is ever simply what it is in terms of a definite object. This is as true of single elements of an order as it is of systems, structures, texts, and most likely, persons. The (always provisional) definiteness and order we establish in our ways of world making is merely a retrospective projection.

"Identity," thus, is always a provisional illusion liable to change by any interfering "event." In this strict sense, a dialectics of the Same and the Other is no longer possible. Where it appears, it is a stasis in a flux, imposed and suffered as an inhibition. Derrida moves beyond a Lacanian notion of an imposed and eventually duped symbolic order as well as a Foucauldian notion of a culture defined by boundaries and their transgression. Paradoxically, in an all-pervading textuality where everything is flux and growth, the difference between otherness and sameness would eventually efface itself in the ongoing movement of *différance*. There is ultimately no need for an otherness that is radically distinct from sameness, for nothing is ever the same. And yet, the notion of otherness persists in the radical otherness of *différance* itself, which opposes its constant movement to all types of identity and presence.

If we want to attribute an implied "ethics" of otherness to Derrida, then we can do so only in the sense that his philosophy defies any stabilization of a same. Derrida recognizes no Other on ontological grounds, but there is, nevertheless, a constant struggle to prevent a living process from freezing into a mortified identity. "The power of textuality to burst through semantic horizons" becomes the site for a struggle to resist the traps of representation as stasis. Derrida's antirepresentational stance or, as Herbert Blau has formulated it, his "almost compulsive assault on representation" (167), may be understood as a paradoxical move to retain the otherness of a continual flow by defying the otherness induced by the stasis of representation—a stasis that, for Derrida, always entails reification or fetishization.

Derrida's position is pertinent for a theory that posits reading as a form of cultural contact, because he criticizes Western philosophy precisely for absorbing otherness into a metaphysics of presence. But how do texts that are themselves readings retain otherness, or, to put it more precisely, how can we read without the violence of reducing otherness? And, finally, do philosophical and literary texts display different relations to otherness? These questions are difficult to address from a Derridean perspective, because Derrida's play of signifiers ultimately effaces the boundaries between a text and its reception as well as between different types of discourse such as philosophy and literature.

Edward Said claims that Derrida's philosophy of *différance* aims at undermining the power texts have over us, alerting us to the fact "that so long as we believe that language is mainly a representation of something else, we cannot see what language does" (*World* 201). According to Said, we react against this power of texts with an impulse to deform them, to perform travesties or philosophical deconstructions. Said thus turns Derrida's terms around, claiming that, far from retaining the otherness of the texts he reads, Derrida performs a deliberate deformation that breaks their power, or, more specifically for Derrida, the grip the metaphysical tradition of philosophy continues to have on Western culture. To illustrate his claim, Said mirrors Derrida's deconstructions in an involuntary travesty of *Hamlet*, performed by a bad theater company, and used by Charles Dickens in *Great Expectations* for a doubly comic effect (*World* 196–201). In reading Dickens's passage, Said argues, we not only laugh at the ham actors who, by performing *Hamlet*, transform the play into a bad comedy, or at the narrator Pip, who is mocked by this very performance in his pretensions to be a gentleman, but we also enjoy the travesty of the play because it loosens the grip the power *Hamlet* has on us and a whole cultural tradition. Even if we concede that "a misreading of texts is made possible by texts themselves for whom—in the best of them—every meaning possibility exists in a raw unresolved state" (*World* 203), what we enjoy in Dickens's travesty is a deliberate playful deformation of the text.

If we revert to the Tiv's reading of *Hamlet*, we may see that Laura Bohannan and her readers probably enjoyed the Tiv's "deformation" of the play on similar grounds. We take pleasure in the twist the Tiv give to Shakespeare's plot precisely because it mirrors our culture back to us as radically other. Pursuing this scenario one step further, we could even assume that, when Bohannan told the story of Hamlet, the Tiv were well aware of the cultural otherness of Hamlet's setting. Might they then not have performed and enjoyed their willful "deformation" with a certain vengeance, precisely because it constitutes such an ironical inversion of the anthropologist's role as witness? In "witnessing" a crucial artifact of Bohannan's culture, the Tiv, unwittingly or not, performed a cheerful travesty of the violence of anthropological readings.

Foucault and Derrida's projects of breaking the power of Western philosophy with its systems of thought and classification, as well as Lacan's analysis of the constraining power of the symbolic order, have inspired critical debates—particularly within French feminism—that call for a revision of their basic premises from a gendered position. Ranging from critical appropriation to outright rejection, French feminists have taken up the challenge presented by poststructuralism and deconstruction, especially their attention to otherness, marginality, deviance, and transgression. Since Simone de Beauvoir's *The Second Sex*, feminist theories have continued to press the issue of woman as other and to refine their theoretical models of otherness. Twenty-five years after Beauvoir and inspired by deconstruction, Luce Irigaray published *Speculum of the Other Woman*, a feminist critique of philosophical and psychoanalytic theories that posit the subject as male and woman as other. In sharp opposition to the Lacanian economy of the phallic gaze—particularly its obsession with the "one," with sameness and its concomitant paranoia of the other (139)—Irigaray envisions "an *other* libidinal economy" (48), derived from women's different relationship to the imaginary and to *jouissance*—an economy that privileges "a heterogeneity unknown in the practice of and discourse about (designated) libido" (48).

Subject to the economy of patriarchal capitalism and its control of maternal spheres, this other economy must, according to Irigaray, remain largely unsymbolized, grasping the feminine only as the unrepresentable, voiced in the dissenting discourse of an *écriture feminine*. Modeled after the operation of the unconscious in language, Irigaray's concept of *écriture feminine* draws on the historical affiliation of the feminine with the unconscious, thus reinscribing the familiar binarism that affiliates woman with otherness and the unconscious. Even though Irigaray constructs woman as irreducibly other, not subjectible to the symbolic and representational strategies that contain "the threat of otherness" (135), every single one of her conceptual moves constitutes itself through an inversion of the values of a rejected male economy of the same. Woman ironically ends up with the same designations attributed to her since time immemorial: the irrational, the unrepresentable, and the unconscious. Moreover, despite Irigaray's critique of Lacan's oculocentrism and simultaneous blindness to any form of radical otherness or heterogeneity, Irigaray's own model remains negatively fixated on oculocentrist predications of otherness, because her indirect affirmation of Lacan's model of the phallic gaze ties her negatively to a French tradition haunted by a paranoia of the other's gaze—a paranoia that Lacan himself had taken over from Sartre.[20]

In "Rereading Irigaray," Margaret Whitford foregrounds a rarely discussed ambivalence in Irigaray's other libidinal economy. While figuring woman as unrepresentable heterogeneity, Irigaray also acknowledges that, due to her negative tie to a presymbolic state of fusion,[21] this very unrepresentability leaves her vulnerable to a psychotic incapacity of symbolization. This is where the utopian project of an *écriture feminine*—however vague it remains in its radical otherness to the symbolic order—becomes crucial. By claiming *écriture feminine* as a space in which women may develop their own symbolic mediations, modes of sublimation, and boundaries, Irigaray ultimately challenges the historical conditions under which the feminine is inscribed within language.

While Irigaray herself does not provide a discursive model for this new textual economy that affirms the capacity of symbolization, Kristeva, in *The Revolution of Poetic Language*, links the maternal economy with the subversive power of poetic language. Distinguishing symbolic, semiotic, and thetic functions in a triadic model of language, Kristeva casts the *semiotic* as "a psychosomatic modality of the signifying process" (*Revolution* 96). Like Irigaray's *écriture feminine*, Kristeva's *semiotic* is linked with the maternal and marked by the heterogeneity, fluidity, and motility of the presymbolic; but, in opposition to Irigaray, Kristeva insists on the inscription of the semiotic in the symbolic. As a figuration, an organized preverbal space or a kinetic functional stage which precedes the establishment of the sign (*Kristeva Reader* 95), the semiotic is necessary to the symbolic order but not identical with it: "Indifferent to language, enigmatic and feminine, this space underlying the written is rhythmic, unfettered, irreducible to its intelligible verbal translation; it is musical, anterior to judgement, but restrained by a single guarantee: syntax" (*Kristeva Reader* 97). Since voice, gesture, colors, tones, and rhythms form the material ground susceptible to semiotization, we could also say that the semiotic creates the mood of a text.

The semiotic space does not yet know an other. Otherness comes into play only with the *symbolic*, which Kristeva, following Lacan, defines as "a social effect of the relation to the other" (*Kristeva Reader* 96-7). A transitional phase between the semiotic and the symbolic, the so-called *thetic phase* (*Kristeva Reader* 98-100), initiates the differentiation of subject and object, and the emergence of the other. The thetic as "the threshold of language" (99-100)[22] operates both as rupture and boundary between the semiotic and the symbolic and posits the subject as signifiable, separate, and always confronted by an other. Like Lacan, Kristeva assumes that the mother "as the addressee of every demand" occupies the place of alterity: "The gap between the imaged ego and drive motility, between the mother and the demand made on her, is precisely the break that establishes what Lacan calls the place of the Other as the place of the 'signifier' " (*Kristeva Reader* 101). The thetic phase thus emerges as "the place of the Other, as the precondition for signification, that is, the precondition *for* the positing of language" (*Kristeva Reader* 102).

What, then, is the revolution of poetic language? "In artistic practices the semiotic—the precondition of the symbolic—is revealed as that which destroys the symbolic" (*Kristeva Reader* 103), Kristeva writes, while at the same time asserting that, in opposition to fantasy or psychosis, "poetic 'distortions' of the signifying chain" do not yield to the "drive attacks against the thetic" but instead lead to a "second degree thetic" (*Kristeva Reader* 103). Poetic language thus uses the semiotic not to refute the thetic (which would amount to a psychotic refutation of language), but to "pulverize" it. Since for Kristeva (as for Lacan) enunciation presupposes "a displaced subject, absent from the signified and signifying position" (*Kristeva Reader* 106), the semiotic helps the subject to emerge within language. While the symbolic order as the place of the Other divides subject and object, the poetic disruption introduces a heterogeneity that allows subject and object to merge in a new synthesis.[23]

Kristeva positions both poetic language and the feminine as a subversive otherness within the symbolic and the Law. In an interview with Xavière Gauthier, she recalls that in our culture "writer and literature in general are considered feminine" (Gauthier 166). Both the feminine and the poetic, Kristeva argues, use the semiotic to reinsert the subject and *jouissance* into the symbolic. Both are a subversive, agonistic "other within," an "internal exteriority."[24]

Yet Kristeva also emphasizes the fundamental ambivalence of the semiotic as the place of *jouissance* as well as of a deadly narcissism or fetishism. Significantly, Kristeva calls her theory of the "subject-in-process" an "ecology," in which a mere rejection or denial of the symbolic turns destructive. Already marked by the symbolic, the semiotic nourishes not only fantasies of unbounded oceanic bliss but also of primordial violence and destruction. As the result of a phantasmatic cathexis of the pre-oedipal mother (*Powers*), violent fantasies recreate the mother as a fragmented body which threatens the subject with annihilation. Such fantasies signal the intrusion of "the *other* gaze" that marks the maternal space with the Law of the symbolic order and constitutes the mother as Other. This phallic gaze creates a phantasmatic mother, product of male fantasies and masculine designation: the phallic mother.

This overview of different French theories reveals an influential tradition that posits the subject as both constituted and simultaneously negated by the gaze of the Other. In this dynamic, otherness always operates as both external and internal otherness. An "internal exteriority" determines the relationship between consciousness and the unconscious as well as the precarious balance between a subject's exclusion from and subversive reinsertion into the symbolic order of language. In principle, anybody may occupy the position of the

Other, but the binary oppositions that constitute the symbolic order figure woman as the primary Other—which, in turn, "feminizes" all other agencies or orders that occupy the position of otherness, be it the racial other, the child, the primitive, the insane, the irrational, the poetic, the unconscious, or simply chaos.

## 6. "Other Scribes, Other Tribes": Cultural Theories of Reading[25]

The strong emphasis in French thought on otherness continues to inform newer theories in cultural criticism whose main paradigm has shifted to culture. Despite cultural criticism's profound suspicion of certain hegemonic tendencies in poststructuralism, deconstruction and first-world feminism, many of its own models nonetheless draw on French thought's pervasive critique of Western culture and its politics toward otherness.[26] Just as French feminism challenges the founders of poststructuralism from the vantage point of woman's otherness, cultural critics now challenge contemporary French theories, including feminist ones, from the vantage point of cultural, ethnic, or national otherness. This history of critical revisions, replete with intertextual appropriations or polemical refutations of theoretical positions, thus reveals its own dynamics of a cultural contact between theories, marked by highly diverse styles of appropriation and ways of dealing with a pervasive anxiety of influence.

Developed under the impact of cultural criticism and its emphasis on culture as the new theoretical paradigm, current theories of reading foreground cultural otherness in the specific sense of other cultures, races, and nations. Drawing their conceptual models from various critiques of Western capitalism, colonialism, and imperialism, they analyze the pervasive ethnocentrism of Western cultures and their destructive forms of cultural contact. Often, however, these theories perceive cultural contact exclusively as a contact between different cultures, thus neglecting to address how the dynamic interaction between different cultural spheres within a culture also shapes its modes of relating to other cultures.

To the extent that anticolonialism and anti-ethnocentrism are the driving force behind the current movement of cultural criticism, it operates with a specific ethics of otherness. "Decolonization" seems to be the pervasive attitude that defines this ethics—be it the decolonization of other cultures, ethnic minorities, women, or the unconscious. The rhetoric of decolonization assumes that the structures and effects of colonialism have so thoroughly marked patterns of cultural contact in general that it makes sense to compare the relationship to cultural otherness in general with the dynamic of colonialism. As in the case of French feminism, we once again witness here the conceptual privileging of one position of otherness—here that of the colonized—as a model for cultural contact in general that may serve as a basis for an oppositional ethics. Within this ethics, however, a tension has developed between ethnically or nationally oriented cultural critics and transnational ones who, following a different ethics of otherness, highlight the increasing globalization of cultures. Paul Rabinow, for example, defines an "ethics of a critical cosmopolitanism" as "suspicious of sovereign powers, universal truths, . . . local authenticity, moralisms high and low" (258). Both trends share the goal of working through the legacy of colonialism and imperialism but differ radically in their politics of doing so.

It is by now a commonplace to say that, since the discovery of the New World, Western cultures have constructed their own image through ethnocentric readings of other cultures. Against this historical heritage of ethnocentric projections, postmodern anthropology and postcolonial cultural criticism in general seek to develop readings of otherness that critically interfere in and disrupt ethnocentric and colonialist perceptions of the other. The rhetoric of a "decolonization of knowledge" (Pratt) indicates that, as Arnold Krupat has claimed, current "ethnocriticism" seeks a "conversation between Western and non-Western perspectives" (29). To pursue this ambitious goal, one of the crucial tasks may be that the protagonists involved in staging such a conversation come to terms with the very nature and ambivalence of projection as a mode of relating to otherness.

A certain reduction of otherness through projection seems inevitable in any cross-cultural "conversation," or, more generally, in any reading of otherness. It is an operation of "making sense" by reducing complexity.[27] Anthropologist Pierre Maranda even stresses projection as the most central mode of reception:

> We phrase our accounts of the "others" so as to make them understandable to other "selves"; we interpret what we see and experience in the light of the ideologies that mold us, as we try to bear witness to the diversity as well as to the permanent structures of mankind. . . . We say that rejection manifests a failure of the reader's accommodation to new parameters. But what is acceptance? Only when one has reduced a society or a piece of literature to congruency with one's own prejudices and stereotypes does one have the feeling of proper understanding. (183)

Here Maranda, however, effaces the difference between literature and anthropology and hence the very otherness of poetic language. One of the most crucial differences between an anthropologist's reading of other cultures and the reading of literary texts results from the fact that cultures are not there to be read by anthropologists, while literary texts are there to be read by readers. Maranda might be right in claiming that, by the mere fact that it entails an uninvited intrusion, any ethnographic reading of other cultures constitutes a form of violence (183), but to generalize this violence for readings of literary texts ignores their very cultural purpose. Literary texts have been written for readers and depend on readings to come alive.

As I have argued, literature itself provides a mode of cultural contact and has done so for centuries. Practiced as a virtual encounter with otherness, reading may, in certain cases, precisely help to reduce the structural or cultural violence of reading the other/Other that is such a central concern in current theories. In addition to offering direct figurations of otherness and cultural contact, literary texts actually deploy complex discursive strategies and aesthetic devices in order to mediate these fictional cultural encounters for their readers. Thus they form part of the cultural politics toward otherness, including the cultural imaginary which they help continually to reshape.

The reduction of a foreign culture or text to one's own prejudices can also hardly exhaust the possible range of cultural relations to otherness that we develop while we grow into a specific culture and learn or even internalize the patterns of its interaction with other cultures. As I have argued earlier, during the socio- and psychogenetic formation of the subject and the ongoing processes of cultural socialization, the mechanisms of projection need to become increasingly refined. In *Dialektik der Aufklärung*, Horkheimer and Adorno see the ability to control projection as a precondition for any distinction between inside and outside or self and other. Without such a distinction there would be no closeness or distance, no self-consciousness and responsibility for others. With the help of such distinctions, on the other hand, both affective and intellectual faculties mature by becoming more differentiated (196–209).

After a certain stage of psychogenetic development, the lack of differentiation is considered to be pathological—as we see when egocentric, narcissistic, or paranoid projections determine interaction with others. At a cultural level, such a pathology may manifest itself as the paranoid projections and annihilations of otherness we saw in the Third Reich, or, more generally, in what Said, in his assessment of contemporary politics, called the "Manichean theologizing of 'the Other' " (*World* 291). Adorno and Horkheimer perceive the differentiation of both the subject and cultural relations according to a relatively linear development of reflexivity and self-reflexivity. The subject is supposed to have the outer world *in* mind, recognizing it at the same time as *other*.[28]

Conceiving reflexivity itself as a form of "conscious projection," Horkheimer and Adorno thus see the pathological element in anti-Semitism not in projective behavior as such but in the lack of "reflected projection." They argue that in the psychohistory of anti-Semitism, projection has largely been misused as a defensive protection of self-boundaries, leading eventually to an attempt completely to destroy Semitic cultures. Based on a paranoid rejection of otherness, the cultural politics of the Nazis might serve as a drastic example. It is no coincidence that the Nazis used their holocaust model of cultural contact also to determine their politics toward literature and cultural objects in general. Their persecution and destruction of "degenerative art" may be seen as an extreme case of rejection by annihilation. Their own cultural fantasies, in turn, propagate the destruction of otherness as a mode of self-construction and preservation. In his two volumes of *Männerphantasien*, Klaus Theweleit, for example, shows how prefascist and Nazi literatures and art built their phantasmatic structures on the rejection and fantasized destruction of otherness.

In general, paranoid projections of grandeur or persecution nourish colonialist, imperialist, racist, or sexist drives to control, subjugate, or destroy otherness. According to Horkheimer and Adorno, such projections have petrified into a dominating cultural, political, and psychological pattern. The very title *Dialectics of Enlightenment* suggests that the authors see these projections as the Other or the political unconscious of the Enlightenment.

But this assessment of Enlightenment rationality retains an unresolved ambivalence. On the one hand, Adorno and Horkheimer perceive increasing reflexivity as a way of differentiating and altering pathological patterns of cultural projection; on the other hand, they show how Enlightenment values have fed into a colonialist and imperialist mentality that denigrates otherness as the irrational, the uncivilized, or the primitive. "Reflected projection" is thus doomed to fail unless one recognizes and deals with the defenses against otherness that reside in the internalized Other. Archaic fears of otherness must be differentiated according to a double strategy that reaches conscious as well as unconscious mechanisms of projection. Self-reflection as a conscious strategy needs to be complemented by a strategy that differentiates unconscious figurations and phantasms of the Other.

## Reading, Otherness, and Cultural Contact

In *The Wretched of the Earth*, Frantz Fanon analyzes the dynamic of unconscious and conscious mechanisms that determine a colonial situation and respective struggles for liberation. Since colonial power is aimed at destroying the otherness of the colonized, the colonized, in turn, may feel that they can only survive by making the colonizer's culture their own. Fanon writes, "He [the native intellectual] will not be content to get to know Rabelais and Diderot, Shakespeare and Edgar Allan Poe, he will bind them to his intellectuality as closely as possible" (218–19). For Fanon, the process of colonization is only successfully completed once the colonized's own cultural values have been relegated to the political unconscious and become internalized as Other. As Fanon shows, the success of any cultural liberation therefore depends upon reaching the fantasies and figurations of the Other in the unconscious. This is why he pointedly invokes the classics of Western literature in order to discuss the formation of internal otherness in a colonized culture.

This dynamic, in fact, also marks inter-European colonialism—as we may see in Joyce's use of *Hamlet* in *Ulysses*. When Stephen Dedalus develops his conception of genius out of "Saxon Shakespeare's Hamlet," he plays out the intercultural anxiety of influence in colonial Ireland. By turning to Homer rather than Shakespeare, Joyce himself, as David Lloyd has argued, transgresses the focus on colonized Ireland in order to unfold "the complexity of the cultural transactions that take place in the thoroughly hybridized culture of 'West Britain,' where Irishmen discourse on English, German and Greek culture while an Englishman, Haines, studies the Celtic element in literature . . . " (101). And when, in *Finnegans Wake*, Joyce cannibalizes the name of the imperial father figure of literature in "shakespill and eggs" (161.31), alluding to Bacon claiming credit for what Shakespeare wrote, he again invokes the anxiety of influence surrounding the classics of literature. His self-ironical aside to the reader—"to understand this as well as you can, feeling how backward you are" (161.33–34)—plays not only with his own marginal status as a colonial subject of Great Britain, but also with his desire to transcend merely local Irish language games toward transcultural perspectives.[29]

A different "anxiety of influence" and negotiation of cultural, national, and linguistic boundaries is also a central concern in current cultural criticism. Arnold Krupat, for example, proposes ethnocriticism as a form of border writing that reappropriates the trope of the *frontier* for "that shifting space in which two *cultures* encounter one another" (5). Compelled by continued "efforts to move back and forth across border lines" (17), the ethnocritic, according to

Krupat, must inhabit "a position at the various frontier points where the disciplines of anthropology and literature, literature and history, history and philosophy meet and interact" (32).[30]

The notion of criticism as a border operation also informs Mary Louise Pratt's concept of the "contact zone." In *Imperial Eyes: Travel Writing and Transculturation*, Pratt revises the history of colonial travel narratives and develops a model of "criticism in the contact zone" that she considers part of "a large-scale effort to decolonize knowledge" (2). Defining "contact zones" as "social spaces where disparate cultures meet, clash, and grapple with each other, often in highly asymmetrical relations of domination and subordination" (4), Pratt treats travel writings as colonial readings of foreign cultures that "produced the rest of the world," contributed to the transculturation of native peoples and subordinated or marginal groups that "select and invent from materials transmitted to them by a dominant or metropolitan culture" (6).

Pratt's project of "decolonizing knowledge" addresses the violent appropriation of otherness in colonial readings of foreign cultures. Implicitly she also explores the status of criticism in the production and dissemination of cultural knowledge. To what extent does "ethnocriticism" remain tied to the colonial project that it criticizes and under what conditions does it really interfere with colonial practices of reading other cultures? Given the fact that even the most basic conceptual categories of ethnocriticism—such as culture, anthropology, literature, and interdisciplinarity—are Western categories, Arnold Krupat, for example, concedes that, in an absolute sense, there can be no discourse of Others that is completely free of violence. But in the pursuit of "noncoercive" cultural work and knowledge, or, more specifically, a "post-colonial, anti-imperialist, dialogical anthropology," Krupat opts for a differential and dialogical model rather than an oppositional one that rhetorically perpetuates what Fanon calls a "manichean allegory" (19).

This debate about ethnographic readings of other cultures challenges literary critics to assess fictional constructions of other cultures or, more generally, literary forms of knowledge in light of how they relate to the colonial project. How does literature contribute to what Pratt calls the "decolonization of knowledge" or what Krupat perceives as a pursuit of "noncoercive knowledge"? Much, of course, depends upon whether one grants that there are forms of knowledge that are less coercive than others in the first place—a problem that remains highly controversial in current debates. This controversy ultimately concerns the status of literary knowledge in comparison to other forms of cultural knowledge. What is the cultural work performed by the invention of specific literary forms or modes of aesthetic reflection? Since there was at all historical times a body of literature that functioned as cultural critique, the history of literature is also marked by devastating critiques of colonialism. The ways in which poetic language and literary form mediate fictional rewritings of colonial histories are crucial for addressing the specificity of literary knowledge. The cultural function of literary form—including what Jameson calls the "ideology of form"—consists to a large extent in shaping literary figurations of otherness—be it an internal otherness or that of other cultures—and thereby determining its mediation to readers. Because they work at a subliminal level, style, formal structures, and literary moods may, in fact, shape experiences of otherness even more deeply than the historical or cultural remoteness of texts.

## 7. The Politics of Otherness in Literary Experimentalism

Precisely this concern with the cultural function of literary form has led me to investigate experimental texts that invent new forms and modes of figuration and expose the materiality of poetic language. With their innovative forms, their self-reflexivity, their hermeticism, or, to use Adorno's term, their "incommunication," these texts insist on the radical othering of poetic language. Their readers' encounter with this otherness may be perceived as a form of cultural contact with other modes of discourse. Just as the formal structures of the eighteenth-century novel were developed in response to the changing modes of communication in the print culture of the time, so the self-reflexive, open, fragmentary, and experimental forms of modern and postmodern texts also react to the changing modes of communication in a global media culture. Adorno, for example, argues that modernism's presumed "incommunication" is foremost a refusal to submit to mass-produced patterns of manipulated speech and to spoon-fed, trivializing, and emotionally empty cultural fantasies. According to Adorno, the negativity of incommunicative forms counteracts the pervading modes of communication and ideologies in modern consumer societies.[31]

If, however, we want to describe this "incommunication" not in opposition to familiar forms of communication, but rather in anticipation of new ones, we will encounter a constitutive "paradox" of aesthetic form. These texts communicate precisely by "othering" the language they use, that is, by abolishing discursive and poetic conventions, by violating language's very structuring principles, by ignoring syntactic and semantic constraints, and by straining the boundaries of understanding. Their love of chaos and anarchy of speech as well as their cult of the hermetic, the obscure, the random, the indeterminate, and the undifferentiated might well be seen as a desire for otherness or for chaos as the Other of order.

Yet, this presumed chaos of experimental poetic language is framed by a rigorous self-reflexivity, an aesthetic paradox that ultimately leads to the emergence in postmodern culture of a new sense of order. The desire to abolish conventional form clashes with the knowledge that ultimately art cannot deny form and literature cannot deny language. Thus, even in their most carnivalesque subversion of poetic expression (Joyce) and their most ardent desire for transforming language into body (Artaud) or silence (Beckett), these texts cannot but produce a new aesthetic order. Throughout the history of literary forms, poetic language itself has reflected on this paradox in endless variations, thus scrutinizing its own conditions and boundaries. Instead of merely symbolizing order or chaos, literature plays a variation of Freud's *fort-da* game, playfully reenacting the paradoxes inherent in such a symbolization.

A similar dynamics operates during the act of reading. Texts that experiment with broken, fragmented forms of poetic language play with new regulations of aesthetic distance, causing readers to alternate between a radical increase and a complete loss of distance. Most significantly, textual plays with the chaos of language are often modeled on the language of the unconscious and the dream, so that the otherness of experimental poetic language becomes affiliated in the game of cultural binarisms with the metonymic chain of chaos, the feminine, and the unconscious. The pleasures of chaos, formlessness, and undifferentiation attune the experimental literary forms to the feminine space of fusion and primordial undifferentiation, eliciting its ambivalent cathexis as *jouissance* or abjection. By simultaneously appealing to unconscious experience and self-reflexivity as the opposite poles of our receptive capabilities, experimental texts also highlight the fundamental ambivalence toward experiences of otherness. Thus it is possible, for example, that we consciously perceive experimental poetic language as radically other, while we unconsciously erase its "otherness" once it is, in Murray Krieger's formulation "absorbed into the poet's (and, ultimately, the critic's) self as subject" (*Poetic* 272).

Such highly flexible and unstable forms of reception have epistemological implications that bear upon the cultural relevance of literary knowledge. Experimental texts require a thinking in open rather than in closed systems which, in turn, tends to increase sensitivity and tolerance for otherness and to decrease cultural paranoia.[32] In *Anti-Semite and Jew*, Sartre, for example, analyzes the compulsive transformation of the phenomenal world into closed systems of thought as a Cartesian desire for the stable, the delimited, and the clear-cut that guarantees continuity at the price of a petrifying destruction of otherness.

In a similar vein, Bateson in *Steps to an Ecology of Mind* emphasizes the mind's tendency retrospectively to project epistemological independence onto partialized closed systems of thought and thus to reduce otherness in our systems of knowledge. According to Bateson, systems of thought or forms of cultural contact that rigidify boundaries in order to maintain internal coherence lead to an increase of outside pressure or, in relation to other cultures, external conflict and hostility, which is ultimately destructive for all agents involved. Conceptually, a dynamic, nondestructive or balancing relationship between cultures in contact, on the other hand, would require a permanent renegotiation of their mutual boundaries, a process resulting in a different form of inner coherence based not on domination but on flexibility and openness to change. In such negotiations the other does not remain completely other, nor does the same remain completely the same.

Literature, especially in its open, experimental forms, seems to be a privileged medium for training negotiations across boundaries that demarcate otherness. This is perhaps literature's most crucial advantage over the occidental philosophical tradition which Levinas sees as haunted by the fear of otherness as well as the fear that the other remains other: "The occidental philosophy is identical with the revelation of the Other; in it the Other which manifests itself as Being loses its Otherness. From its beginnings philosophy is terrified by the Other that remains other . . . " (*Spur* 211). By contrast, the experience of literature retains the paradox of otherness that Winnicott describes as crucial for the transitional space. Different from systematic interpretations of the other, literature provides, at its best, a heteronomous experience that achieves a movement to the other that never returns to the same. While thus reflecting the irreducible heteronomy of the Other, literature may nonetheless also be absorbed and interiorized as Other. Interpretation may emphasize either heteronomy or interiorization. In each case, it would need ways to translate otherness into language without obliterating it—the problem and struggle with language that Derrida's philosophy pushes to its extreme. "Is there a meaning of meaning that does not culminate in a transformation of the Other into the Same?" has also been a central question in Levinas (*Spur* 214). This question addresses the very status of the subject in its own speech. Poetic language may produce readings and interpretations that deal with, reflect, or even thematize the paradoxes inherent in experiences of otherness and cultural contact. Levinas sees this responsiveness as a responsibility with respect to the Other: "The I is infinitely responsible with respect to the Other," and "this responsibility expels the imperialism and egoism of the I" (*Spur* 225).

As a medium of cultural contact, the experimental forms of poetic language are instruments in an aesthetic experience that may well form a countersocialization—as long as literature retains its subversive potential. What Hartman says about theory and interpretation is true for literature itself: "it lives within what it criticizes and tries to isolate certain antibodies" ("New" 101). A theory of reading based on a model of cultural contact sharpens the sensitivity for such antibodies and enforces the resistance to destructive forms of cultural contact while enhancing the capacity for nondestructive ones. The radical problem has become survival (Blau 162)—not only in the ecology of the earth, but also in the ecology of encounters with other cultures, the ecology of mind, speech, and voice, or the increasingly marginalized space of reading.

# NONSENSE, DREAM, AND CHAOS:
# THE OTHERNESS OF LITERARY LANGUAGE

# NONSENSE AND METACOMMUNICATION
## *Alice in Wonderland*

THE HISTORY OF nonsense literature is intrinsically linked to the history of literary realism. With the latter's insistence on the validity of the quotidian as an aesthetic object, nineteenth-century realism led to a radical redefinition of the traditional notion of mimesis. The novel is supposed to portray the life of its hero within a realistic fiction of the social world. Even the so-called psychological novel with its attempt to evoke the "inner lives" of its characters is still concerned with realism and mimesis.

The Victorian genre of nonsense literature, by contrast, emerges at the beginning of a far-reaching break with the mimetic tradition. Writers begin to free the materiality of language from meaning and reference. Caring more about sounds than sense, they play with words and create silly puns or discover the pleasures of children's sound games in order to produce nonsense. Long before the surrealists used automatic writing in their attempt to gain access to the unconscious, Lewis Carroll experimented with this very technique of automatic writing in order to disrupt the willful control of speech in his literary production of nonsense (Gardner 8). Surprisingly enough, Carroll's break with the mimetic tradition anticipated many new literary techniques developed later during the proliferation of multiple forms of experimental literature in the twentieth century—ranging from surrealism, Dada, High Modernism (especially James Joyce and Gertrude Stein) to the manifold simulacra of postmodernism.

Like all experimental literature, literary nonsense seems to draw its energies from an antimimetic effect. Refusing to serve as a "mirror of nature," it thrives in the delirious space of the looking-glass world in which language no longer "re-presents" but mocks its very foundations and speaks on its own against rhetorical conventions, rules, and codes. Literary nonsense uses the excess of the signifier over the signified—which has always characterized the poetic use of language—in order to disturb and to recreate the relation between words and worlds and to fold language back upon itself. Rather than referring to imaginary objects and worlds, this language refers to linguistic and mental relations (Sewell 1–6). It unsettles mental habits formed by rhetorical conventions and thus induces the pleasures of both a temporary relief from the boundaries of internalized rules and an increased flexibility of mind.

And yet, this antimimetic core of literary nonsense is not predicated upon a rejection of narrative—a trend developed later in experimental literature and appropriated by certain literary theories. Even though the narratives of *Alice in Wonderland* and *Through the Looking Glass* follow a dynamic of their own and are more fragmented than their realistic counterparts, it is no coincidence that Lewis Carroll, the "double" of Charles Lutwidge Dodson, a Victorian mathematician of Christ Church, Oxford, has created two of the most unforgettable imaginary worlds.

I am interested here in this nonmimetic if not antimimetic relationship between words and worlds and the statement it makes about our mimetic mental habits. I therefore propose to analyze Carroll's texts as an eccentric form of literary communication, a communication which celebrates the excess which literary language is able to produce in relation to a signified imaginary world, a narrative or "mere nonsense." This reading will explore the cultural function of literary nonsense within the larger framework of an "ecology of mind and language," by folding the delirious space of nonsense back upon the "potential spaces"[1] which it dynamically mobilizes in the reader: the dream and logic. I will end with a playful construction of a "culture contact" between two imaginary worlds that share a delight in the effects of surfaces: Victorian nonsense and postmodernism. If we filter our most cherished (theoretical?) constructions of postmodernity—schizophrenia and simulacrum—through Carroll's looking glass of nonsense, we might perhaps discover a tacit complicity of these categories with a tradition of thinking in terms of mimetic representation, which we otherwise claim to have abandoned.

*Alice in Wonderland* begins with a dreamlike displacement of its main character. During a free fall through the rabbit hole Alice loses the ground of her own culture and lands in a "Wonderland" whose inhabitants, a weird and colorful bunch of creatures, animals, cards, legendary beings, and all sorts of nonsense characters, have their own anthropomorphic culture, live and dress like humans, and speak their language, but ostensibly disregard its conventions and rules. Seven-year-old Alice encounters this world as alien, nonsensical, unpredictable, and threatening—especially since she herself, shortly after her arrival, changes so profoundly that she is confused about her "sense" of herself.

## Nonsense and Metacommunication

*Alice in Wonderland* and *Through the Looking Glass* belong to the Victorian genre of nonsense literature, a genre whose very label indicates a refusal to make sense, while at the same time engaging in aesthetic communication. The denomination "I am nonsense" provides a metacommunicative frame which claims that the refusal to make sense is meaningful. We are thus faced with the aesthetic paradox of literary nonsense as sense.

The following reading highlights a possible aesthetic experience of nonsense located in a realm which engages dream and metacommunication. This space could also be viewed as profoundly "nonmimetic," as a space which carefully avoids the middle ground of an imaginary world constructed according to conventions of realism or verisimilitude. Critics have often compared the surface phenomena of Carroll's textual Wonderland with the dream, the fairy tale, or the projection of an alternative world whose meaning is constituted through its differences from conventional systems of meaning in our quotidian world. As we can infer from the designation "nonsense," these differences lie less in the order of things than in the order of sense—that is, the symbolic order.

"Where there is sense there must be perfect order," says Wittgenstein—an assumption immediately and immensely complicated by Carroll's texts (98). This very assumption, in fact, remains controversial to this day, when the most diverse theories of language have challenged not only the codes and conventions of symbolic orders but the status of order itself. The most profound challenge concerns the very notion of referentiality in language and—as a side effect—some of the most basic categories in literary criticism, such as mimesis on the one hand and realism on the other.

Nonsense is a sense produced by a disorder in the system of meaning. According to Rudolf Arnheim, disorder results not from a lack of order, but from a collision between different systems of order within a larger system. Nonsense can be defined accordingly not as a lack of sense, then, but as a collision of systems of meaning—a collision which invites a new relationship between the involved systems or even causes them to collapse.

In both *Alice in Wonderland* and *Through the Looking Glass* the plot is framed by a form of culture contact.[2] At a superficial level, the cultural systems brought into contact are the culture of a Victorian girl and the cultures of Wonderland as well as the looking-glass world. But there is also a contact between cultural subsystems, such as that between formal logic and the symbolic order, or the language of the dream or schizophrenia and so-called ordinary language. In her attempts to mediate her own cultural presuppositions with those she encounters in the foreign culture of Wonderland, Alice becomes a pilot figure for the reader. Throughout the texts her perspective maintains a constant awareness of both cultures and their differences. Far from observing a fusion or amalgamation of different cultures or a blurring of the boundaries between them, we thus experience in Carroll's textual world a sequential chain of collisions which maintains and even highlights the boundaries, while at the same time challenging them in the production of meaning. Gradually Alice develops a perspective which can change instantly and at will between her own and the "alien" cultural system.

However, her acculturation is a merely pragmatic one; her sense of the other culture as irreducibly alien remains intact and continues to determine her responses. She learns to speak and to act "inside" while observing from the "outside." Without ceasing to perceive the otherness of Wonderland as bizarre, she nonetheless begins to experience otherness as the norm of an "inverted world." Most often the effects of otherness are produced by a particular use of language, namely, a complex game of "referentialities" in which the characters constantly choose references which violate the conventional use of a word or a phrase.

Carroll's texts also play with certain "mimetic effects," that is, with specific similarities to forms of alternate consciousness such as the dream or schizophrenia. At the beginning and the end of *Alice in Wonderland* the narrator evokes the dream as a metacommunicative frame. The fiction of a completely alien and nonsensical world is thus mediated by a familiar framing perspective. Like the dream, Carroll's Wonderland displays a proliferation of rhetorical condensations and displacements, as well as a high degree of visual language. Free from the constraints of linguistic codes or a mimetic reality principle, the narrated events dispense with the familiar relationship between cause and effect as well as time and space. Surprising—yet smooth—metonymic transitions govern a set of narrative sequences in which actions or dialogues are constantly disrupted, while seemingly unmotivated shifts are taken for granted.

The plot is governed by phantasms of changing bodies: Alice's first culture shock consists of the sudden changes of her size, and further transformations of bodies occur throughout both texts—prominent examples include a baby that transforms into a pig, an egg that becomes Humpty Dumpty, or a cat that melts into a mere grin. Thoughts materialize as images, and wishes are instantly fulfilled: the Cheshire Cat can make itself partly or wholly invisible, while insects are visible from afar. Time, personified and treated like a bodily creature, may simply stop moving. Often Alice's adventures recall typical nightmares—such as her falling into a deep hole, her being trapped in a tiny space or barred by a locked door. As in a dream, language is both malleable and concrete; words are condensed, dialogues stripped of their pragmatic function, meanings are displaced metonymically, and references are suspended or transformed. Released from its ties to the pragmatics of a world of familiar causes and effects, language becomes a material which is formed and used according to different rules that must be discovered as we go along.

But a close reading reveals that Carroll's texts are very different from a quasi-mimetic representation of a dream. The dream model, in fact, turns out to be a deficient if not deceptive framing device—deceptive, however, in a significant way. While dream elements indeed help to constitute the textual world, they are organized and shaped such that they do not create a dream but nonsense. This nonsense is mediated by Alice's subject position, which combines the role of an active agent exposed to the hazards of culture contact with that of an observer who, instead of becoming absorbed by her dream world, stays at a safe distance. In order to gain a primary orientation to her new cultural environment, Alice uses the whole arsenal of her Victorian school wisdom—preferably logical operations and rational argumentation. Logic, or more precisely the logic of a child, is called upon to keep her from dissolving into the dreamlike dissolutions and transformations of Wonderland. But it is precisely with this logic that she produces nonsense.

Thus dream and logic become the first two signifying systems that collide in Carroll's text. Alice's precocious references to her Victorian book learning and her diligent "logical" argumentations themselves appear nonsensical within the cultural context of Wonderland. The wrong conclusions typical for the mechanically applied logic of a child enforce this effect. For example, Alice imagines that after her free fall through the earth, she will meet people on the other side who walk on their heads. This fantasy of a world turned upside down is at one level, of course, nothing but the literalization of an idiomatic image extrapolated from the logic of her own perspective. At another level, however, the same image playfully evokes an ironic concretization of a non-Euclidean space.

But perhaps more important than the rational result of such mental operations is the abstract trace of an effaced emotional cathexis. Each contact with a foreign culture threatens one's own constructions of a cultural identity, all the more so when, as in the case of Alice's Wonderland, the foreign culture is based on modes of thought that resemble the dream. Alice has a fundamentally ambivalent experience of this dreamlike structure. While its negative effects appear to be a loss of self, its positive lures are the wish fulfillments of fairy tales. Her first experience in Wonderland is a sudden transformation of her body in which fairy-tale elements are mixed with characteristics which define a schizoid dissolution of the self. As in a fairy tale, food and drink display the labels "eat me" and "drink me." As we know from fairy tales, such oral seductions always contain the threat of black magic, that is, of the use of a poison or potion which leads to an unwanted transformation. After succumbing to this oral temptation, Alice shrinks to the size of a mouse, or grows instantaneously into the tops of the trees.

At the basic structural level of bodily transformations, these corporeal changes resemble schizoid sensations of the body, ranging from a dissociation of body from self to the independent development of distinct body parts which are then personified and perceived as foreign to the self. This "disorder" in the relationship between parts and whole also entails a loss of control over bodily functions, as exemplified by Alice's perception of her feet being so distant from herself that she plans to send them Christmas presents in order to make them favorably disposed toward her.

Alice reacts to these diverse images of a loss of self and body with a double strategy of rational distancing. In her favorite game of being two persons, she enters into a rational discourse with herself in which she tries to convince herself that in her transformed body she can logically no longer be "I" but must be an other. Through this paradoxical construction, which follows the rules of logical nonsense games cherished by little children, Alice nonetheless secures her "I" in a double way, a strategy which appears as a completely formalized reflex of a possible psychic economy of such pseudo-logical operations. If Alice were right, the threatening changes in her new cultural environment would no longer affect her, but the "other." At the same time, however, Alice also manages to maintain herself linguistically, since the act of saying "I am Not-I" presupposes within the logic of language an "I" which sustains its linguistic boundaries.

The collision of dream and, by extension, schizophrenia and logic, characterizes not only the actions of literary characters, but also the fictional construction of the textual world and the devices that generate nonsense. Like the dream, schizophrenia, too, provides only certain structural affinities or, more precisely, a negative foil for the nonsense world. Nonsense absorbs crucial features of both the dream and schizophrenia, such as the condensation and flexibility of its images and the freedom from logical constraints. However, the precise operations of nonsense mark a clear distinction from the unboundedness of the dream or schizophrenia. Critics who have compared Carroll's Wonderland or his looking-glass world with the dream or a schizoid world have often emphasized structural affinities between the two at the expense of the distinctive features of nonsense (see, for example, Empson). Such equations tend to turn the dream into a referential world and nonsense into a mimetic effect. They thus totalize dream and schizophrenia as modes of experience which Carroll does evoke, but only to transform their characteristics into the decidedly different effects of nonsense. After all the dream is, as Elizabeth Sewell has convincingly argued, only an opponent in a game that nonsense plays with logic.

The characters in Wonderland or in the looking-glass world show a tenacious insistence on logical operations which even exceeds the one displayed by Alice herself. The caterpillar, for example, challenges Alice's logical construction of her identity with a different logic. Its simple question "Who are you?" is only a pretext for a quasi-philosophical dialogue about the linguistic and psychological foundations of the self. The caterpillar's discourse reveals that Alice can say "I," but only at the price of losing her identity. Asked to explain what she means when she says "*I* am no longer *myself*," Alice answers, "I can't explain myself because I am not myself, you see." The caterpillar's laconical answer "I don't see" is characteristic in its insistence on a literality which is, of course, nonsensical, given the familiar rhetorical use of "I see." But this "nonsense" is inspired by an implicit philosophical reflection of a formal "symbolic logic"—a reflection which plays with the tension between pronoun and speaker-reference.

Due to the nonsense characters' fanatic insistence on literality, Alice increasingly loses the rhetorical securities of her own symbolic order. This insistence on literality harbors at its core the dream of an absolutely unequivocal language, a language that is either completely formalized or else establishes an absolutely mimetic relationship to the world. Carroll's texts show that any dream of a totalized mimesis, that is, a dream that attempts to efface the difference between map and territory or signifier and signified will in fact produce nonsense. This is epitomized in Humpty Dumpty's absurd request that a name must mimetically represent the shape of a person—a request in which he consciously uses the dream of a mimetic equation between word and object in order to assert his power over the discourse with Alice.

As Alice's internalized tacit rule of using language and rhetoric conventionally—that is, nonliterally—becomes problematic, the links between sound and sense emancipate themselves from the conventional linguistic code. The newly generated forms, however, continue to reflect back upon these conventions and their cultural implications. Poems, for example, turn into parodies of Victorian education. Unmoored from their coded signification, free to follow an economy of pleasure and desire, sounds can generate significant displacements and ambiguities. The ethic of the duchess—"Take care of the sense, and the sounds will take care of themselves"—is obviously not shared by most of the Wonderland characters. They rather invert this ethic, an inversion which, for that matter, is in perfect tandem with the fact that the duchess's formulation itself is a sonorous echo of the English proverb "Take care of the pence and the pounds will take care of themselves" (see Gardner 121).

Under close scrutiny it becomes quite obvious that the characters' obsession with referentiality and literality serves—as in the case of Humpty Dumpty—a much more mundane purpose than the pursuit of a puristic philosophy of language. One aim of their unconventional use of language, especially their mania for contesting and arguing, as well as their competition as smart alecks—seems to be to control language and communication. They entrap Alice in weird language games, the rules of which change not only from character to character, but from case to case. The most salient common feature of these language games is, in fact, the characters' insistence that they determine the rules of the game and, whenever necessary, that they be able to change them or spontaneously invent new ones. Despite his preposterous request for mimetic name-shapes (ironically replicated and subverted, for that matter, in the tail-shaped tale), Humpty Dumpty, for example, has developed his own absurd philosophy of a private language, according to which the meaning of a word can be defined independently from a cultural context or a linguistic convention—a philosophy which guarantees him absolute sovereignty over language and communication. The fact that he personalizes this language—assuming that verbs are proud and have a temper while adjectives can be manipulated at will—only adds to his imperial pose as a master of language, since it feeds into his general fantasies of controlling inferior beings.

Linguistic imperialism and power is also the motif of numerous language games played by other characters. Mutual understanding and exchange as a basis or a motif of communication is replaced by the overarching goal of using or twisting specific rules and arguments in order to win the language game. To this end, the characters develop their own rhetorical system whose favorite figure appears to be metonymy. Alice can hardly start a conversation without her "opponents" changing the conversational frame, preferably by a metonymic displacement which allows them to criticize her inadequate use of language, thereby forcing her to engage in a metalevel of conversation which focuses on its very rules. Alice's "inadequacy," however, is the result of the deliberately "foreign" gaze of the other characters who, by ignoring Alice's linguistic and cultural context, are able to reveal linguistic ambiguities which would dissappear within the adequate context.

The characters' "language game" is thus less a Wittgensteinian "language game" than a competitive rhetorical game based on restrictive rules and oriented toward a winner. Within the frame of this game, communication is most successful where it would fail according to the rules of so-called ordinary language or communication. The winner in this language game is the one who most successfully outsmarts the other with linguistic puns or other tricks. "Language game" thus primarily means a game *with* language. But in order to outsmart the other rhetorically, one must know his or her linguistic and cultural conventions and rules, allowing one then to focus on their weak spots. The "weakness" of language which the characters exploit for their own purposes of asserting a linguistic imperialism results from the very fact that language generates a nonmimetic referential system full of ambiguities. "Weakness" in language is produced by words which allow for a double or multiple meaning, rhetorical figures of speech or idiomatic phrases which play with double meanings, homophones or homonyms—in short, all imaginable ambiguities of language. The structural foundations of such ambiguities are precisely those domains that deviate from the characters' nonsensical insistence on a mimetic equation between words and objects and form the core of Carroll's nonsense, namely metaphor, metonymy, and metacommunication.

*Alice in Wonderland* is, then, a text about literality. Strictly speaking, the characters' language games place a taboo on metaphor. In all of their dialogues, the characters in Wonderland seem to obey the tacit rule that one must—literally—say what one means and mean what one says. They, in fact, use this very rule strategically in order to produce deliberate "misreadings" of Alice's metaphorical speech. Moreover, they indulge in metonymic language games and in displacements of a word from its context in order to take advantage of the thus-produced linguistic ambiguity. Whether the characters insist upon a literality that defies linguistic conventions or upon a linkage between sound and sense that defies context, they invariably blame Alice for ambiguities and require that she adhere to a literality which they themselves are far from applying. Their insistence on literality plays out the ideal of symbolic logic: the notion that there could exist a logically constructed language so formalized that it would be completely free of ambiguity.

From a different perspective, this ideal of symbolic logic converges with the

# Nonsense, Dream, and Chaos

ideal of mimetic unequivocality. In both cases language would provide an absolutely infallible map for reading the world. The characters oppose the ideal of such a formalistic or else a completely "mimetic" language to the ambiguities of so-called ordinary language. If each word and each utterance had only one logical or one mimetic reference which would remain the same through all possible uses, there would be no metaphorical or metonymical speech, since metaphor and metonymy play with multiple meanings and displacements of meaning. The characters thus challenge what belongs to the most habitual forms of rhetoric, namely, to say one thing and to "mean" another.

The second dimension of Carroll's nonsense, metacommunication, functions in a similar way. Metacommunication emerges in the space between map and territory and presupposes an acknowledgment of their difference. In the characters' dialogues, metacommunication follows as a logical consequence of their verdict on metaphor. At the very moment that characters render the tension between "saying" and "meaning" explicit, they simultaneously discard the initial frame of communication and establish a metaframe within which they communicate about communication. Whether through their obstinate insistence on literal meanings, or their sophistic game with metonymic displacements, or their playful shifts from one level of communication to another, they always seek to destroy an established frame of discourse—in most cases the one established by Alice. The dialogues thus become "metalogues."[3]

The master of this strategy is Humpty Dumpty, who already sets up his questions as linguistic traps:

> "How old did you say you were?" ... "Seven years and six months."—
> "Wrong!" ... "You never said a word like it!"—"I thought you meant 'How old are you?' " ... "If I'd meant that, I'd have said it." (265)

Such strategies of argumentation lead to an artificial metalinguistic discourse which takes advantage of our unconscious use of habitual forms of speech. According to Saussure, we acquire the use of such forms of speech as a kind of tacit knowledge that never becomes conscious. When we turn this tacit knowledge into an object of metacommunication, we create an artificial practice of speech which precludes any spontaneous communication. Under certain conditions, the only possible escape from internalized patterns of communication is to establish a metacommunication about the conditions and patterns of communications (Bateson et al.). But to shift systematically and regularly to a metacommunicative level and to consciously bring to mind and challenge the tacit rules of speech—as the characters in Wonderland do—

means to give up any regular communicative exchange. In this sense, the characters resemble a driver who consciously reflects every single act of steering a car and becomes incapable of driving.

The characters' metacommunicative language games thus unsettle the referential relations within speech. Its pragmatic dimension is shifted toward the games with language and the strategies of metacommunication as such. In conjunction with the characters' insistence on literality and univocality, this metacommunication sharply distinguishes the language games from the dream, which ignores the logical exclusion of contradiction and hierarchical distinctions among different levels of communication. The dream acknowledges only its own frame, which marks a different mode of consciousness and experience. Within this frame, the dream elements interact with each other in a highly flexible and nonhierarchical way, thus producing the condensations and displacements that characterize the dream's mode of representation.

Alice, however, does not dream; she rather falls with her waking consciousness into the different culture of the Wonderland which has many resemblances to but as many differences from the dream. One of the most crucial differences is its inhabitants' obsession with logic. As we have seen, Alice's adventures in Wonderland are based on a collision between these different orders. The order of the dream collides with the order of logic, and both are mediated through but also collide with the order of Alice's Victorian culture—which by now forms a kind of impossible or lost middle ground. Alice measures the speech of the characters in Wonderland according to the norms of her own symbolic order. But in its confrontation with the different order of dream and logic, this very order is in a way threatened by its own extreme poles, namely, its origins in the dreamlike primary processes of early infancy and its utopian ideal of univocality and the self-identity of formalized logic.

During Alice's adventures in Wonderland, the collision of her symbolic order with dream and logic performs a parody of this symbolic order by turning it into nonsense. At the same time, however, dream and logic form a complementary challenge for Alice, since she must reconcile both their order and the new order of Wonderland with her own symbolic order. On the one hand, the affinities between Wonderland and the dream force Alice to learn how to de-differentiate her own system of order, to deal with condensations and displacements and to tolerate the dissolution of familiar boundaries and identities or unities. On the other hand, the affinities with logic and especially the taboo placed on metaphor and idiomatic speech force Alice to satisfy the requirements and differentiations of a metacommunicative language game which

questions the very premises of her own discursive practice. From both directions, the dream as well as logic, the means of communication are "distorted"
(in the double sense of a productive *Verfremdung* and a practical disturbance
of communication). Both threaten to undermine communication, since both
the refusal of metacommunication as well as the reduction to metacommunication generate a communicative aporia. Paradoxically, however, the insistence
on literality, which ultimately plays with a refusal of metacommunication, produces a veritable proliferation of metacommunication. This convergence creates the discursive energies of Carroll's nonsense.

These considerations return us to the affinities I emphasized at the outset
between nonsense and the dream or schizophrenia. Both the dream and schizophrenia are characterized by a certain literality of words and language. Freud
has characterized the schizophrenic's use of language as a confusion between
*Wortvorstellung* (the representation of a word) and *Dingvorstellung* (the representation of a thing). For the schizophrenic, the word *is* a thing. But this is
precisely why the schizophrenic is threatened with a dissolution of the boundaries between self and world. Language no longer mediates between interior and
exterior spaces or self and other; it *becomes* other and turns into an object that
invades the self and effaces its boundaries. Carroll's text not only plays with
literality, but activates it in conjunction with the typical fears and dissolutions
of schizophrenia: fantasies of distorted and fragmented bodies, confusions and
discontinuities between parts and whole, autonomous functioning of organs,
distortion or reification of language—in short, with all those forms of
dedifferentiation which also characterize the primary processes. The decisive
factor, however, is how the text molds and integrates these forms of dissolution.
For like the dream, schizophrenia in Carroll's text is only an agent in a language
game, the effects of which are derived from asserting the hegemony of logic
within a cultural frame.

Literality is an important strategic element in these logical games, since the
ideal of a formal logic is oriented toward the univocality of a completely unambiguous meaning. Because it effaces any ambiguity between signifier and
signified, a literal meaning would fulfill this ideal. But the literality of a logician
is very different from that of a schizophrenic; furthermore, the literality played
out by the characters in Wonderland draws upon both systems without fitting
into either one of them. The crucial difference between the use of literality in
nonsense and schizophrenia lies in the fact that for the schizophrenic the word
becomes an "object" invested with materiality, depth, and a phantasmatic cor-

poreality, while for the nonsense characters the word is an empty literal surface, a mere container of meaning that resembles a "thing" only in the sense of its own reification. Both nonsense and schizophrenic discourse efface the rhetorical space between signifier and signified, then, but they do so in very different ways.

In *Logique du Sens*, Gilles Deleuze has outlined the basic differences between Carroll's nonsense and schizophrenia. The comparison between these categories has been inspired by what Deleuze calls "traps of resemblance" (113). For Deleuze, Carroll's language is a surface effect, while the language of schizophrenia—exemplified by Artaud's polemical rewriting of Carroll's *Jabberwocky*—inscribes itself into the depth of the body and absorbs its cathexis. Schizophrenia remains the "other" of nonsense, but an other that is never allowed to penetrate through the surface of nonsense. Deleuze reads Artaud's remark "there is no soul in Jabberwocky" ("il n'y a pas d'âme dans Jabberwocky") as an indication of the general emotional emptiness and flatness of Carroll's text (114). This quality distinguishes it dramatically from the impassioned discourse of the schizophrenic which, emptied of meaning, pursues less the recuperation of meaning than the destruction of the word (118). The effects of this schizophrenic discourse reach below the surface of language and, in fact, destroy the surface of language: "Non-sense no longer releases any surface-meaning; it absorbs and swallows all meaning both at the level of the signifier and at the level of the signified" (122). The schizophrenic's destruction of the word also effaces its linguistic functions: "Not only is there no longer any meaning, but there is also no longer any grammar or syntax and ultimately even no more literally or phonetically articulated syllables" (122). Deleuze asserts how, by contrast, Carroll depends upon a strict grammar. As I argued earlier, Carroll also depends on maintaining the boundaries between self and other or a word and its meanings—including those boundaries which his characters challenge for their own strategic purposes. This is why Deleuze plays Artaud's depth off against Carroll's superficiality, and why he follows Artaud in rejecting Carroll's safe distance from the schizophrenic other that haunts his text. Artaud attributed this distance to an "English snob" about whose text he remarks, "This is the work of a man who ate well and one feels this in his writing" (qtd. in Deleuze 114).

This juxtaposition between Carroll and Artaud may be given another turn. A decade and a half after the publication of Deleuze's critique, Jean-Jacques Lecercle used Deleuze's reading of Artaud against Carroll in order to charge

Deleuze with being a "Romantic philosopher." In *Philosophy through the Looking Glass*, Lecercle writes:

> One might say that, in *Logique du Sens*, Deleuze is turning into a Romantic philosopher, abandoning the classicism of the historian of philosophy and finding his own critical way by crossing the frontier with literature in style, content and general attitude. Of course, Deleuze's Romanticism is, at best, odd. In the broadest possible terms, one can describe Romantic theory and practice as based on a contrast between poetry, or the language of emotion and subjectivity, and science, or the language of rational argument and objectivity. (Lecercle 114)

If we draw out the implications of Lecercle's argument we might conclude that what Deleuze criticizes in Carroll through Artaud is that Carroll, the scientist, has won over Carroll, the poet—even when the scientist Dodgson relinquishes his logical rigor to Carroll, the poet. In this respect, nonsense would be generated through a tension with poetry, a tension brought about by another collision between two signifying systems and rhetorical practices, namely, the two cultures of science and poetry. But Lecercle reminds us also that Carroll's nonsense does not leave us indifferent and that in order to account for its pleasures we must understand its grounding in what Lecercle calls *délire*.

While Deleuze foregrounds the contrast between schizophrenic discourse and nonsense, *délire* rather emphasizes the link between the two. Deleuze defines the relationship between signifier and signified according to a dialectic of lack and excess. Lecercle discovers this dialectic as a central characteristic of nonsense:

> too much signifies, and too little is signified; The abundance of words balances the lack of meaning. After all, *délire* is first characterized by logorrhea, an unceasing flow of words, indicating that communication is no longer possible. (107)

In this respect, delirious speech could be characterized by its severing of any mimetic ties to the referential space of the "signified." And yet, in Carroll these ties are never really given up. Instead of logorrhea or a free flow of words or sounds, we have a sequence of constant disruptions of the signified which, rather than a flow, creates a movement of violent shifts—shifts of the kind enforced by the nonsense characters when they require Alice to abandon the frame of familiar rhetorical conventions. Lecercle addresses this problem when he discusses the paradox of nonsense, namely, the proposition "I mean not to mean." Conceptually, such paradoxes can be solved using the theory of logical types, that is, by distinguishing levels of text, the framing and the framed. Le-cercle, however, argues that literary paradoxes of this kind cannot be solved by the theory of logical types:

> Yet, clearly, this does not work for the kinds of texts which are classified as literary, or for our delirious tradition. They resist the distinction, they delib-erately blur the frontier, they organize a game of mirrors in which the question of who speaks, and at what level of signification, can never be satisfactorily answered. (110)

Lecercle sees the literary paradox of "I mean not to mean" rather solved by the effects of *délire* in language:

> So the absence of intended meaning, the lack of a signified, is balanced by an excess of signifiers which in turn creates meaning. . . . In the excess of signi-fiers, language speaks on its own. Deleuze's conception enables us to under-stand this genesis of sense, the presence of *délire* as a necessary part of lan-guage. (111)

I believe that we may push one step further than Lecercle. I would argue that Carroll often produces this excess of signifiers precisely by engaging the theory of logical types, that is, more concretely by having his characters dis-tinguish between levels of text and between framing and the framed. Rather than residing in "the preverbal psychic expression of somatic drives" (Lecercle 111) as it does in schizophrenic discourse, *délire* in Carroll resides in the effects of a pastiche of the theory of logical types, in the characters' deliberately in-appropriate distinctions between levels of texts and in malicious confusions between framing and the framed. One could say that Carroll contains the ef-fects of schizophrenic *délire* within the surface of a language which is not a mirror of nature but a mirror of rhetorical conventions gone mad.

In this respect, the specific ways in which Carroll's texts play with affinities to the dissolutions of schizophrenia are strikingly relevant, because of their communicative structure. One could read this structure as an early literary re-sponse to a very specific form of cultural schizophrenia.[4] The very same lin-guistic operations that form the core of Carroll's nonsense—namely, metaphor, metonymy, and metacommunication—coincide with what Freud, Bateson, Lee, and others have identified as the specific failures of schizophrenic communi-cation (see Bateson et al.). These theories argue that, unable to identify meta-phors, the schizophrenic takes them literally and treats them as reality. Moreover, the double bind of schizogenic communication places a taboo on meta-communication.

This taboo placed on metaphor and metacommunication also characterizes the communicative patterns that the characters in Wonderland impose upon Alice. And yet, they treat the rhetorical conventions of metaphor and meta-communication in a decidedly different fashion from the schizophrenic. While the latter is unable to identify these modes of speech, Carroll's characters use them obsessively in order to claim univocality or in order to introduce ever new metacommunicative frames. This is why, instead of producing the discourse of a schizo, they simply produce nonsense. On the other hand, as we have seen, this very nonsense draws some of its energies from playing with affinities to schizophrenic discourse. In this respect Carroll's nonsense appears as an abstract parody of schizophrenic discourse, achieved by its logical inversion.

Alice is right, then, to complain about the characters' strategies to drive her insane. However, as the Cheshire Cat pointedly remarks, everybody is insane in Wonderland. The cat's attempt to logically prove its own insanity confirms this statement—albeit against the grain of the logical argument—since it uses a pseudologic that turns out to be the classical parody of logic.

> "A dog's not mad. You grant that?"—"I suppose so," said Alice. "Well, then," the cat went on "you see a dog growls when it's angry, and wags its tail when it's pleased. Now I growl when I'm pleased and wag my tail when I'm angry. Therefore I'm mad." (89)

The Cheshire Cat's proof of its own madness consists in a distorted syllogism which, in turn, typifies "schizophrenic logic."[5] Paradoxically, the proof therefore turns out to be both right and wrong at the same time, since the *wrong* logical conclusion is evidence for what had to be proved in the first place.

The flawed argumentation of the Cheshire Cat exemplifies the characters' logical games and metacommunicative abstractions in general. It reveals that, while formally being an instrument of differentiation and abstraction and thus generating a counterbalance to the dedifferentiations of dream and schizo-phrenia, the metalogical games in fact turn out to be a mere inversion of the same rhetorical and cultural problem. Both the characters' logic and metacom-munication are full of confusions of logical types and wrong logical conclu-sions as well as systematic confusions of levels of communication. This "false logic" paradoxically produces displacements and distortions that in some re-spects resemble those of the dream. In a similar way, the obsessive games of shifting the frame of communication ultimately generate a general dissolution of frames. Logic and metacommunication thus lose their absolute polarity with the dream or with schizophrenia. Their opposition is effaced by nonsense.

How then does this nonsense affect Carroll's readers, who are both outside the frame of Wonderland and outside the frame of Alice's own symbolic order? What is the language game that the text plays with its readers? While at first glance this game may resemble the language games played by the characters, its effects accomplish yet another inversion. Like Alice, Carroll's readers must experience the inadequacy of their communicative competence and discover the rules of a "foreign" language game. They must expose themselves to the diverse processes of dissolution and dedifferentiation as well as to the effects of a flawed logic and a renunciation of metaphor.

But in contrast to Alice, the reader may experience these games as a source of pleasure, since they appear in the "tamed" form of a narrative that is framed as nonsense. According to Freud, the pleasures of nonsense result from the fascination with what is prohibited by reason (*Reiz des von der Vernunft verbotenen*), ("Witz" 119). Nonsense reopens those pleasurable sources of language, which tend to seep away once the dominance of the function of judgment is established within language (123). In order to rejoice in this pleasure we must, as Huizinga has argued, slip into the soul of a child and prefer the wisdom of a child to that of an adult. Originally written for children, Carroll's nonsensical language games share basic features with childhood games. They develop within a closed psychological frame in which primary and secondary processes may playfully interact or merge with each other.

Carroll's game is a game with language that uses linguistic rules and rhetorical conventions as its elements in order to generate an artificial speech located in a realm that partakes of the primary undifferentiation of the dream, the secondary differentiation of the symbolic order, and the tertiary differentiation of symbolic logic. Aesthetically, this game draws upon all three of these domains and plays with transgressing the boundaries between them. Carroll's pleasure is based on making mockery of restrictive systems of order—the symbolic order of Victorian culture, the codes of language, and the formalistic order of symbolic logic alike. In this respect, nonsense creates affinities not only to play but also to the joke. Like the joke, nonsense draws its effects less by engaging our reflective consciousness than from a spontaneous if not unconscious insight. In many ways, its comic effects resemble those of the joke. In both cases, a sudden insight may open a channel to the unconscious. But this is also the point at which they differ. While the joke makes its point by playing with an unconscious understanding of social taboos or cultural repressions, nonsense plays with internalized rules of language, rhetorical conventions or modes of thought. The latter are also unconscious—not in the sense of a dynamic repression but in the sense of habitual modes of thought or unconscious rules of language which, according to Saussure, never reach consciousness, even though they are acquired culturally.

This difference between nonsense and the joke also accounts for the fact that nonsense does not share the cathartic effects of the joke. Nonsense may once in a while generate laughter, but, as Sewell has argued, laughter is not essential to it. Its pleasures derive from a less dramatic subversion of our categories and habits of thought. Both the joke and nonsense challenge the symbolic order: the former by mobilizing unconscious desires or fears, the latter by questioning our very systems of meaning. If during this process nonsense establishes, as in Carroll's case, a secondary closeness to the unconscious it is because the latter uses any rupture of the symbolic order and any deviation of the code for its own purposes. In Carroll's case the links to the unconscious are further enforced by the previously described affinities to the dream and schizophrenia. Logic and pleasure principle meet in a space where the pedant's delight in the controlling functions of order, categorization, differentiation, and segmentation implodes, transforming into the complementary delight in chaos and subversion. Nonsense rediscovers those pleasures in language which the child knows before it must succumb to the function of judgment and the dictates of linguistic codes (Freud, "Witz" 119).

In contrast to the joke, the pleasures of nonsense are not consumed by a spontaneous insight. Instead of an affective catharsis, nonsense rather generates an impulse further to reflect upon or reconstruct what offered itself to a spontaneous understanding. This in fact happens in a very specific sense. As we have seen, the characters' language games are governed by metacommunication. If these games generate an impulse in the reader to reflect upon their conditions and effects, that is, an impulse to "understand" nonsense, then we can say that Carroll invites the reader to enter into a metacommunication with the text itself. Strictly speaking, this communication is a metacommunication about metacommunication. Apart from illuminating the functioning of language, the conditions of successful or unsuccessful language games or the internalized rules of language, nonsense also reveals the functions of metacommunication as such. While for the characters metacommunication is a strategy to win the language game against Alice, it produces a double effect on the reader: during a spontaneous reception, the reader enjoys the cunning of language and the symbolic order, but during a metacommunication with the text, s/he may turn nonsense into sense. The history of literary criticism on Carroll testifies to this second form of response. Carroll's texts have not only become classics of children's literature but also standard works which to this very day are referred to by philosophers, mathematicians, linguists, and literary critics who have followed their invitation to metacommunication (see, for example, Gardner).

The metacommunication with the reader gains a specific relevance in relation to the "other" of Carroll's text, namely, dream and schizophrenia. With its framing label "I am nonsense" the text creates a receptive disposition that the dream ignores and which is precluded from schizogenic communication. If the schizophrenic were able to identify metaphor and metonymy or use metacommunication, s/he could escape the traps of a communicative double bind. With its self-designation as nonsense, literary nonsense by contrast offers already an invitation to metacommunication. The reader thus is compelled to activate precisely those modes of consciousness which the dream and schizophrenia lack. One could even be tempted to speak of a schizoid experience with built-in therapy. Like Alice, the reader must perform acts of both differentiation and dedifferentiation. Nonsense generates pleasure by a curious admixture of both receptive activities.

It is true that literary nonsense breaks through conventional frames; but instead of succumbing to the anarchy of unboundedness, it replaces them with different ones which often result from a privileging of rigid linguistic rules over more flexible rhetorical conventions. Precisely in this respect, nonsense may teach us an important lesson about the "ecology of signs" since it illustrates that the overly rigid use of linguistic rules and the attempts to eliminate the ambiguities of language do not strengthen but, on the contrary, undermine its communicative functions. Nonsense, one could say, thus beats the system with its own means by imploding it from within. Rather than resulting from a rebellion against law and order, dissolution and anarchy are produced by an overly rigid insistence on rules.

Nonsense stretches the receptive dispositions of readers in two directions. The formal dedifferentiations with their affinities to the dream and schizophrenia appeal to the unconscious, while the metacommunication increases self-reflexivity and the conscious awareness of tacit rules and conventions of speaking. In this respect, Carroll's text anticipates certain features of the highly experimental texts of modernism. Nonsense forms an alliance between dream and logic in order to challenge the boundaries of so-called ordinary language. But at the same time, nonsense is never truly subversive in a radical sense. The formal procedures of nonsense contain and neutralize its subversive potential. The threatening aspects of a schizophrenic dissolution, for example, are not only contained aesthetically but also psychologically. Nonsense even plays dream or schizophrenia and logic off against each other: logic domesticates the dream, even as the dream undermines the rigid boundaries of logic. Neither one is allowed to dominate the other. Their collision transforms both into nonsense.

This chain of arguments leads us back to Sewell's thesis introduced at the beginning of this essay: that literary nonsense refers to mental relations rather than to a world of objects. We may now specify this perspective and say that rather than "referring" to mental relations in a quasi-mimetic way, nonsense establishes a metacommunication about mental relations. The difference lies in the fact that nonsense operates at a higher level of abstraction—even when it is most playful and paradoxical.

This metacommunicative aspect of literary nonsense will be reactivated in multiple ways by the later forms of experimental literature which—as Michel Foucault and Hans Blumenberg have pointed out—are characterized by an aesthetic coexistence of an opening of language toward the unconscious (the dream) and a high degree of formalization (logic). Historically, we will see a change in literary experiments with the boundaries of language. The aesthetic potential of dream and logic will be freed for literary experiments with more serious cultural claims than Carroll's nonsense games. While Carroll developed his nonsense techniques at a time when realism was at its height in British literature, in later experimental literature both the opening of literary language toward the unconscious and its abstract formalization broke with the conventions of mimesis and literary realism by creating new spaces of literary communication. This literature insisted on "making sense" with literary forms of speech that resisted specific cultural codifications. These literary experiments still rely on self-reflexivity and metacommunication, but less in order to obtain a secondary stabilization of their communicative systems than to reflect the blind spots of these systems.

Klaus Reichert has argued that Carroll's nonsense can be read as an anticipatory parody of modernism (7–39). The textual adventures in Wonderland may seem like a parody of the fragmented, playful, yet also highly self-reflexive devices of literary modernism. Elizabeth Sewell points out that nonsense is produced by a segmentation and fragmentation of elements that pertain to an indivisible whole. If we then read nonsense as an anticipatory metacommunication about literary devices developed later, nonsense may reveal an important insight into the aesthetic coexistence of an opening of literary language toward the unconscious and its self-reflexive formalization. In finding ways to communicate how these different aspects belong together and cohere in a larger cultural context, the new experimental forms of literature have made use of Carroll's devices. But they also have moved beyond the mere production of nonsense in order to enter into a literary language game which expands the boundaries of a codified symbolic order as well as a long tradition that valued literature mainly for its mimetic functions.

We might well argue that Carroll marks the beginning of those far-reaching challenges to our cultural notions of mimesis and representation which culminate in what we have come to call the simulacra of postmodernism. But then we seem to have come full circle: if our conventional rules and perceptions fail to distinguish the signifier from the signified or the simulated from the real, are we then not exposed to confusions between map and territory or words and objects similar to those experienced by Alice in Wonderland? The "surface-intensities" which Fredric Jameson invokes as characteristic of postmodern experience, in fact, recall the *délire* of nonsense. But if the simulacrum is postmodernism's privileged form that displaces "re-presentations," have we then not entered a phase of inverted mimesis?

I would prefer to turn the question around and ask whether the privileging of the category of the simulacrum in current critical theories is not indicative of the fact that we tacitly continue to harbor a notion of mimesis at the core of our critical apparatus. The same could, in fact, be argued for the category of postmodern schizophrenia. Our inclination to posit and then tag the fragmented and hallucinatory surfaces of postmodern culture with labels such as "simulacrum" and "postmodern schizophrenia" betrays a desperate urge to "reterritorialize" them within a space that is radically "other," yet at the same time uncannily familiar. The designation of "simulacrum" allows us to harbor the illusion that we are always elsewhere and that the realities we inhabit are "only" simulated—albeit with the perfect mastery of a mimetic artist. The designation of "schizophrenia," on the other hand, helps us to evaluate the overwhelming sensation of increasing intensities and fragmentations with reference to a familiar "pathology" which remains nonetheless irreducibly other.

Our critical approximation of either Victorian nonsense literature or postmodern culture with the pathologies of schizophrenia may then be seen as a "mimetic fallacy," a move to recuperate these forms of literary practice for a tradition from which they have broken away. This mimetic fallacy enacts a critical evasion, sparing us the pains of actually encountering them on their

Nonsense, Dream, and Chaos

own terms. In his introduction to *The Annotated Alice*, Martin Gardner writes, "The last level of metaphor in the *Alice* books is this: that life, viewed rationally and without illusion, appears to be a nonsense tale told by an idiot mathematician" (15). In this formulation, both life and nonsense lose their cutting edge. By sheer coincidence, this "idiot mathematician" may then well have anticipated some of the most pertinent features of a "postmodern simulacrum of schizophrenia"—but the willful simulation also saves him and us the tortures of a schizophrenic experience.

Regarding this tacit sibling rivalry between mimesis, simulacrum, and schizophrenia, it seems interesting that, historically, Deleuze played out the depth of Artaud's modernist "discourse of the schizo," while the postmodern literary forms engage instead in the play of simulacra and surface-effects. Could it be that what some critics call "postmodern schizophrenia" is a form of pastiche whose affinities to the phenomenology of schizophrenia are based on what Deleuze calls "traps of resemblance"? And, in consequence, does what Jameson calls the "waning of affect" in postmodern culture not rather resemble the "safe play" of nonsense than the existential abyss of schizophrenia? Or do I with this construction fall into the same kind of Romanticism that Lecercle criticized in Deleuze? But if, on the other hand, this were true, then we could expand Reichert's statement and say that Carroll's nonsense may also be read as an anticipatory parody of postmodernism and its enchantment with simulacra and effects produced at the surface of language.

# 3

# JOYCE, CAGE, AND CHAOS

## *Finnegans Wake, Roaratorio,* and French Feminism

### 1. "Ownconsciously grafficking": Framing Chaos in Joyce and Cage

while that Other by the halp of his creacive mind offered to deleberate the mass from the booty of fight our Same with the holp of the bounty of food sought to delubberate the mess from his corructive mund, with his muffetee cuffes ownconsciously grafficking. (300.19–24)

IN THIS CANNIBALIZING pastiche of Yeats's *A Vision,* Joyce playfully opposes the order of the Other with his "creacive mind" to the order of the Same with his "corructive mund." "Mund," or mouth and voice, as the protagonist speaking the "order of the Same" both corrects and corrupts the protagonist who acts in the order of the Other, the active, reactive, and creative "creacive" mind. Language thus performs a corrective, corruptive translation of mind's creations, reducing their otherness to the order of the Same. Language and mind, Same and Other, no longer merely represent, mirror, or refer to each other, but pertain to different orders, thus contaminating and "othering" each other.

As this Joycean punning indicates, the ways of perceiving, understanding, and imagining order have dramatically changed during the course of the twentieth century. Marked by the impact of psychoanalysis, the beginning of the century was captivated by the new order of the unconscious. Via the dream and the somatic semiotics of the hysteric body, Freud had discovered that the unconscious had its own "order of the Other" with alternate modes of inscription. The unconscious is, as Joyce put it, "ownconsciously grafficking," thus becoming readable and accessible to specific forms of communication such as transference. No longer merely irrational or sheer chaos, the unconscious becomes visible in its agonistic, yet dynamic relation to consciousness, and ac-

knowledged as a vital force in shaping "civilization and its discontents." According to Hans Blumenberg, Freud's theory that human desire and civilizing
processes alike are governed by the death drive is modeled after the scientific
principle of entropy as a force that works toward the gradual dedifferentiation
of all order (see also Wilden 125–52).

At a planetary level, the popularization of the Second Law of Thermodynamics and the principle of entropy created an apocalyptic cultural mood
dominated by the powerful image that the universe is running downhill—an
image that virtually produced a phantasma in the popular mind. We recall here
that Joyce's epigraph, in fact, also invokes a planetary level, namely, Yeats's vision: "The first gyres clearly described by philosophy are those described in the
*Timaeus* which are made by the circuits of 'the Other' (creators of all particular
things), of the planets as they ascend or descend above and below the equator.
They are opposite in nature to that circle of the fixed stars which constitutes
'the Same' " (McHugh 300). The discovery of entropy replaces this image of
the universe as a site of eternal order and of a harmonious relation between
fixed stars and circuits of moving planets with that of a universe threatened
by increasing dedifferentiation and the gradual disappearance of its harmonious orders.

At a sociopolitical level, the first half of the twentieth century is marked by
the trauma of two world wars and the establishment of mass warfare. Above
all, it was fascism and the concentration camps that shattered forever the Enlightenment vision of an evolutionary progression of rationality, humanistic
values, and political order. Joyce's emphasis on transnationalism and cultural
hybridity must be read as his political stance against colonialism, especially in
relation to Ireland as a colonized nation, and against the rise of nationalism all
over Europe.[1] Among many critics who read *Finnegans Wake* as a manifesto for
transnationalism and transculturalism, Philippe Sollers is perhaps the most
outspoken in calling the *Wake* "the most formidably anti-fascist book produced between the wars" (189).

This brief sketch evokes the cultural mood in which Joyce creates his own
monumental vision of order and chaos in *Finnegans Wake*—a text which, under
the strong impact of Freud, explores the dream, the unconscious, and the dark
side of human civilizations, orders, languages, and cultures. Determined by a
pervasive distrust of civilization and progress, the cultural mood that surrounds Joyce's own "Work in Progress" is deeply modernist. *The Education of
Henry Adams* is a prototypical work at the onset of modernism, symptomatic

of the popular dissemination of entropy and the simultaneous propagation of an experimental narrative space as a negentropic principle. Similarly, Joyce uses poetic language as a negentropic device. Even when its entropic forms mimic the alleged "chaos" of the unconscious or of a civilization under distress, artistic creation, in this age of suspicion, is comparable to a dose of negentropy in a universe running downhill.

The second half of the century discovers the other side of "chaos," its creative potential, beauty, and "hidden order." Anton Ehrenzweig, for example, theorizes the unconscious as a scanning instrument in creative production far superior to consciousness, rational reasoning, and normal perception.[2] Political theorists and cultural critics develop a radical critique of Enlightenment rationality and its dependence on a Cartesian-Newtonian concept of order, and finally, scientists discover the new paradigms of chaos and complexity which are soon imported into other disciplines such as feminist theory and literary criticism. The cultural mood behind this new revaluation of order is truly postmodern. At best it remains reminiscent of the deep ambivalence underlying the cultural history of order and chaos; at worst, it naively celebrates chaos with the same amazement and wonder that accompanied the early colonialists' discovery of the New World.[3]

Rereading *Finnegans Wake* with the tools provided by chaos theory and its new conceptual perspectives, one is immediately struck by such amazing affinities that one feels Joyce has anticipated a new cultural sensibility that found its theoretical match only much later. Because chaos theory allows one to access a new "order" in chaos and complexity, it also helps one to understand why Joyce is about more than mere chaos. One could say that Joyce trains our ability to perceive and play with order in chaos before a theory becomes available that may account for this type of reception. On the other hand, chaos theory may also show why certain nonlinear and playfully experimental readings of the *Wake* are more attuned to its enfolded order and the new sensibility it anticipates than readings that try to work with conventional notions of order. My own reading will first explore the *Wake* in conjunction with John Cage's musical response *Roaratorio* in order to contrast two different modes of experiencing "chaotic" otherness according to the two different orders of textual and musical production. In this context, I perform a transcoding between chaos theory and the aesthetic experience of *Finnegans Wake* and *Roaratorio* that allows one to see how Joyce and Cage train our senses to perceive chaos as more than mere noise or contingency. Finally, I will loop back to the *Wake* and read its chaos as "gendered chaos," thus drawing out the cultural implications of French feminism's reception of chaos theory for a feminist reading of the *Wake*.

## 2. Joyce, Chaos, and Cage: Inhabiting Postmodern Schizospheres

The great fall of the offwall entailed at such short notice the pftjschute of Finnegan, erse solid man, that the humpty-hillhead of humself prumptly sends an unquiring one well to the west in quest of his tumptytumtoes. (3.18–21)

This sentence on the first page of *Finnegans Wake* introduces the fall of Humpty Dumpty into the schizosphere of Joyce's chaosmic sounddance. When the *Wake* was published in 1939, it caused a colossal earthquake among readers and literary critics trying to come to terms with the otherness of a poetic language whose surface is crisscrossed by faults and fractures, a disturbing play of bumps and effects of the seeming randomness of perturbing words. Units of words are broken up and glued together with fragments of other broken words; yet, the new surfaces of word fragments do not touch everywhere. Fissures and gaps remain—as you can easily hear when you try to pronounce the word "pftjschute." With these gaps Joyce created "Finnegans Quake," an "*earth-quake*" that causes words to shift tectonically, and finally to flow, introducing a fluid motion into language that releases tensions and blockages—just as an earthquake causes a motion of fluids below the earth's shattered crust. Because they prevent us from smoothly gliding over the surface of phonetic writing, Joyce's cracked and fluid words cause a quake for the ear, thumping our eardrums and driving us to play their percussive offbeats out loud in the mind's ear.

According to what legend can one map this unstable territory? Its cartography must accomodate change over time, since *Finnegans Wake* occupies a temporal zone that at once contains a multilayered history of past epistemologies and anticipates future ones. One of the most far-reaching effects of Joyce's earthquake is, in fact, the creation of turbulence in time, its reversal or dechronologization, and the anticipation of future events in language, theory, and what is left of "real life."

Joyce's anticipatory use of chaos theory merits further exploration. In the forties, not long after the publication of the *Wake*, scientists discovered that the particular mathematical pattern created by the distribution of large and small earthquakes coincides precisely with the scaling pattern that governs the distribution of personal incomes in a so-called free-market economy. But only in 1978, nearly 40 years after the publication of *Finnegans Wake*, did they find a theory able to explain this striking coincidence. Christopher Scholz, a Columbia University professor investigating earthquakes, read Mandelbrot's *Fractals: Form, Chance and Dimension*, a text that shares Scholz's—and, for that matter, Joyce's—postmodern obsession with surfaces.

Scholz discovered that the faults and fractures on the surface of the earth were astonishingly self-similar not only to the fluctuating patterns of the stock market, but also to the shape of Mandelbrot's fractals and, we could add, to the faults and fractures created by Joyce on the surface of language. Mandelbrot showed that patterns with complex boundaries between order and chaos proved to be fractal, as did the mathematical objects that subsequently provided the key to nonlinear dynamics (Gleick 114).[4] From a certain perspective, fractal shapes may engender a territory so random and chaotic that the observer seems to be placed in the position of a "schizo" unable to provide an adequate map. In true postmodern spirit, Scholz called this ragged territory "schizosphere" (105)—not unlike those critics who, unable to provide a map for reading the *Wake*, had declared Joyce's text to be a prime paradigm of postmodern schizophrenia. Scholz, however, discovered in Mandelbrot's fractal geometry such a map for describing precisely the random and chaotic fractures in the structure of the earth and other chaotic objects. Fractal descriptions, then, were designed to provide what the schizo lacks, a map to account for seemingly chaotic shapes such as the "bumpiness" of the earth's surface and the gaps that remain when broken surfaces come together—gaps which then control the flow of fluid through the ground. Again, Scholz named the effect of these gaps in the schizosphere of the earth very aptly—and with a Wakean intuition—"the Humpty-Dumpty-Effect" (Gleick 106)—which brings us back to Joyce's "humpty-hillhead tumptytumtoes."

Beyond these nominal interfaces, Joyce's anticipation of chaos theory runs at a deeper structural level than the mere production of a Humpty-Dumpty effect. He equally shares its preoccupation with infinity, recursion, and self-similarity. "In the mind's eye, a fractal is a way of seeing infinity," writes Gleick in *Chaos: Making a New Science* (98). Joyce wants his text to contain the whole universe with all its recursive times (*recorso*) and histories. He also wants the whole of the *Wake* to be contained in each of its self-similar parts. His ideal reader is supposed to grasp the text both in recursive loops of readings and in a holistic perception of the whole text in each part. If one wants to imagine a fractal text that entails the "infinite self-embedding of complexity" (100), *Fin-*

*negans Wake* comes as close to it as possible. The *Wake* enfolds words into words that enfold other words, and all these imaginary word-worlds enfold narratives within narratives of other narratives, or characters that are the effects of other characters, and so on ad infinitum. Joyce even seems to tease us about this infinite process of self-embedding when he deposits the Great Letter in the muddy surface of his text. The Great Letter is figured as a miniature of *Finnegans Wake* which, in turn, contains the Great Letter which contains *Finnegans Wake* which contains the Great Letter which contains *Finnegans Wake*. . . . Chaos theory has termed this well-known *mise-en-abîme* "self-similarity." Defined as symmetry across scale, self-similarity "implies recursion, pattern inside of pattern" (Gleick 103). "Fractal meant self-similar," writes Gleick, recalling the endlessly mirrored mirror or the Russian dolls as the favorite examples of a "symmetry across scale" that produces the infinity effects of fractals. The *Wake* drives this dream of infinite self-similarity to its extreme: as an enfolded replica of *Finnegans Wake* which, in turn, is figured as a text able to store all texts, sounds, and signs of all times, past and future, the Great Letter also embodies, somewhat self-ironically, the *Wake*'s dream of being a written hologram of a self-similar universe.

Joyce's self-ironical deposition of the Great Letter in the "mudhill" of *Finnegans Wake* plays also with the difference between geometric fractals and the ragged and seemingly random structures of fractals with higher complexity. The *mise-en-abîme* of the Russian doll or the Great Letter produces a geometric fractal with perfect symmetry across scale, which is much less experimental and exciting than the fractals that incorporate random perturbations into self-similarity. The *Wake*'s fracturing processes are more complex because the *Wake* does not simply "mirror" or reduplicate itself infinitely. One could say that the Great Letter is related to the *Wake* as a geometric fractal such as the snowflake is related to the fractal complexity of a universe.

What Mandelbrot in *The Fractal Geometry of Nature* called "scaling," in fact, also operates as a more complex mode of Joycean self-similarity than the *mise-en-abîme* produced by the Great Letter. In fracturing hundreds of foreign languages, for example, Joyce uncovers self-similarities between them, while at the same time re-covering them in his scaling processes. The self-similarity thus created is more complex than the infinite self-mirroring of the same object. The same is true for Joyce's creation of self-similarity between layers of narratives borrowed from different cultures, mythologies, and literatures and enfolded into the narrative of HCE and ALP. Since fractals are generated by recursion, a process that generates pattern inside of pattern and complex boundaries between order and chaos (Gleick 103), the fractal thus provides a compelling—as well as aesthetically appealing—model for describing not only the order enfolded in the irregular and fragmented forms, the jagged and broken-up words of *Finnegans Wake* (Gleick 114), but also the multiple symmetry produced across the different scales of the *Wake*.

In 1988, Hugh Kenner introduced the fractal as a new trope in literary criticism—in a reading of Ezra Pound, whose theory of music Kenner identifies as a theory of fractals.[5] Kenner demonstrates the persistence of scaling processes in twentieth-century literature, music, and art (721–30). According to Kenner, self-similarity in literature occurs whenever we find structures repeating themselves on varying scales or motifs recurring in similar sequences but on different scales. Kenner utilizes Mandelbrot's distinction between two types of self-similarity, that is, between "scaling" and "scale-bound" objects, to discuss two corresponding variations of literary self-similarity.

The distinction between scaling and scale-bound works also affects their aesthetic experience. Scaling works engage their recipients very differently from scale-bound works. Scale-bound works "can please as a whole but have nothing new to offer in close-up" (Kenner 723). Their structure can be disclosed in an overview and mapped onto precise planes, while their form can be explained with a schema. As the quality of the scale-bound work resides in its macrostructure, you are not rewarded when you dwell on detail: "Close up, see less" (723). "Scaling" works, on the other hand, reward both closeness and distance. " 'Scaling' connotes interesting detail at varying ranges" (725). Complex scaling processes organize details into larger forms, defined in turn by the contour of the details. Seen from this perspective, *Finnegans Wake* can be said already to explore the limits of scaling processes within poetic language. Scaling in the *Wake* becomes another mode of enfolding the whole in its parts. Or, as Kenner phrases it, "Small units, when they have integrity, imply wholes" (728).

The fractal and related techniques of scaling may also account for the strange attraction of *Finnegans Wake* and its persistence through time. Even though the fractal appears as a chaotic shape to our perceptual habits/prejudices, it was discovered as a "natural shape"—that is, a "harmonious arrangement of order and disorder as it occurs in natural objects" (Gleick 117), an arrangement that possesses aesthetic appeal and beauty. The striking affinities between the new mathematical aesthetics of fractal geometry and changes in literature and the arts in the second half of the century suggest, according to

Gleick, that fractal shapes correspond to a new cultural sensibility (Gleick 116). N. Katherine Hayles and others even argue that these affinities reveal a new epistemological configuration and structural paradigm of postmodernism.

Why are we so drawn to fractal shapes, and what turns the reading of fractal texts into a new type of aesthetic experience? The shapes that express the non-linear dynamical processes at work in the *Wake*'s language, the infinite flow of sounds jelled into the physical forms of words made of words, and the particular combinations of order and disorder typical for them can be described as enfolding the whole universe of postmodernism before it imploded into the social schizosphere, disseminating its fractal semiosis into literature, the arts, music, architecture, cityscapes, television, and computer screens. In terms of changing social and cultural formations, the attraction of fractals is undoubtedly linked to a new sense of motion and speed in postmodern culture, and to related changes in the experience of time. Numerous critics have claimed a shift from temporal to spatial models of thought as a common feature of postmodernism. Yet, rereading *Finnegans Wake* with chaos theory, we also detect a different insertion of time into new spatial forms.[6]

This new sense of time may be linked with the earlier observation that *Finnegans Wake* inserts motion into language. Fragments of potential meaning speed through the phonetic spaces of the *Wake* with such velocity and in so many directions that we can duly speak of a turbulent text. While reading *Finnegans Wake* we may initially experience nothing but disorder at all scales: phonetic, semantic, syntagmatic, narrative, and temporal. This text is so unstable, its motion so random, that the order of the book in general is at stake. How are we supposed to read a book that presents itself to us as sheer alterity? When the *Wake* was first published its readers virtually had to discover new modes of reading. Instead of reducing the *Wake* to familiar parameters, the challenge was to appropriate its radical otherness on its own terms. This meant finding the unfamiliar, yet decipherable, order that was inscribed into its "chaos." In this respect, the experience of reading the *Wake* is not unlike that of a scientist exposed to turbulence. As we know, however, turbulence drains energy, and for some readers the disturbances of reading grow catastrophically. For a long time, it was also thought that turbulence resists analysis. No wonder that readers of the *Wake*, just like scientists in the face of turbulence, have gone out of their way trying to resist the text's turbulence by undoing its condensations, closing the gaps between words, deciphering passage for passage, and restoring a conventional narrative.

Thus the *Wake*'s history of reception has in its beginnings been a history of appropriating its otherness according to familiar notions of order, an attempt to restore the order of language and the word, of narrative, history, and time. Postmodern theories, including chaos theory, by contrast, call for a model of reception that resists the reduction of textual otherness to familiar parameters. Yet meeting the "chaos" of the *Wake* on its own terms does not mean remaining engulfed in the trivial contingencies of mere disorder, but discovering a new order not scaled to customary perceptions, senses, or reading habits.

On the other hand, turbulence also resists stasis. The turbulent motion within the words of *Finnegans Wake* renders a plasticity to its linguistic space that makes it seem squeezable (an effect of condensation), and stretchable (an effect of displacement). In representing the turbulence of certain chaotic systems in topological form, chaos theorists uncovered a stretching and squeezing process that forms "strange attractors." The latter constrain disorder and channel it into patterns with a "common underlying theme" (Gleick 152).[7] In the long run, a dynamic system settles down to an attractor (Stewart 109). Strange attractors are "strange" because they combine properties that seem mutually exclusive: on a microscale, trajectories diverge exponentially, producing irreducible unpredictability; on a macroscale, though, these trajectories continually fold back on themselves and form a clearly discernible pattern that occupies a bounded region of phase space. Each point on the strange attractor defines the qualitative behavior of the whole system. In *Finnegans Wake*, the enfolded narrative of HCE and ALP, which runs through the turbulent currents of poetic language and reappears on different scales, functions as such an attractor. Like strange attractors, this narrative is hard to detect on a microlevel because its perception requires a holistic perspective of the whole system. Most importantly, however, the *Wake*'s formal properties seem to induce a corresponding mode of reception. As readers we depend upon strange attractors such as this narrative or other self-similar recursions that guide us through the turbulence of fluid sound- and wordshapes and lure us with the aesthetic appeal of familiar forms in a world of chaos.

The "strange attractors" in *Finnegans Wake* can thus be said to entice its readers to a holistic perception, a global qualitative definition of the textual process, the "ph(r)ase space"[8] of the *Wake*. "Phrase space" is not meant as a mere Joycean pun. It refers back to the way in which Joyce maps time and speed onto the surface of language. The strange attractor in chaos theory channels the "chaos" of a multidimensional space, whereas the strange attractor in *Finnegans Wake*, the underlying "themata" of HCE and ALP, channels the "chaos" of multidimensional, overlaid, and condensed narrative strands from different historical and textual spaces. In both cases the effect is one of a containment of time—namely, infinity—in a finite space.

Gleick quotes physicist David Ruelle as saying that strange attractors are "psychoanalytically 'suggestive' " (133). We may, in fact, unconsciously perceive certain strange attractors in dynamic systems and react to their aesthetic appeal, that is, to a syncretistic experience of order in chaos. In our literary adaptation, strange attractors are not merely properties of a system—their "attracting" power does not simply settle a chaotic system into a patterned behavior. Rather, strange attractors function here as focal points that draw our unconscious attention to a (textual) pattern that is not consciously accessible. This process is what Anton Ehrenzweig, in *The Hidden Order of Art*, calls "unconscious scanning."[9] The presence of strange attractors is, then, what distinguishes the chaos of a text like *Finnegans Wake* from pure contingency and noise. In order to become an aesthetic object in the strong sense of the word— an object with a persistent appeal and a strong holding power—a chaotic text thus needs not only an enfolded order but also strange attractors able to draw the reader's attention to this order.

From this perspective, we can further qualify the earlier remarks on scaling. Scaling appears as a literary technique of organization which inserts self-similarity on varying scales and thus installs strange attractors in the form of recursive structures or rhythms that are similar to each other without duplicating themselves.[10] The strange attractors produced by scaling thus reside no longer in the thematic resonance of dispersed narrative traces, but in the formal and rhythmic resonance of self-similar structures.

It becomes clear now why the scales of a text like *Finnegans Wake* depend upon "the viewing points of beholders"—a quality which Kenner attributes to scaling objects in general (724). The ability to read or listen across scales, and the sensitivity to self-similarity and strange attractors, must first be acquired and can, in fact, be trained by a text like *Finnegans Wake* whose implied reader seems to be—to modify Hugh Kenner's remark on Pound—"fishing for fractals" (728).

To develop this attunement to self-similarity we must learn both to shift between varying scales of attention and to develop a syncretistic attention which grasps the varying scales in a processual continuum or even simultaneously as a whole. This mode of reading stimulated by the *Wake* allows one further to qualify the distinction between scale-bound and scaling. Readers may easily reduce *Finnegans Wake* to a "scale-bound work" if they keep their attention focused on specific scales like the meaning of words, the underlying narrative, the macro-organization, etc. As Hugh Kenner has pointed out, "lit-crit is more at home with the scale-bound" (723). The early history of the *Wake*'s reception is characterized by such a focused or scale-bound attention. Joyce's implied reader, however, reads the text as a "scaling work" with an unfocused syncretistic attention, swiftly moving across varying scales and unconsciously scanning self-similarities and strange attractors (see also Schwab, *Subjects* ch. 5). Just as the fractal model allows one to account for the specific aesthetic experience of texts dependent on self-similarity and strange attractors, the categories of "scale-bound" and "scaling" are useful for differentiating between types of aesthetic experience.

John Cage envisioned *Roaratorio*, his musical response to *Finnegans Wake*, as a kind of circus with a "plurality of centers" (Cage 107). He also expressed his hope that his listeners would find some way to penetrate the noise, as if they would be drawn to these centers. Could we say that these centers function like "strange attractors" in Cage's "noise"? To be sure, at a microscale, the trajectories of the multilayered soundsystems that Cage produces with the help of chance operations diverge exponentially, thus producing unpredictability and seeming randomness. Cage's assumption about audible "centers" of noise, however—which many of his listeners have confirmed—seems to suggest that there is something comparable to "strange attractors" at work which channel the seeming randomness into a pattern. And indeed, one could say that, at a macroscale, the different trajectories of Cage's soundsystems fold back on themselves, forming centers with distinct patterns. *Roaratorio*, I would argue, draws its most intense effects precisely from this combination of properties that seem mutually exclusive, its ability to convey a discernible pattern within what seems to be utter randomness.

Cage wanted *Roaratorio* to be "free of ideas" (83), full of "poetry and chaos," to oppose "law and order" (85). Chance operations like the I-Ging or the recording of random noises at places mentioned in *Finnegans Wake* replace a consciously determined order with a nonintentional, randomly produced one. In order to reduce the number of listed places, Cage used the I-Ging chance operations to select 626 places—a number corresponding to the number of pages in *Finnegans Wake*. Understood as liberating processes, chance operations are meant to free musical production from the constraints of convention and musical theory. "I wanted to make a music that was free of melody and free of harmony and free of counterpoint: free of musical theory. I wanted it not to be music in the sense of music, but I wanted it to be music in the sense of *Finnegans Wake*. But not a theory about music. I wanted the music to turn itself toward *Finnegans Wake*" (89). One could also say, as N. Katherine Hayles argues in her analysis of Cage's work, that the goal is to free music from merely anthropocentric connections: "Yet the point is not to deny connection, since conjunction is a kind of connection. Rather it is to subvert the anthropomorphic perspective that constructs continuity from a human viewpoint of control and isolation" ("Chance Operations" 228).

Chance operations determine everything in *Roaratorio* down to technical details such as the stereo position and length of each sound, or, as Cage explains, "how it would come in, whether it would fade in, whether it would switch on, whether it would roll in, what its dynamic level would be, or levels, it could have one, two or three levels, and then how it would die away: whether it would fade away, roll off or switch off. All this was done with chance operations" (103). This shows that, despite its seeming randomness, *Roaratorio* is, of course, a highly deterministic work, albeit only in the sense that chance operations *determine* every single one of its structures. What produces the sense of randomness, then, is—like *Finnegans Wake*—not the lack of structures but their overdetermination.

And yet, like *Finnegans Wake*, *Roaratorio* depends on "strange attractors" that constrain randomness by channeling it into a pattern with a common underlying "theme." Not every overdetermined text or randomly produced music would appeal to us by generating an attractive chaos; on the contrary, most chaotic productions would certainly leave us cold. Formal constraints are crucial to distinguish Joyce's and Cage's works from mere chaos, noise, randomness, or contingency. Or, to put it differently, formal constraints generate the differential qualities that turn these "chaotic" productions into works of art. I would further assume that in a work of art self-similarity and strange attractors are linked to formal constraints. However, since all the soundtracks in *Roaratorio* are recorded over each other with the different layers melting and flowing together, its strange attractors are hard to detect. Like condensation in *Finnegans Wake*, the layering of sounds in *Roaratorio* inserts motion and speed into discrete sounds, so that their discreteness disappears into a flow that produces noise. Both Joyce and Cage deliberately insert noise into their "sounddances." Joyce echoes noises of Irish pubs, fragments of words picked up from the buzzing of voices and lifeworld noises, or distorted echoes of remembered words from foreign languages and cultures. Cage records random noises from scattered places, or from a randomly re-collected arsenal of musical instruments and technological sounds found in *Finnegans Wake*. In both Joyce and Cage such "quoted" noises often draw their effects from sudden flashes of recognition, faint memories of repetitions, distant echoes of familiar themes, rhythms, or melodies. Whenever turbulence suddenly settles down to a fragile equilibrium, it becomes possible to hear with another ear that perceives ordered soundwaves within chaos, or merely the sounds of silence.

The concern with noise and its vanishing Other, silence, is another pointedly postmodern issue that Cage shares with Joyce. The new space or schizosphere of noise and silence explored in postmodern artifacts may also be seen or heard as another effect of motion and speed. The concern with noise reflects the awareness of lost silence and clarity in the universe of sound, a sound pollution resulting from the speed, multiplicity, and technological amplification of sounds in technologically oversaturated schizospheres. Cage evokes the brittle ecological balance between sound and noise when he says, "A fugue is a complicated genre; but it can be broken up by a single sound, say from a fire engine" (19). "True, the fugue's principle is self-similarity: subject and countersubject reintroduced, restated," writes Hugh Kenner (727). But what happens when, as Cage points out, self-similarity is disrupted by noise? Noise accounts for the difference between the self-similarity produced by Joyce and Cage and the self-similarity of a fugue or of the exotic fractal images produced by computers. The latter immediately lure their recipients with a bizarre harmony, while Joyce and Cage deliberately expose them to painful noise before revealing their self-similarity. If self-similarity is not displayed "harmoniously" as in a fugue or a fractal image, it must be discovered within the "noise" produced by the condensation of different scales such as the soundtracks in *Roaratorio* or the word traces in *Finnegans Wake*. When discrete scales are layered, condensed, or melted together into one continuum, the "scaling object" becomes overdetermined and assumes a degree of complexity that makes it extremely hard to discern its enfolded self- similarity. In *Roaratorio* self-similarity may, for some listeners, remain buried in noise and never reveal an attractor. In this case, the piece would present itself as irreducible alterity. If, on the other hand, a listener is able to release control and listen to the piece with unfocused attention, then she shifts to that receptive attitude that Cage calls "letting sounds be." Hayles compares this type of reception to the solving of a Zen koan:

Confronted with such a text, the reader struggles to correlate differences so that they become significant, until finally the mind is swamped with the enormity of the task and comes to rest. At this point the text can begin to function like a Zen koan, releasing the initiate from the circle of her assumptions by posing a question that cannot be answered unless she is willing to relinquish the primacy of human intention. Letting sounds be, Cage calls this receptive condition, and he strives to achieve it with language as well as with music. ("Chance Operations" 236)

These reflections might inspire a more general conclusion about the aesthetic experience of otherness. The alterity of pieces like the *Wake* or *Roaratorio* is not absolute in the sense that we may find it in the works. Like otherness in general, it is sensitive to the attitudes, interests, learned patterns, perceptive habits and moods with which those exposed to it approach it. Similar to so-called counterchanges—pictures such as the famous duck-rabbit that may be perceived in two ways depending on shifting viewpoints—the *Wake* and *Roaratorio* may be read in two ways: as exposing alterity, noise, and chaos or as revealing a deeper order. Often this shift in perspective coincides with a shift from focused to unfocused attention (see also Schwab, *Subjects* ch. 5). In a way, this shift resembles the cultural shift in sensitivity to order and chaos marked by chaos theory. It is foremost a theory that induces shifts in perspective, reading chaos in seemingly ordered objects and order in seemingly chaotic objects. The cultural affinities between Joyce, Cage, and chaos might thus lie in their insistence that chaos is no longer the mere Other of order.

This shift in the perception of order is intimately tied to the use of technology—not only the technology of computer-generated fractal images in chaos theory, but also the advanced technologies of writing and composing. Both Joyce and Cage take up the challenge presented by the accelerated motion and speed of emerging schizospheres of sounds. Keenly aware that the littered, high-speed soundscapes are effects of new technologies, they nonetheless both renounce a nostalgic technophobia. Instead of turning technology into the Other (of "natural" or "human" sounds), they explore its new spaces and its effects in the realm of language, sound, and silence. By enfolding silence within noise, Joyce and Cage convey that we may well get lost in the new schizosphere of ragged sounds and words, and hear nothing but noise unless we recover a different form of silence from within by developing a new sensitivity of reading and listening with unfocused attention, attuned to the syncretism of fractal forms.

In addition to "thematic noises" such as the random noise picked up from the environment and incorporated into *Finnegans Wake* and *Roaratorio*, both works generate noises of their own, noises born out of their density, complexity, and overdetermination. Cage reports Frans van Rossum's concern that, because of its overwhelming number of sounds, *Roaratorio* might result in "white noise." Cage's ironical reply—"no Frans, if it's going to be noise it will not be white but black—or some other color than white" (97)—alludes to his conviction that the "coloring" of noise, its musical coloration, will have the effect of a strange attractor. The point ingrained in Cage's humorous remark is that the noise engendered by *Roaratorio* is other and more than the transmission noise in the telephone lines or the hiss from a generator commonly referred to as white noise. It is the noise produced by several multitrack machines, a nearly unbearable multiplicity of sounds coming together and forming a soundspace where noise and information are no longer binary opposites but one and the same. The medium of noise does not interfere with information, but is the message, and, at the same time, information does not release an immediately discernible "message," but noise itself becomes a new code that generates its own meaning.[11]

How, then, are we to listen to this noise in *Roaratorio*? Since we cannot—as in *Finnegans Wake*—turn to the strange attractor of an underlying narrative, we must undergo the pain and torture of "black noise," of sounds polluting each other, in order even to accede to the other colors of Cage's noise. The pain of turbulence from magnified and condensed technological versions of roaring real-world noises is an indispensable initiation into *Roaratorio*.[12] Listening to Cage might then also paradoxically stimulate our senses to hear what we have made ourselves deaf to under normal conditions: the roaring noise of a world in chaos that mirrors us. "We are submerged to our neck, to our eyes, to our hair, in a furiously raging ocean," writes Michel Serres, "[w]e are the voice of this hurricane, this thermal howl, and we do not even know it. It exists but it goes unperceived. . . . We have eyes in order not to see ourselves, ears in order not to hear ourselves" (77). The mutual exclusiveness of roaring noise and silence thus collapses. We hear what our ears are deaf to: the roaring noise that surrounds us and the silence within. *Roaratorio* thus plays, like *Finnegans Wake*, with the coincidence of opposites, the *coincidentia oppositorum*. There is, of course, a dose of mysticism in these artistic games that both Joyce and Cage affirm with a vengeance against the hegemonic law and order of reason.

Thus Cage playfully links the new sciences and technologies with ideas from Eastern philosophies, carrying out his chance operations in the spirit of the Zen Buddhist idea of "purposeful purposelessness." In this way he hopes to open his music to a plurality of centers that unconsciously appeal to the mind like strange attractors (see Cage 21, 127).[13] These multiple centers emerge like clusters of soundsense within the turbulence of noise; they surface like eddies of familiarity, echoes of melodies or harmonies, memories of sounds never consciously "heard" as sounds. They flash into consciousness with the speed of a lightning flash, or they simply emerge with the uncanny quality of unconscious resonance. When we grasp these flashes in *Roaratorio*, we have gained an exemplary experience of the whole work.

Nonsense, Dream, and Chaos

These flashes of insight, produced by the capacity to perceive hidden self-similar structures and enfolded orders, might in fact be a crucial activity in unconscious scanning. During our unfocused attention to *Roaratorio*'s turbulence, its colored noises may transmute into meditative silence. Silence then appears as a strange attractor—the eye of the storm—within the multiplicity of sounds produced by technological turbulence. "What silence is," says Cage, "is not the absence of sounds but the fact of having changed one's mind to be interested in the sounds that there are, to hear them" (45). And then he adds, "the purpose of music . . . is to sober and quiet the mind thus making it susceptible to divine influences" (159).

Listening for the first time, nothing seems harder to imagine than a piece like *Roaratorio* produced or used for this purpose. And yet, Cage is precisely interested in the paradox of silence born out of turbulence, believing in our unconscious response to this silence as to a strange attractor. Heinrich Vorweg's speech given in 1979 at Donaueschingen during the presentation of the Karl-Sczucka-Prize for *Roaratorio* testifies to this qualitative shift in reception, this settling down of our attention to the strange attractor of silence within turbulence:

> *Roaratorio* runs for an hour, and as a rule my faculty of conscious perception, when detached from its accustomed patterns of reference, slackens after 12 to 15 minutes. Quite unexpectedly, however, the sound world of *Roaratorio* carried me through. What had been a close attentiveness turned, in an easy transition, into an almost unrestrained, surprisingly clear and pleasant appreciation of the listening matter. That was second dimension of my experience. My listening grew—I can't think of another paraphrase—into an unhoped-for meditation on a truly human course of the world. (167)

Vorweg's "second dimension" of aesthetic experience is precisely the new type of unfocused "scaling" attention that Hugh Kenner calls "transient, recurring, enduring" (729). Unfocused attention receives a text or piece of music as a truly "open work," that is, a work without the norm of completeness. During unfocused attention, the reading/listening may simply stop at a given point, since each part may provide an exemplary experience of the whole. "Self-similarity in general confers the liberty to stop without incompleteness" (729), writes Kenner. "One could work on the whole work from the beginning in such a way that from the moment the work began it was at all times and at anytime finished," says Cage about *Roaratorio* (161). This is yet another aspect of the containment of infinity in a finite space. Kenner's conclusive assertion about "scaling works" is valid for both *Finnegans Wake* and *Roaratorio*: "They aren't 'unfinished,' nor is the fractal composition of mountains, islands, clouds" (729). Not unfinished, but infinitely self-similar. This is why our reading/listening can become exemplary at any given time and then simply stop or go on endlessly shifting from scale to scale or containing them all ad infinitum.[14]

Finally, we may add that unfocused attention does at the level of reception what Cage does with his random operations at the level of production: both unfocused attention and random production free the mind from the restrictions of a censoring consciousness and from the habitual attention to conventional codes, familiar forms and sounds, rhythms and melodies. Setting us free for new modes of perception, unfocused attention also helps to forgo or undo the conditioning effects of our own cultural tradition. This, in turn, becomes the basis for attuning us to the otherness of cultural productions such as the *Wake* or *Roaratorio*. In a similar vein Gerald L. Bruns writes about Cage's ethics:

> Certainly a crucial link between poetry and ethics lies in allowing words . . . to live their own lives; it means listening, not tuning things out but letting them take us along. This does not mean, Cavell says, that we should stop making sense, rather it means being attuned, open and responsive. (220)

In this respect both the *Wake* and *Roaratorio* train us to do what Joyce and Cage do in the production of their works. This training also means attuning us to a radical otherness. Unfocused attention is decidedly "noncentric" in the most encompassing sense: it precludes focusing on the centrisms that still haunt our global world—be they ethnocentrism, sexism, racism, nationalism, or religious fundamentalism. In this sense, too, Joyce and Cage work against cultural hegemonies, while producing their transnational global effects from within the richness of local noises. Joan Retallack argues that the practice of reading initiated by Cage "enacts a tolerance for, and a delight in complex possibility," and concludes that such a practice "could have real social consequences" and "change the social climate" (268). Or it could, as Marjorie Perloff and Charles Junkerman argue, "avoid what Wittgenstein dismissed as 'transcendental chit chat'—the making of large and hence questionable generalizations, designed to 'explain' the universe" (12).

Reading Joyce with chaos theory, I have mainly emphasized the decentralizing strategies of the *Wake* and chaos theory's ability to attune us to its textual otherness or "chaos." So far I have not addressed the fact that Joyce's textual universe is deeply gendered, nor the fact that, as many critics have pointed out, in our culture chaos itself is encoded within the chain of cultural binarisms as the feminine opposite of masculine order. In this context, it is particularly interesting to see that French feminists have not only taken *Finnegans Wake* as a privileged example of *écriture feminine*, but have also displayed a special interest in the epistemological shift in the sciences toward fluid epistemologies. Irigaray and Kristeva, for example, address the question of a feminization of culture from within a larger historical shift toward fluid epistemologies and experimental aesthetic or discursive practices. What French feminists find attractive in both the fluid epistemologies and modernist experimentalism is their politics of heterogeneity and heteroglossia, a politics that is polemically turned against notions of identity and unambiguous sexual definition, or identity politics more generally.

In "Woman can never be defined," an interview in *Tel Quel* in 1974, Julia Kristeva warned against certain feminist demands to revive a "kind of naive romanticism, a belief in identity" (Gauthier 138). Since Kristeva models her own political stance on the politics of the literary avant-garde—namely, experimental modernists like Joyce who explore open and fluid forms of poetic language and dissolve identity at the level of voice, form, epistemology, and genre—she draws mainly on male writers in theorizing the "revolution" of poetic language. Not without a certain historical irony, it is thus male avant-garde writers who figure most prominently as models for the new *écriture feminine*. The latter is not tied to biological gender, but is explicitly based on structural effects of linguistic differentiation and sexual differentiation within cultural codes rather than gender and sexual difference.[15] The emphasis in French feminism on stylistic and formal aspects of speech and writing only reflects the assumption that, historically, open, chaotic, fluid, and nonlinear styles and forms of language have been encoded as feminine. Considering these affinities between Joyce, French feminism, and chaos theory, I will dedicate the second part of my reading of *Finnegans Wake* to Joyce's figuration of woman in chaos.

## 3. "Should Ladies Learn Music or Mathematics?" Feminists' *Wake* Meets Fractal *Wake*, or, Refractions of French Feminism and Chaos Theory

Once we tune our "eye-ears" (482.35) to the "feminine libido" (123.08) of *Finnegans Wake*, we may read it as a "proba-possible prolegomena to ideareal history" (262.03-08) of "bysexicle" (115.16) relations. The *Wake*'s answer to the question that serves as title of this section—"Should Ladies Learn Music or Mathematics?"—is "both," since woman in this text is to man not only what sound and music are to sign and writing, but also what space is to time and geometry is to history. Woman appears in carnivalesque archetypes as the Gran Geamatron (257.05), combining geometry with the archetypal earth mother, or as Frivulteeny Sexuagesima (298.25), combining frivolous, teeny, and vulva with the archetypal sexual being. Woman meets man in binary oppositions such as "Father Times and Mother Spacies" (600.02), "woman formed mobile or man made static" (309.21–22), or "Preausteric Man and his Pursuit of Pan-Hysteric Woman" (266.Margin). Joyce's "charactures" mock these binaries with questions such as "Is the Co-Education of Animus and Anima Wholly Desirable?" or "Why hidest thou hinder thy husband his name?" Psychoanalysis is an easy target when it comes to carnivalizing sexual tropes on this "map of the souls' groupography" (476.33) or in this "psychical chirography" (482.17–18). Jung and his concept of animus and anima are caricatured in Anna Livia's casting as "annyma" and in her daughter Issy's ironical remark that she follows the "law of the jungerl" (268.F3), insinuating there might be a streak of "primitivism" in Jung's archetypes of young girls.

Myriad puns on age-old gender binarisms, sexual fantasies, and fears of women are subverted, inverted, and distorted or collapsed into each other. If the "ideal reader suffering from an ideal insomnia" (120.13–14) reads these ironical invocations of worn-out gender binarisms in *Finnegans Wake* as marking the intersection between gender and textual politics she will become "cryptogam of each nightly bridable" (261.27). But what does it mean to be "cryptogam," or "When is a Pun not a Pun?" (307.02–03)? Can "cryptogamy" be read as a cryptic feminine writing that emphasizes the secret, the unspeakable, the crypt, and the womb—that is, all that has been incorporated and buried within the womb of language from the time of "ancient tongue" (270.17–18) to that of "postconditional future" (270.1)?

Approximately 30 years after the publication of the *Wake*, French feminists discovered *Finnegans Wake* as a text that not only exemplified but directly inspired their concept of an *écriture féminine*. Playing out the resonances and correspondences between Joycean poetics and feminine writing, French feminists celebrate Joyce to this day as one of its most radical practitioners. In an interview with Xavière Gauthier in 1974, Julia Kristeva says:

For at least a century, the literary avant-garde (from Mallarmé to Lautréamont to Joyce and Artaud) has been introducing ruptures, blank spaces, and holes into language. It is what Mallarmé called 'the music in letters': Maldoror's explosive *Chants* or the multiplied condensation of myths, philosophy, history, and verbal experience in *Finnegans Wake*. All of these modifications in the linguistic fabric are the sign of a force that has not been grasped by the linguistic and ideological system. This signification renewed, 'infinitized' by the rhythm in a text, this precisely is (sexual) pleasure (*la jouissance*). (Gauthier 165)

Interestingly, Kristeva draws out precisely those features as feminine *jouissance* that also pertain to the shapes of fractal chaos: the introduction of ruptures, blank spaces, and holes into language, and the "infinitizing" self-similarity of rhythm. Reading Joyce's "woman formed mobile or man made static," in light of Kristeva's quote, as an index to the textual politics in *Finnegans Wake*, we may say that Joyce feminizes poetic language by endowing it with a mobility hitherto unknown—a mobility that plays through the age-old binarisms of our culture. In a politics of otherness, binary oppositions work generally by culturally privileging one of the binary chains, thus creating, for example, the familiar gender hierarchies that assign an inferior status to whatever appears on the "feminine" side. Joyce invokes the whole range of binaries that have traditionally aligned woman with otherness, the body and pleasure (*jouissance*), darkness, the dream, the unconscious, the unbounded, the fluid, the irrational, the chaotic, and, of course, the poetic. But the carnivalesque condensations of binary oppositions undermine the boundary that constitutes them, thus defying the unequivocal construction of identities. Binary oppositions become the prime material for puns that often invert their implicit values and expose their function as cultural stereotypes.

Simone de Beauvoir was the first radically to denounce that all constructions of otherness in Western culture are gendered feminine. Following this tradition, French feminists focus their own politics of otherness on inverting the old values of binary oppositions. Affirming woman's affiliation with otherness, the body, the unconscious, and the "chaotic" forms of fluid epistemologies, they celebrate a language modeled precisely on the experimental forms that were culturally introduced by the (predominantly male) canonical modernists.

Among the codes of the feminine reappropriated by French feminism, the most controversial was certainly the binary chain of woman, the body, pleasure, and desire. "Writing with the body" programmatically reclaimed the subversive energies of female sexuality (*jouissance*) and especially those of its cultural formations that had been labeled as female pathologies: narcissism and hysteria. *Finnegans Wake* practices a quite different "verbivocovisual" form of "writing with the body." Reactivating the sensual dimensions of language—the "chimes of sex appealing" (268.02–03)—Joyce "feminizes" the "body of language" in its materiality of speech/sound and writing/script. While French feminists have reappropriated the language of the hysteric in their notion of "writing with the body," Joyce has given us an image of "writing in the womb": the "Uteralterance of the Interplay of Bones in the Womb" (293. Left Margin.22–25). Does this feminine speech of the "Pan-Hysteric Woman," where "flash becomes word and silents selfloud" (267.16–17), reappropriate the hysteric's lie or confirm the old stereotype "She'll confess it by her figure and she'll deny it to your face" (271.14–15)?

For Joyce and French feminists alike, "writing with the body" is first and foremost a textual practice, a cultural intervention addressed toward systems of representation based on binary oppositions. The affiliation of *écriture feminine* with Joycean poetics suggests that, apart from representing a feminine strand of modernism, Joyce also heralds a more general "feminization of culture." But what does "feminization" mean in this context? Undoubtedly, Joyce's poetics of mobility and openness, as well as his linguistic exploration of the dream and of chaos, belong to—if not anticipate—an increasingly pervasive trend in the culture at large toward thinking in the "fluid epistemologies" of complex, open, dynamic, and chaotic systems. As we have seen, this type of thought has historically been encoded as feminine because its most basic characteristics stem from the "feminine" side of the binary system.

At stake for feminists is thus the question to what extent this general cultural shift indicated a genuine feminization of culture. In contrast to the widely analyzed feminization of culture in the eighteenth century—a process marked by a new politics of the emotions labeled "cult of sensibility"—this new "feminization of culture" would be grounded in the forms of language and the epistemology of textual spaces. As we may infer from *Finnegans Wake*, mathematics and music meet in these textual spaces to produce "a rhythmatick" (268.8) that is filled with ruptures and blanks, a "music" taken from "gramma's grammar" (268.17) in the form of textual rhythms, alliterations, and rhymes or carnivalesque words that "entwine our arts with laughter" (259.7–8).

This is the larger framework from within which French feminists—particularly Irigaray, Kristeva, and Cixous—have read Joyce's poetic language as *écriture feminine*. My own retrospective reading of French feminists' Joyce engages the recent interest in literary studies in chaos theory, which shares with Joyce and the French feminists the fascination with ruptures, blank spaces, holes, noise, turbulence, and chaos. The links between Joyce, French feminism, and chaos theory are, in fact, forged by the theorists themselves. Luce Irigaray and Julia Kristeva, for example, connect their epistemologies explicitly—if critically—with the sciences. The problem of differentiation and undifferentiation in relation to chaos and order is crucial in Joyce, French feminism, and chaos theory alike. Kristeva, Irigaray, and Cixous, for example, see the gendering of language as a process of differentiation from within. At stake are, on the one hand, the effects of gendered cultural codes that are traceable within the forms of language and, on the other hand, aesthetic or discursive practices that work through, appropriate, or alter these codes. Kristeva, for example, argues that "the subject experiences sexual difference, not as a fixed opposition ('man'/ 'woman'), but as a process of differentiation" (Gauthier 165).

Kristeva's notion of "differentiation" may serve as a conceptual linkage between the Joycean practice of writing and the "fluid epistemologies" to which it has been connected. Kristeva sees "sexual differentiation as interior to the praxis of every subject" (Gauthier 166), including the praxis of theoretical discourse: "If we call the moment of rupture and negativity which conditions and underlies the novelty of any praxis 'feminine,' we understand that this moment is also present in the elaboration of theorems, theories, and science. No 'I' is there to assume this 'femininity,' but it is no less operative, rejecting all that is finite and assuring in (*sexual*) *pleasure* the life of the concept. 'I,' subject of a conceptual quest, is also a subject of differentiation—of sexual contradictions" (Gauthier 167).

Given the fact that the avant-garde aesthetic practices Kristeva chooses as her examples—the most radical among them being Joyce's *Finnegans Wake*— are largely based on processes of dedifferentiation, her emphasis on *differentiation* may, at first glance, seem surprising. In fact, if we view Kristeva's arguments in light of her own distinction between symbolic, semiotic, and thetic functions of language, we could argue that the specific mark of sexual differentiation in writing is precisely dedifferentiation, that is to say, the irruption of the feminine within a symbolic order that is encoded as masculine. Accordingly, Kristeva links the semiotic inscription of sounds, rhythms, and intonations with the maternal. Marked by the psychogenetic experience of symbiotic undifferentiation, the maternal sphere is, in other words, what knows no distinction between subject and object or self and other. Since language, however, develops in opposition to primordial undifferentiation, the inscription of the semiotic in language paradoxically results in an internal differentiation, an inscription of sexual difference that is not marked by gender but by mnemonic traces of the culturally gendered space of the semiotic.

Kristeva understands Joyce's practice of writing in terms of this concept of the semiotic. Dedifferentiation is the most obvious textual strategy that opens up Joyce's poetic language and generates the mobile and fluid forms reminiscent of the dream, the primary processes, or the semiotic in Kristeva's sense. Joyce's crossing of boundaries between words and languages on the one hand, and voice and writing (*écriture*) on the other, generates dedifferentiation as a structural effect within a gendered cultural code in which man figures on the side of differentiation and the symbolic—"static" sign—and woman on that of dedifferentiation and the semiotic—"mobile" sound.

Many critics have commented on the fact that Joyce reactivates the oral within the written or the spoken word within writing. But Joyce also precludes any nostalgic return to the paradise of undifferentiated voices before the fall of language into writing: "as they warred in their big innings ease now we never shall know" (271.23-24). Instead, his condensation of sounds and signs explores the potential of sounds within signs and, conversely, of signs within sounds. This is why his writing merges the opposition between the symbolic and the semiotic, or between sign and sound, within the intermediary function of the thetic which, according to Kristeva, inscribes the semiotic into the symbolic functions of language.

We could thus argue that along with the conventional distinction between writing and speech, the *Wake* also complicates the cultural affiliation of man, the "penman," with rhetoric and writing, and woman, "storiella" (267.07), with storytelling and the semiotic sounds, the "Singalingalying" (267.07) of nursery rhymes.[16] From the perspective of Kristeva's model of poetic language, Joyce privileges the semiotic over the culturally dominant symbolic functions of language and thus enforces those aspects of language that operate beyond signification, that is, the traces of our earliest perceptions and unconscious memories of language formed before we have learned to understand its codes and to speak. Since in patriarchal cultures the formation of the semiotic occurs at a time when the mother figures most prominently in the infant's life, Kristeva also describes the "semiotic" as the space of a linguistic inscription of the maternal. In Kristeva's theory we find thus a concrete psychogenetic explanation for the gendering of linguistic codes and of different dimensions of language.[17]

Many of Joyce's puns, his casting of men as mountains and women as rivers and, most importantly, the rhythms and moods of his different chapters, seem to confirm these different gender inscriptions in language. The feminine rhythms of Anna Livia Plurabelle, to take the most familiar example, are generated with tropes and forms that mimic the myriad fluid shapes and murmurs of rivers. And yet, the text plays across the boundaries that separate these binary oppositions in order to merge them or expose them as what they are: cultural constructions and stereotypes. Woman in Joyce does not remain fixed within her place in (prelinguistic) paradise where she is seduced by the (rhetoric of the) snake—"Eat early earthapples, Coaz Cobra to chatters. Hail, Heva, we hear! This is the glider that gladdened the girl" (271.24–26). Joyce has maliciously exchanged one stereotype for another: it is Eve who coaxes the snake into chatters, seducing by gossip rather than high rhetoric. Neither does woman remain fixed within the semiotic (in Kristeva's sense) or the Wonderland of a narcissistic mirror phase: "Though Wonderlawn's lost us forever. Alis, alas, she broke the glass!" (270.19–21).

Ironically, in reading *Finnegans Wake*, we can therefore no longer conceive "mobile woman" and "static man" as a fixed opposition that operates according to a clearly demarcated sexual or gender difference. With the whole text being mobile and fluid, the boundaries between female and male characters become unstable and flexible, too. Female characters in the *Wake* may temporarily assume solid shapes or turn into men—as, for example, when the two washerwomen turn into tree and stone or into one of the many textual incorporations of Shem and Shaun. Sexual differentiation appears, then, less as an effect of gendered characters—an effect that Joyce ironically dismisses as "She's her sex, for certain" (250.01)—but as an effect of differentiation within a fluid process of speech. The *Wake* may destroy the binarisms of the many cultures it invokes, but their effects—and here concretely the effects of "mobile woman" and "static man"—continue to operate within the text across different scales: at the level of character-effects, allusions to sexual difference, gender and gender wars reaching back to Adam and Eve, allusions to the tradition of romantic love in literature from Tristan and Iseult to the present. Moreover, the sexual differentiation of epistemologies and textual practices—static male epistemologies (the penman) versus fluid female epistemologies (whispers and gossip)—are, in turn, grafted onto the sexual differentiation of geographies and territories—mountains versus rivers, etc. The *Wake* very early refers to self-similarity across scales with the apt word "multiplicables" (4.32), which simultaneously invokes algebra, geometry, sexual reproduction, and aesthetic repetition.

This may lead us back to the questions posed at the beginning: How do the theoretical discourses of French feminism of twenty years ago relate to theoretical discourses today? Can we discern conjunctions, conjectures, and disjunctions that stimulate new readings of the *Wake*? Differentiation may again be taken as the key issue: in traditional epistemologies, differentiation is affiliated with order and dedifferentiation with chaos and entropy. Debates about order and chaos in *Finnegans Wake*, its self-proclaimed "chaosmos," have never ceased to mark the reception of this text. On the scale of obsolete static binary oppositions, order has, of course, been posited as (male-gendered) rationality and chaos as (female-gendered) irrationality. This is the conjunction where French feminist readings of Joyce have recently merged with readings from chaos theory. Their shared emphasis is what Gleick called "the demon of nonlinearity" (Clarke 89), or, to put it differently, Joyce's irreducible heterogeneity, his irregular, fragmented, or chaotic shapes that nonetheless reveal certain patterns of self-similarity or symmetries across scale—in short, his fractal forms.[18]

What happens when French feminist Joyce meets fractal Joyce? Luce Irigaray has argued that, historically, the symbolic order of language has maintained a tacit complicity with the sciences and especially the (meta)physics of solids, and that "the properties of fluids have been abandoned to the feminine" (Irigaray, *This Sex* 106): "What structuration of (the) language does not maintain a 'complicity of long standing between rationality and a mechanics of solids alone?' " (Irigaray, *This Sex* 107). Against this trend, Irigaray posits a feminist epistemology that draws its rhetoric from the scientific model of fluid dynamics, nonlinear dynamics, and their fractal dimensions. However, this gendered perspective of the sciences is deeply ambivalent because the "fluidity" of women has been, as Irigaray points out, an attribute produced within the binary logic of the epistemologies produced by patriarchal systems. In *Chaos Bound*, Hayles also invokes the affinities between chaos theory and cultural codes of the feminine: "Chaotic unpredictability and nonlinear thinking . . . are just the aspects of life that have tended to be culturally encoded as feminine" (173). But at the same time Hayles criticizes feminism's all too easy alliance with chaos theory at a time when chaos theory itself remains nearly exclusively a male domain.

Most of the analogies between chaos theory and feminism are structured around issues of differentiation and fluid boundaries. And yet, Irigaray and Hayles remain ambivalent toward the feminine/fluid and woman/chaos analogies. Similarly, in "Resistance in Theory and the Physics of the Text," Bruce Clarke cautions us to take the affinities between chaos theory and French feminism as experimental heuristic moves instead of stable identities that essentialize the locally feminine. Taking up the "feminine/fluid analogy" as an instance of the "politics of discursive isomorphism," he nonetheless ventures a perspective of chaos theory as "feminism for physics," speculating that we may currently witness a "reformulated scientific and critical rationality, a postmasculine rationality that establishes relations with rather than annihilates that which resists it" (92).

It seems tempting to develop a postmodern reading of *Finnegans Wake* as an aesthetic practice pertaining to a new space of postmasculine rationality. Yet, here we might also take Joyce's text as a corrective for a certain resistance in chaos theory to ambivalence. Theoretical abstractions tend to ignore the vicissitudes of local specificity. By contrast, the imaginary embodiment of certain figures of thought in literature highlights their sensitivity to environment or context. Joyce's isomorphisms, for example, remind us that "postmasculine" is not necessarily "feminist." Humor, irony, carnival, even sarcasm create a very distinct mood in the *Wake*, a practice of deterritorialization[19] that resists totalization and closure, insisting on a fundamental ambiguity in its textual politics. One may therefore easily connect but never reduce the *Wake* to any fluid language or theory (including future ones)—be it the dream, the dissolutions of the schizo, or the plays of nonsense; be it deconstruction, schizoanalysis, French feminism, chaos theory, or weak thought (Borradori, Introduction, p. 13).

On the other hand, the "politics of discursive isomorphism" performed by critics who make Joyce's text interact with different theories are very much in the spirit of Joyce's own operations: they play with analogies and reveal or build correspondences between disparate spheres. *Finnegans Wake* and its orbiting theories—including French feminism and chaos theory—will continue to interact without ever being reducible to each other. In order to retain the fluidity owed to the spirit of the *Wake*, a theory may never be taken as the one and only adequate framework that accounts for Joyce's aesthetic practice, lest it share the fate of "man made solid," succumb to gravity (loss of humor), and fall—like Adam, Finnegan, and Humpty Dumpty, whose fall is invoked at the beginning of Joyce's text. Or, if the theory happens to be feminist, it will fall as "Eve takes fall" (293.32). Theories aware of their own historical and cultural provisionality, on the other hand, attest to the *Wake*'s power to remain mobile and reach across the boundaries of confined historical times, politics, religions, cultural codes, discursive practices, and theoretical models. This different relationship to history is perhaps the most crucial difference between literary and theoretical discourses and in this sense we may well say with Joyce, "let us leave theories there and return to here's here. Now hear" (76.10–11).

What we hear when we focus on the "here's here" are sounds and rhythms that connect us with all times and places, including ever new theoretical ones. Here comes everybody and throws something else into this huge whirlpool of potential readings. The very multiplicity and diversity of Joycean readings is a direct result of Joyce's politics of otherness. What Clarke says about chaos theory, that it "establishes relations with rather than annihilates that which resists it" (92), is also true for Joyce and his implied politics of reading otherness. There might be a long way to go from here to a concrete feminist politics; yet the question of epistemology has been crucial for any politics and urgent enough to forge conceptual alliances between Joyce, French feminism, and chaos theory.

We will never overthrow patriarchy with the *Wake*, but we might use it to mock patriarchal or patriotic moods and the rationalist confinement to linear thought, bounded forms and dogma of whatever kind, including theoretical ones. If Joyce promotes a politics, it is a politics of otherness that defies the hierarchies of binary oppositions while exposing their cultural power, their grip on the mind in the form of stereotypes and archetypes. We may learn from Joyce to loosen this grip through a specific humor that restores or creates complexity, ambiguity, and openness—even in relation to feminism and its politics of otherness.

Regarding what I called fluid epistemologies, we may also learn from the emphasis Joyce places on the dark side of fluidity. Both French feminism and chaos theory present a very aesthetic fluidity: flowing streams, clear water, bizzare but beautiful fractal forms. Even bodily fluids appear in aesthetic sublimation. Cixous, for example, romanticizes the maternal body in images of writing with the flow of the mother's milk or the intimacy of menstrual blood. Joyce, by contrast, also incorporates unsublimated fluids, uncontrollable bodily substances, and monstrous excesses. Monstrosity inspires his figuration of characters and use of language. Interestingly, monstrosity is also another cultural encoding that fractal shapes and women share with each other. After pointing out that, among other things, fractal shapes had been called "hydralike" (5), Mandelbrot uses the rhetoric of monsters for his own enterprise of studying irregular forms: "as the classical monsters were defanged and harnessed through my efforts, and as many new 'monsters' began to arise, the need for a term became increasingly apparent" (4). Similarly, many critics have treated the irregular and excessive forms in *Finnegans Wake* as monstrous. As if to support this monstrous feminization of language thematically, Joyce's text abounds with invocations of archetypal female monsters and monstrous archaic mothers. Allusions to primitivism such as the "law of the jungerl" further extend the "monstrous" to animalistic aspects of human sexuality and feminine libido. Monstrous, voracious, and excessive, human sexuality, and feminine libido in particular, become a site of the abject, of defilement and filth, of spilled bodily fluids, repelling smells, and uncontrollable waste.

In "Wasted Words," Clara McLean analyzes Joyce's obsession with and ambivalence toward bodily fluids and waste. As Kristeva argues in *Powers of Horror*, bodily fluids, too, have been encoded as feminine, that is, as ciphers for the abject female body or for an abject maternity, the monstrous body of the archetypal great mother. In *Male Fantasies*, Klaus Theweleit emphasizes the destructive impulses toward this abject female body and its overdetermined and overcoded figuration in a militarized culture. *Finnegans Wake*'s figuration of bodily fluids emphasizes both their liberating and threatening aspects: they are, as McLean points out, "both life and waste, sustenance and poison (McLean n.p.)." This is the challenge that the *Wake* presents to our current fascination with fluid epistemologies: to insist on their dark, monstrous, and abject side as what is repressed in the current fluid epistemologies and to remind us of the stakes in encoding this abject side as feminine.

French feminism has taken up and reevaluated cultural fantasies of abjection and female monsters, among them those of writing monsters. Christiane Rochefort's question "Are Women Writers Still Monsters?" recalls that not long ago female writing performed a monstrous transgression of cultural boundaries, a usurpation of the Word, man's exclusive possession. Kristeva links phantasms of the monstrous archaic mother with abjection, cast in an ambiguous opposition to the *jouissance* of *écriture feminine*. Abjection is the Other of *jouissance*, its dark side, a "jouissance in which the subject is swallowed up but in which the Other, in return, keeps the subject from foundering by making it repugnant" (*Powers* 9). Itself rooted in the abject, artistic experience is, according to Kristeva, also a means of purifying the abject. Kristeva reads *Finnegans Wake* as a text that purifies the abject by transposing its thematic occurrence into a formal dimension, a way of speaking: "The abject lies, beyond the themes, and for Joyce generally, in the way one speaks; it is verbal communication, it is the word that discloses the abject, and that is what Joyce seems to say when he gives back to the masterly rhetoric that his *Work in Progress* constitutes full powers against abjection. A single catharsis: the rhetoric of the pure signifier, of music in letters—*Finnegans Wake*" (*Powers* 23). If rhythm and music are thus, as Kristeva says, "the only way out, the ultimate sublimation of the unsignifiable" (*Powers* 23), then both Joyce and Cage achieve their cathartic release of the abject into language not by negating but by embracing it, thus recovering a *jouissance* that spits out the swallowed subject in a thunderous torrent of sounds and words.

# WITCHES, MOTHERS, AND MALE FANTASIES:
## THE OTHERNESS OF WOMAN

# 4

# SEDUCED BY WITCHES

## *The Scarlet Letter*

No play is deeper than its witches.
—Herbert Blau, on Arthur Miller's *The Crucible*

IN 1692, over a period of three months which has become famous as the New England witch craze, Salem, a little town in Massachusetts, which also happens to be the birthplace of Nathaniel Hawthorne, witnessed twenty-one executions on account of witchcraft. Another 150 accused, including a four-year-old girl, were held in chains for months. Women were not the only ones to die at the gallows. Among the twenty-one victims—seventeen of whom were female—were two men and two dogs. This happened at a time when the witch craze in Europe was already nearing an end, and even in New England the legal proceedings of the witch trials had begun to be challenged.

A century later, this period of the witch hunts resulted in a flood of adaptations in American nineteenth-century literature whose trail of influence reaches well into the present. I will present a contextual reading of Nathaniel Hawthorne's *The Scarlet Letter*, choosing this historical frame and its fictional adaptations as the horizon of interest. I would like to show that even though *The Scarlet Letter* does not, like some of Hawthorne's other texts, directly focus on Salem witchcraft, it is deeply affected by its larger cultural impact. In order to grasp the textual traces of this impact, my reading reaches beyond literary history proper in order to unfold a pyschohistorical criticism. From this perspective, Hawthorne's text appears as a cultural critique that does not so much concentrate on a historical period as on the effects of a cultural internalization of certain patterns of interpretation, in this specific case the witchcraft pattern.[1] This pattern had been formed during the Middle Ages and was used as the basis of direct social action until about the end of the seventeenth century, that is, the time of the Salem trials. At that time, however, the pattern was already dissolving gradually, and in the eighteenth century it disappeared from the surface of social semantics.[2] But due to the fact that the witchcraft pattern had been internalized, it lived on in displaced forms as a part of the political unconscious.

To put it more concretely, I am concerned here not with the literary depiction of historical witches but with an internalized pattern of witchcraft which was effective on a much larger scale in the cultural representation of women in general. The witch appears, in this perspective, as Other in the cultural production of female subjectivity. *The Scarlet Letter* offers a prime example that allows one to trace this cultural phantasma of the witch. While undercutting the stereotypical literary figuration of historical witches, the highly overdetermined narrative of Hawthorne's romance also reveals the fundamental ambiguities of the witchcraft pattern.

My analysis proceeds in three steps. First, I address the cultural use of the witchcraft pattern as a mode of interpretation and action. Here I focus on male phantasms of seduction or, more precisely, on fantasies of women seduced by the devil. Staged as public spectacles, the witchcraft trials allowed these fantasies to be acted out collectively. In this context the gaze becomes crucial—be it the public gaze of the Puritan community in its cultural function, or the phantasmatic cathexis of the witch gaze, namely, the evil eye. In a second step, I point out how conventional literary witchcraft narratives reenact a specific witch stereotype by displacing it onto various phantasms of seduction.[3] Usually such narratives create a romance, figuring a witch who weaves her black magic into certain family ties, always plotting seduction. These romances function like a Freudian "family romance" in inciting their readers to act out the cultural phantasm of the witch in the reading process. Third, I read *The Scarlet Letter* as a narrative that, instead of fictionalizing historical witches, reveals the witch stereotype as a cultural pattern of interpretation used by the New England Puritans against deviant women in general.

Since its cultural formation in the Middle Ages, the witchcraft pattern had been used to symbolize and interpret the relationship of historical subjects to what was perceived as "external nature" or society. For example, women who provided traditional medical care as midwives and healers were increasingly cast as witches by a gradually professionalized male system of medicine. But, at the same time, the witchcraft pattern was also used to express a cultural relationship to "inner nature," that is, to specific psychological states, particularly fear and desire in relation to women. Thus it was for example able to absorb and externalize the male fear of seductive women on the one hand, and of strong, independent women on the other. In each case, the creation of a witchcraft pattern as a constitutive element of the social semantics of the time reveals a pervasive cultural attempt to overcome or subdue nature—be it figured as external or internal, as wilderness, native Indian, untamed and earthbound woman, or female desire and power. Moreover, the witchcraft pattern functioned on the basis of a double code, according to which all *visible* signs of the phenomenal world gained their deeper meaning as manifestations of an *invisible* world ruled either by divine or diabolic powers.

Any epistemological framework according to which the essential meaning of the world is concealed behind its visible representations requires a special code that allows the members of a community to read the manifestations of the invisible world. Otherwise, the social semantics of this community would cease to function as a reliable system of orientation. In Puritan New England the logic of the Covenant provided such a code, allowing one to interpret signs of grace (see Miller). This code remained, however, highly problematic and unstable since there was always the suspicion that the devil or his allies, the witches, aimed, in their perfidiousness, at outwitting precisely this system of interpretation provided by the Covenant. Devils and witches were supposed to do what God did not do: use signs to deceive and also to seduce. Their cunning was believed to undermine the reliability of the Puritan search for redemption, confronting it with a semantics of deceit and a rhetoric of seduction. Therefore the invisible diabolic world was believed to have its own code figuring visible and readable symbolic objects and signs of witchcraft. Be it the flight on the broomstick or the suspended gait, tearlessnes, or the evil eye, the repertoire of witch attributes and the signs of the witch code were precisely delineated. Perceived as visible signs of the invisible world, they could accordingly be used to persecute the carriers of the signs and thus bring the invisible world under control. Thus, the signs of the witch code were not merely seen as the stereotypes transmitted by deranged imagination, but also as symbolic vehicles used to control the invisible world through the coding of visible objects.

This is how gradually a negative fixation on the gaze evolved, and in Puritan New England this fixation was reinforced even more by the Calvinistic search for signs of redemption. The public sphere was organized according to an overall cultural attempt to expose the invisible world to the gaze. In addition to the precise coding of visible manifestations of witchcraft, the Puritan community also established ritualistic forms of publicly exposed punishment in which bodies were inscribed with visible signs of offenses against the divine order. Thus, paradoxically, the gaze as medium of interpretation became a guarantor, albeit an ambivalent one, of a reality that was actually invisible.

Accordingly, the witchcraft trials and executions were staged as institution-alized visual spectacles in which the community actively participated. In Puritan New England, the function of these spectacles was even enhanced by the fact that they were the only allowed form of festive gathering. Those members of the community who believed themselves to be bewitched by the accused—mainly women—performed their symptoms of affliction during the public trials under the community's gaze. Carried to the brink of insanity, their ecstatic convulsions betrayed an erotic semantics of the body and visually demon-strated the art of witchcraft through encoded gestures of demonic possession. In fact, the bewitched imitated and outdid the gestures displayed by the al-leged witches. If the latter, for example, crossed their fingers while pleading innocent, the victims would throw themselves immediately to the floor with splayed arms and spastic movements. The body became the stage for a specta-cle of seduction in which the gestures performed by the alleged witches were taken to devalue the spoken word, that is, the affirmations of innocence. A cul-turally encoded body language was turned into a visual (dis)play that split off from and devalued spoken language. Whatever the alleged witches would say, the community would reinterpret and challenge through a reading of their bodies.

These trials left the accused virtually no choice but to assume the role of a witch. This is why the puritanical cleric George Burroughs could claim during his own trial that in fact one had to be a witch to prove that one wasn't one. Burroughs thus referred to the split in social semantics and the paradox inher-ent in the historical "reality" of witches according to which one in fact had to admit to being a witch in order not to hang as one. In this paradoxical language game any plea of innocence was construed as an indication of firm adherence to the devil's Covenant. As a sign of repentance, however, official admission could prevent a death sentence. In both cases the "reality" of witchcraft was taken as a given. The "witch" herself had, in fact, been forced to cooperate ac-tively in establishing a social consensus.

In the historical context of the Salem trials, the witchcraft pattern thus served publicly to reaffirm the reality of witchcraft—a reality that had long since become precarious. On a more subliminal level, however, the public trials staged an erotic spectacle of seduction and punishment, acted out collectively on the basis of a shared tacit knowledge concerning the highly ambivalent status of the witch within Puritan ethics. In this sense the witchcraft pattern provided a tangible symbolic framework for a concrete social practice that al-lowed one to ward off both the internal and external attacks on Puritan beliefs.

How, then, does this witchcraft pattern change once witchcraft is no longer part of the official social semantics? Nineteenth-century New England literature saw a flourishing literary discovery of witchcraft as a favorite Gothic and romantic theme. The historical drama of the Salem witchcraft period revealed itself as an exotic heritage whose ambivalence could be reenacted under new historical and epistemological premises. One of the crucial aesthetic challenges for the nineteenth-century writers lay in the fact that the secular perception of what is assumed to have been the historical reality of the witch hunts had changed in the meantime. In retrospect, only the *belief* in witchcraft and the witch craze were considered real. In contrast, the invisible world and all its manifestations were seen, according to the new cultural code, as imaginary projections of the historical protagonists. The retrospective view thus added its own interpretation to the concurrent one, thereby doubling once again the already double-edged semantics of witchcraft.

There is an abundant corpus of fictional literature that deals explicitly or implicitly with New England witchcraft. The roughly forty works which are direct literary renditions of the Salem events exceed the narrow scope of Gothic literature.[4] The most important ones range from Lydia Maria Child's *The Rebels: Or Boston before the Revolution* (1825); John Neal's *Rachel Dyer* (1828); Whittier's *Legends of New England* (1831); Longfellow's *New England Tragedies* (1868); Esther Forbes's, *Mirror of Witches* (1928); up to Arthur Miller's *The Crucible* (1952).[5] It seems to me that all these texts fail to solve aesthetically the crucial problem of the period, namely, that, retrospectively, the status of what was considered to be reality or imagination had changed. But this failure is in itself highly significant, because it reveals the persistence of both the seductive power of the witch and the desire for "displaced" witch hunts. Although the historical interest in the witch craze is central to these texts, their precarious proximity to melodrama and to the Gothic novel allows one to surmise that they are, in fact, whetting quite a different appetite, which thrives less on the historical interest than on the witch as feared but seductive object of desire. The latter, however, remains precariously close to the witch stereotype used during the actual persecution of witches. The aesthetic problem nineteenth-century writers of literary witchcraft narratives faced was one of cultural politics: if they wanted to avoid merely reenacting the old stereotype under a fictional guise, they had to find a form that undermined the witchcraft pattern.

It is no coincidence that the literary interest in witchcraft arose in America almost simultaneously with the demand for a "genuinely American literature."

Aesthetically, this demand remained, however, oriented toward the English model. Walter Scott had already discovered the thematic reservoir with which to realize this demand: the historical past, on the one hand, and the miraculous, on the other. Significantly this discovery was made along the path of the Gothic novel. The New England witchcraft episode seemed ideally to meet this double interest in the historical and the miraculous, endowing America with its own piece of a belated Middle Ages that could simultaneously satisfy the hunger for history and the desire for the supernatural. Witchcraft literature is, in fact, nostalgic about this past inasmuch as it reenacts the witch stereotype and its inherent pattern of seduction and punishment on the basis of a romantic, or even more narrowly Gothic, imagination of femininity.

Indeed, this promising historical material seems to resist an aesthetic treatment that avoids the lure and entrapment of the Gothic. Even when literary figurations of witchcraft are explicitly framed as historical novels, they still draw on the Gothic imagination as their basic source of aesthetic effect. The Gothic novel's romantic interest in the occult, however, collides with the presentation of witchcraft as a historical event: the heritage of the Enlightenment obliges the nineteenth-century writers to present the witches as innocent victims, thus setting a trend toward demystifying the occult. This is why, aesthetically, historical witchcraft fictions are torn between two genres and desires: the Gothic novel and historical fiction. Instead of being one or the other, they are, in most cases, a literary compromise with a built-in disappointment. Their dilemma is that they cannot afford witches historically or ethically and yet are aesthetically dependent on them.

The aesthetic compromise of literary witchcraft narratives is usually based upon the age-old ambivalence toward the witch as a symbolic figuration of woman as Other—lure and abjection. This fundamental ambivalence is retained throughout the historical transformations of the witchcraft pattern, thus testifying to the persistence of a split figuration of otherness within cultural language games. Once the supernatural lost its claim to reality status in the wake of the Enlightenment, one might have assumed that the witchcraft pattern would disappear from the codes that regulate social and cultural activities. This was true, however, only insofar as this pattern vanished from the surface of public discourse. Yet, far from losing its symbolic value, the witchcraft pattern now became interiorized and would henceforth form part of the political unconscious. One could see this cultural interiorization of the witchcraft pattern as pertaining to the same process that psychohistorian Norbert

Elias describes on a larger scale as the gradual cultural transformation of outer into inner restrictions.

When, about 130 years after its dismissal as a pattern of sociocultural organization and interpretation, the witchcraft pattern reemerged in the guise of fiction, this interiorization had already been achieved. Hence the fictional witchcraft literature needed to account for the changed cultural status of the witch. In a certain sense, the aesthetic experience of witchcraft narratives had to allow, in other words, a deliberate and artful return of the repressed political unconscious. But in order to avoid simply reenacting the old pattern, these narratives would aesthetically have to work through the unconscious fascination with the witch. Historically, moreover, the belief in witches also needs to be interpreted as ideological construct. In fact, nineteenth-century writers and historians alike focus on socioeconomic and psychological motives which, at the time of the witch craze, were not accessible to public knowledge. Socioeconomic explanations, for example, point to the emergence of a specialized male medical system as one of the crucial factors in the labeling of women healers and midwives as witches. Psychological explanations, on the other hand, foreground the deeply rooted fears of and ambivalence toward women. Retrospectively, however, one can of course also see how these very motives already belonged to a tacit knowledge enacted during the witch trials—especially considering their eroticized subtexts.

Both the historical and the fictional witchcraft narratives of the nineteenth century thus attempt to reconstruct or act upon the presumed political unconscious of the witch craze. Nineteenth-century narratives, in other words, scrutinize the multiple motivations for the persecution of witches that were supposedly repressed in the official cultural code of the time. Accordingly, the historical or aesthetic function of these narratives lies in the fact that they recuperate for the realm of public discourse and communication parts of what was repressed in the past. How they attempt this recuperation varies of course greatly from text to text. While the historical witchcraft narratives must "rationalize the irrational," the fictional texts—in a romantic countermotion to the Enlightenment—discover in this very irrationality a source from which to draw their aesthetic and psychological effects.

The aesthetic use of the irrational or the miraculous produces, however, problems of a particular nature for the witchcraft fictions. Along with and partly as a reaction to the cultural desymbolization and interiorization of the witchcraft pattern in the wake of the Enlightenment, phantasms of the witch

survived in cultural clichés and stereotypes that were able to absorb the repressed irrational desires and fears connected with the witchcraft pattern.[6] Fictional witchcraft narratives tend to draw their effect from reviving or acting
out such phantasms. This is why, instead of critically exposing or undermining
the split language game that characterized the witch craze, these narratives so
often reproduce it aesthetically—albeit in various displacements. This dynamic
can be illustrated by retracing a basic scheme in these texts.

Most strikingly, the nineteenth-century witchcraft narratives perform a reevaluation of values, a new investment in the figure of the witch that draws
mainly on Enlightenment and Romanticism. Women, who during the actual
witch hunts were supposed to have been seduced by or to have sold themselves
to the devil, are now figured retrospectively as victims of an age blinded by the
witch craze. In their romantic figurations, these women are finally allowed to
unfold in uncensored form the erotic charm of their seductive play, formerly
considered to be a sign of their sinful nature. From the perspective of historical
fiction, these very women form the core of a plot that figures well-known historical protagonists from the Salem witchcraft trials.

To take a famous example, in John Neal's *Rachel Dyer*, Rachel is figured as a
strong, mysterious, and attractive woman, whose fate is sealed because she carries the very stigma that had historically belonged to the repertoire of signs
revealing an allegiance with the devil: a deformed body. Her sister Elizabeth,
by contrast, is portrayed as a beautiful, fragile, child-woman. Both women love
the male hero of the novel, the Reverend George Burroughs, historically one of
the two men put to death during the Salem trials. The choice of Burroughs as
male hero in Neal's novel is itself highly significant since Burroughs figures as
the Other of colonial history: son of an English Quaker woman and an American Indian father, this mixed-blood character invokes the Quakers' heretic belief and Indian devil worship in one person. Moreover, in his public defense of
the two Dyer sisters, this Byronic hero of a witchcraft romance also acts as an
enlightened skeptic. He finally dies at the gallows, together with Rachel, while
Elizabeth is saved. A dense network of historical allusions forms part of an
intertextual web of family relationships between various historical figures used
as characters in other New England witchcraft fictions. Rachel and Elizabeth
Dyer, for example, are daughters of the legendary Mary Dyer who, before her
execution, uttered the curse on the Salem judges and their descendants to
which Nathaniel Hawthorne refers in his introduction to *The Scarlet Letter*.
Moreover, on her way to the gallows, Mary Dyer was accompanied by Ann
Hutchinson, the heretic who founded the Antinomian sect. Ann Hutchinson,

in turn, plays a crucial role in *The Scarlet Letter*. Thus, the two Dyer sisters, and later Hester Prynne, are linked to the first sectarian movement that offered women an alternative to the misogyny and sexual repression of Puritan orthodoxy and could therefore recruit large circles of women.

Beneath the surface of the fictionalized historical events, the protagonists of the Romantic New England witchcraft fictions reactivate all-too-familiar phantasms of the witch. In virtually all of these texts the relationships are dominated by familial organization and reveal fantasies of a wish-family strikingly similar to those in the Freudian family romance. The witch is the center of desire in these fictional elective families, or, more precisely, it is always one of two witch types: the beautiful wild witch (who will become the model for Hester Prynne) or the child-woman witch—a classic model of which is Doll Bilby figured in Esther Forbes's *A Mirror for Witches*, about whom the narrator says that she "with more than feminine perversity preferred a Demon to a Mortal Lover," and who destroys all the men who fall prey to the magic of her seduction. Significantly, both stereotypes underlying the witchcraft pattern coincide with the two complementary male fantasies of female seductresses. A third type of witch—the most common historical victim—may, in the fictional texts, occupy only the position of a peripheral figure: the old or deformed witch possessing magic powers, who comes to represent, in fact, the inverse of seduction.

In addition to these pure types, we find, of course, female characters who are condensations of different types—for example, Rachel Dyer, who is a condensation of the strong, mysterious witch and the deformed witch. In contrast to the third type of the old or deformed witch, the seductive women, stigmatized as witches and desired by the male protagonists, are at the same time classified as antagonists to the "normal" woman. By a curious inversion, however, it is now the "normal" woman who must assume the very negative feminine attributes that had been formative for the witch stereotype. We thus encounter in these Romantic texts both a significant displacement and a reproduction of the witch stereotype: these fictions reevaluate the historical witches by romanticizing the two seductive types, while at the same time displacing the pattern of the third and nonseductive witch type onto the normal woman. Be it as the frigid or infertile wife, prototype of antiseduction, or as the jealous mother, the normal woman is unwittingly stylized as the affective driving force behind the witch craze. Thus she is used not only to reproduce the old pattern of male fear of women, but also to serve as a scapegoat who can absorb the displaced guilt stemming from the witch craze.

We can find this schema even in Arthur Miller's *The Crucible*—a play that was obviously not conceived as a romantic adaptation of the historical material, but as a historical projection of the McCarthy era. Miller's drama relies much more heavily on the documented witchcraft trials than do the earlier adaptations. Witchcraft itself is presented under a rationalizing perspective: the "bewitched" young girls suffer from adolescent hysteria; behind the accusations lie dramas of jealousy and revenge, as well as political or economic interests. All the more interesting is the fact that the classic witch family romance remains intact. The play's hero is the historical John Proctor, whose identity is threatened by two women: by his wife Elizabeth, who is portrayed as the frigid, cold woman and by her opponent, Abigail Williams, a nymph who seduces Proctor and blackmails his wife as a witch. Thus the conventional phantasms underlying the witchcraft pattern are preserved: the nymph incorporates the seductive child-woman witch; the hysterical woman is a descendant of the possessed woman; and the frigid wife is figured as a contrasting social paradigm of antiseduction, itself a threat to masculinity. While Miller's play is supposed to show that there are no witches, but only witch hysteria, it also reveals, if read against the grain, how the phantasms that underlie the witchcraft pattern have survived as phantasms of male fear and desire.

It is precisely this witch family romance that, in the fictional witchcraft narratives, functions as a literary compromise, making the old witch phantasms aesthetically palatable. Even if the romanticized (or, as in Miller, "hystericized") witches function, in one way, as a demystification of the historical witches, their aesthetic effect is drawn from the phantasm of the desirable, but also threatening, witch who, because of her seductive powers, retains an aura of the supernatural, even in a disenchanted world. Since, moreover, the distribution of negative and positive witch phantasms is preserved by stigmatizing the normal woman—thus maintaining the two polar evaluations of femininity —these texts do not overcome the witchcraft pattern, but only achieve an inversion of the manifest and the latent cultural codification of the witch. While, in the historical context, the cultural cathexis of the witchcraft pattern was governed for the most part by fear of the witch, the literary texts now invert this cathexis by focusing on the complementary fantasies and desires that had been concealed in the historical context. Nevertheless, the old fear lurks beneath the surface, since even after the pattern of desire and seduction has surfaced, the men who are the objects of seduction perish along with their objects of desire. To make matters worse, the driving force seen behind the destruction of the male protagonists is now the old witch disguised as an ordinary woman.

The aesthetic and psychohistorical weakness of this type of fictional witch-craft narrative, the witch family romance, rests on the fact that it reevaluates the witchcraft pattern, yet leaves its underlying phantasms intact. Thus it merely transposes fixed cultural clichés into literary fictions that reveal the persistence of the witchcraft pattern in the political and cultural unconscious.

This is the specific context in which I see Nathaniel Hawthorne's texts making an ambiguous if not ambivalent intervention. Even though most of his texts do not belong to the direct renditions of the Salem events, seduction in New England Puritanism is one of their prominent themes. Quite often Hawthorne treats his subject by invoking an aura of witchcraft, or even by revealing a subliminal persistence of the witchcraft pattern. As I am less concerned here with the fictional representation of historical material than with the literary reproduction of a witchcraft pattern, it turns out that those of Hawthorne's texts in which witchcraft as such is displaced from the center of the plot are the most interesting. *The Scarlet Letter* seems to me paradigmatic not only in exposing the witchcraft pattern in a displaced context, but also in displaying devices that undercut its aesthetic reproduction. In "The Custom-House," his introduction to *The Scarlet Letter*, Hawthorne presents himself as the descendant of two notorious persecutors of witches and heretics, William and John Hathorne. The latter is said to have been the harshest judge of the Salem trials. Nathaniel Hawthorne declares himself to be superstitious enough to see his fictional dealings with witchcraft as an answer to the curse which the famous heretic Mary Dyer leveled against the Hathorne family. It is to Hawthorne's credit that he did not give us yet another spectacular dramatization of the witch craze, but a fictional analysis of the witchcraft pattern in a broader framework not limited to the empirical witch. In *The Scarlet Letter*, historical witchcraft is only the background for a far more pervasive use of the witch stereotype. It is this stereotype that becomes the actual subject of the novel.

Hester Prynne, the protagonist, is indicted not as a witch, but as an adulteress. The prominent drama of seduction has been displaced from a supernatural to a secular stage. Even so, the basic traits of the stereotype remain obvious. At the onset of the novel's familiar plot, Hester is established as an outcast woman. The scene opens with the traditional Puritan performance of public punishment. Exposed to the gaze of the collected community, Hester stands at the pillory bearing the two emblems of her disgrace: sewn to her dress the scarlet letter *A* for adulteress, and in her arms her illegitimate daughter Pearl. Since Hester does not name the father, the Reverend Arthur Dimmesdale, the parishioners suspect a diabolic paternity. Hester's exposure to the humiliation of the public gaze coincides with the arrival of her husband, who had been presumed dead after his disappearance, and who, through secret gestures, now commits Hester to silence about his identity.

The network of family and love relationships is thus concealed from the public but revealed to the readers—a device designed to create a complicity with Hester, who is the only one to know all the threads of the network. Following this scene, Hawthorne's readers become witness to a drama of revenge which could—as far as the plot itself is concerned—easily occur in a Gothic novel. In silent revenge, Hester's husband, a doctor with the allegorical name of Chillingworth, himself suspected of witchcraft because of his affiliations with the Indians and their use of herbal plants, moves into Dimmesdale's house under the pretense of investigating the reverend's "heart problems."[7] Dimmesdale will perish under Chillingworth's penetrating gaze because he has concealed his guilt from the community. In contrast, Hester lives with Pearl at the edge of town and learns to outgrow the role that the stigmatic *A* has imposed on her by changing its symbolic cathexis not only for herself but also for the community.

Like the conventional witchcraft narratives of the time, Hawthorne's novel is based on the scheme of a complicated family romance. Not only are the entanglements of family and love relationships similar to those in a traditional witchcraft narrative, but there are also secular representations of the three types of witches which together form the witchcraft pattern. While Hester is figured according to the image of the beautiful, wild witch, her daughter Pearl is stylized as the child-woman witch. The third type of the old and ugly witch is represented by Ann Hibbins, a peripheral character modeled after one of the historical witches who was hanged for witchcraft in Salem in the year 1656. However, while the conventional witch family romance uses the witch to seduce the reader into acting out the passions that she represents, Hawthorne reveals these passions to be the result of a repressed desire that has historically lent its energies to the formation of a culturally shared witchcraft pattern. Hawthorne's text thus scrutinizes a social semantics in which the stereotype of the witch transmits cultural norms of femininity via the repression of sensuality and desire. In so doing, *The Scarlet Letter* foregrounds the dominance of the gaze in the historical formation of the witchcraft pattern.

The gaze, in fact, becomes the organizing principle for the whole text: as puritanical gaze, it steers the dynamics of the narration; as the gaze of the narrator, it inserts a normative perspective to guide the readers' responses. Thematically, the gaze is revealed as a medium of social formation, be it through the dynamics of seductive or of punitive exposure to the gaze, or even—as in Hester's interaction with the community—through a dialectic of seduction and punishment. Finally, as aesthetic device, the gaze is used as metaphoric visualization, as an exposure of images to the gaze of the reader. All the central symbols in *The Scarlet Letter* are visual images derived from the puritanical gaze-mediated code. The gaze of the scopophilic community, fixed on the marked woman and her child, appears as a social ritual staged in order to establish the power of social consensus via visual interactions. The letter *A*, which Hester is forced to bear her entire life, imposes upon her a visible codification of her body. Under the Puritan gaze the letter becomes a vehicle that enforces her new identity as adulteress. Hester is deindividualized, reduced to a mere representation of sin until she learns to deallegorize and resemanticize the symbol *A*.

Hester's interiorization of the Puritan gaze also becomes identity forming for her daughter. Pearl does not see herself mirrored in the eyes of her mother but in the golden reflection of the scarlet *A*:

> The very first thing which she had noticed, in her life, was—what?—not the mother's smile, responding to it, as other babies do, by that faint, embryo smile of the little mouth. . . . But that first object of which Pearl seemed to become aware was—shall we say it?—the scarlet letter on Hester's bosom! One day, as her mother stooped over the cradle, the infant's eye had been caught by the glimmering of the gold embroidery about the letter. (110–11)

As Pearl's "mirror stage" is thus determined by the scarlet letter, she will have internalized its phantasmatic cultural significance, the witchcraft pattern, long before she grows up to understand its codified meaning. Hester in fact reinforces this pattern through her interactions with her daughter. In keeping with current superstitions of the time, Hester does not see herself mirrored in the eyes of her daughter. Instead she sees Dimmesdale's image, which, as in a dream, is very tellingly condensed with the image of the devil:

> Once, this freakish, elfish cast came into the child's eyes, while Hester was looking at her own image in them . . . suddenly . . . she fancied that she beheld, not her own miniature portrait, but another face in the small black mirror of Pearl's eye. It was a face, fiendlike, full of smiling malice, yet bearing the semblance of features that she had known full well, though seldom with a smile, and never with a malice, in them. It was as if an evil spirit possessed the child, and had just then peeped forth in mockery. Many a time afterwards had Hester been tortured, though less vividly, by the same illusion. (120)

This reflection not only reveals that Hester herself has unconsciously linked her own stigma to the witchcraft pattern, but also shows that she transfers it to her own daughter. Pearl develops as an elfin, witchlike girl, persecuted by the suspicious gaze of the community as much as of her mother, who fears in the daughter the stigma she herself bears. In tracing Pearl's development and her interaction with Hester, the text introduces a dimension that undermines the historical polarization of supernatural reality and sensual manifestation: the sociopsychological genesis of a "witch" according to the witch stereotype. This process is mediated by a gaze that condenses the psychological function of the mirroring process between mother and daughter with the social function of the gaze in the Puritan cultural code. Pearl's gaze is figured as carrying the stigma of "a born outcast" (117) since her early infancy. "It was a look so intelligent, yet inexplicable, so perverse, sometimes so malicious, but generally accompanied by a wild flow of spirits, that Hester could not help questioning, at such moments, whether Pearl was a human child" (116).

When Pearl screams as a reaction to being persecuted by the other children, the narrator, who in another context openly talks about "Pearl's witchcraft" (118), describes her "shrill, incoherent exclamations that made her mother tremble, because they had so much the sound of a witch's anathemas in some unknown tongue" (117–18). Thus it is Pearl, more than Hester, who embodies the phantasmatic cathexis of the scarlet A—to a point that even the townspeople consider her as "a demon offspring" (122). Pearl clearly assumes and spitefully plays the role of a witch-child whenever she communicates about her missing father or about the scarlet A which, for her, also symbolizes the absent father. The text leaves no doubt, however, that this role is assumed in a collusion between mother and daughter. The mother turns the child into a mirror reflection of her own fears, a literal embodiment of the witch stigma: "It was the scarlet letter in another form; the scarlet letter endowed with life! The mother herself—as if the red ignominy were so deeply scorched into her brain, that all her conceptions assumed its form—had carefully wrought out the similitude; lavishing many hours of morbid ingenuity, to create an analogy between the object of her affection, and the emblem of her guilt and torture" (125).

Thus, the crucial irony in Pearl's stigmatization lies in the fact that Hester is the active agent who unconsciously transfers to her daughter what she herself tries consciously to control: namely, the social construction of her identity according to the witchcraft pattern. By assuming the role of a healer, Hester manages, in relation to herself, to use the social stigma against itself, thus inverting its ambivalent social cathexis. Under the gaze of the community, the adulteress transforms into an angel. Decisive for Hester's liberation from the witch stereotype is the ambivalent function of the letter *A* and Hester's use of the mobility of the signifier, its double symbolic potential, and hence its reversibility.[8] While the exteriority and physical visibility of the letter affixed to the body is supposed to codify this body for the gaze, it also enables Hester to find a partial redemption. By turning a stigma into an adornment, a crime into a virtue, Hester inverts the letter's codified meaning. As soon as Hester learns to understand the letter as carrier of the Puritan code rather than as emblem of disgrace, she can distance herself from this code and finally even develop her own free heterodox philosophy.

This process, which she experiences as a new realization of her forcefully derealized personality,[9] also reflects back on her social existence. What saves Hester as a person is the *A* as letter, because she can reverse its codified meaning. She does this by using all its ambivalence. From the outset she not only bears it as an emblem of shame but also wears it proudly as an item of seduction. She achieves this through her artful embroidery, which reworks the letter into a brilliant jewel. This in itself is a spiteful violation of the Puritan sumptuary laws that restricted any rich and decorative display:

> On the breast of her gown, in fine red cloth, surrounded with an elaborate embroidery and fantastic flourishes of gold thread, appeared the letter A. It was so artistically done, and with so much fertility and gorgeous luxuriance of fancy, that it had all the effect of a last and fitting decoration to the apparel which she wore; and which was of a splendor in accordance with the taste of the age, but greatly beyond what was allowed by the sumptuary regulations of the colony. (80)

By embroidering her stigma as a seductive jewel "which drew all eyes" (81), she plays with the duplicity within the Puritan law, thus manipulating the imaginary cathexis of the letter by the community, while at the same time removing herself beyond its reach. The scarlet letter thus "had the effect of a spell, taking her out of the ordinary relations with humanity, and enclosing her in a sphere by herself" (81). In a similar way, Hester uses the silence imposed on her by law by sustaining it with such exotic grace that it envelops her in an aura of mystical saintliness. The emptiness of both sign and silence seduces the community into filling it with projections of their own fears and desires. Thus Hester uses both the ambivalence of the letter's symbolic potential and the emptiness of her proud silence to assimilate the witch to her cultural counterpart: the image of the saint. She supports this assimilation by performing the original social activities of the historical witch as healer, midwife, or advisor to suffering women. The mutual exclusiveness and irreconcilability of opposites may be sublated in the letter *A*. Witch or saint, adulteress or angel—even the community is drawn into the current of its own phantasms and puzzles over the true meaning of the letter. As the title suggests, a story is mediated through a letter, and the ambiguity of this letter illuminates the ambivalence of the Puritan code. Since the *A* can carry meanings that are socially accepted as well as others that are rejected, one could even say that the letter reflects the split Puritan language game. Thus it allows the witchcraft pattern to appear in its ambivalent double-edgedness.

Already in Hawthorne's autobiographical satire, "The Custom House," which introduces the romance, the red embroidered *A*, unearthed from a file cabinet, assumes a dual function. On the one hand it is invoked as a historical relic that ensures authenticity; on the other it figures as a magic object, making its finder feel as though it were burned into his skin. The narrator's epiphany thus invokes the unbroken power of this magic object—and hence of the old stereotypes—some two hundred years after it was in use.

The dual function of the letter as a historical relic and a magical object is rooted in the narrator's notion of history. Under the impact of transcendentalist aesthetics, Hawthorne's historical consciousness is decidedly subjective. The narrator's voice incorporates this notion of aesthetics, cherishing the romantic notion of liberating the real from the distortions of the factual. His personal insertions not only mediate diachronically between the different perspectives of the seventeenth and nineteenth centuries, but also provide synchronic references that will remain implicit in the novel's plot itself.

This strategy of synchronic mediation is further elaborated in the many references throughout the text to the heretic Ann Hutchinson, whose story mirrors Hester's fate on a more political level.[10] Female heretics like Ann Hutchinson can be seen as the philosophical sisters of witches, judged and persecuted on the basis of the very same stereotypes. Like Hester Prynne, Ann Hutchinson was in the Boston jail, where a rosebush is said to have "sprung up under the footsteps of the sainted Ann Hutchinson, as she entered the prison-door" (76). Like Hester Prynne she had established close ties to a leading cleric, John Cotton, who later publicly disavowed her—as Dimmesdale disavows Hester. Significantly, in order to describe Ann Hutchinson's heretical writings, the witchcraft specialist Cotton Mather used the metaphor of an illegitimate child of orthodox belief begotten by the devil. These heretical writings, in turn, are mirrored in Hester's secret philosophy. But while both of these women's philosophies form part of the larger historical context of protest movements against orthodox Puritanism, Hester, unlike Ann Hutchinson, does not openly protest. The narrator attributes this silence to the existence of Pearl.

Yet, had little Pearl never come to her from the spiritual world, it might have been far otherwise. Then, she might have come down to us in history, hand in hand with Ann Hutchinson, as the foundress of a religious sect. She might, in one of her phases, have been a prophetess. She might, and not improbably would, have suffered death from the stern tribunals of the period, for attempting to undermine the foundations of the Puritan establishment. (183)

As these foundations are sternly patriarchal and misogynist, Hester's secret heresy is, at its core, a feminist heresy, which the narrator describes while simultaneously asserting his own antifeminist bias:

The whole system of society is to be torn down, and built up anew. Then, the very nature of the opposite sex, or its long hereditary habit, which has become like nature, is to be essentially modified, before woman can be allowed to assume what seems a fair and suitable position. Finally, all other difficulties being obviated, woman cannot take advantage of these preliminary reforms, until she herself shall have undergone a still mightier change; in which, perhaps, the ethereal essence, wherein she has her truest life, will be found to have evaporated. (184)

What is for Hester a necessary condition to "make existence worth accepting" for women is for the narrator an evaporation of woman's "ethereal essence." In this view, a true woman is neither witch nor heretic. Hawthorne has his narrator reject Hester's secret affinities to both of these roles as deviations from true femininity. Again it is Pearl who seems to prevent Hester from choosing the other alternative for dealing with her social stigma: the active assumption of the witch role. Ironically, the historical witch Ann Hibbins, Governor Bellingham's sister, brings this alternative into play while addressing Hester after her encounter with the governor:

"Wilt thou go with us to-night? There will be a merry company in the forest; and I wellnigh promised the Black man that comely Hester Prynne should make one."

"Make my excuse to him, so please you!" answered Hester, with a triumphant smile. "I must tarry at home, and keep watch over my little Pearl. Had they taken her from me, I would willingly have gone with thee into the forest, and signed my name in the Black Man's book too, and that with mine own blood!" (139)

The fact that Hester is mirrored by two historical women who evoke, in their function as mythological figures, two rejected possibilities of dealing with her social stigma, adds to the already overdetermined function of the letter *A*. Ann Hibbins embodies the stereotype of the aged witch who tries to use Hester's stigma, the scarlet letter *A*, as an item to seduce Hester to join the Covenant with the devil. Ann Hutchinson, on the other hand, persecuted as a heretic and venerated as a saint, embodies the witch stereotype as much as its social counterpart, the stereotype of the angel. Adulteress or angel, witch or saint, Ann Hibbins or Ann Hutchinson—all of these cultural stereotypes stem from the secularization of mythologies and are cited in the text to mirror Hester, albeit only in order to lend her psychological depth in contrast to the historical cliché.

Along with the historical witch stereotype, the text also undermines the conventional forms of its nineteenth-century literary revitalizations. While Hawthorne's characters and plot are staged as reflections of historical figures and events, they also function as intertextual quotations of characters from the Gothic novel. Behind the individual makeup of the characters, there is always an ironical quotation of the genre. Be it Hester as the dark, wild beauty, Dimmesdale as the hero who is seduced by her, or even Chillingworth as the classic villain, they all echo their Gothic counterparts. Ann Hibbins imbues this device with traces of a carnivalesque parody of history. The historical witch is transfigured into an ironic quotation of the literary stereotype of the old witch. By using the conventional clichés of the code of witchcraft, she tries to seduce Hester to participate in the Witches' Sabbath or to inscribe her name in the Black Book. Thus the woman who, in the historical context, was executed as a witch, is ironically used, in *The Scarlet Letter*, as a character who provides comic relief for the tragic development of the plot. With well-calculated irony, the narrator leaves it up to his readers to decide the undecidable, namely whether to read Hester's encounters with Ann Hibbins as a quotation of historical reality, as parable, or as historical allegory. Decisive for the strategies guiding aesthetic response is the fact that it is precisely the historical witch who appears as the ironic quotation of the witch stereotype.

The literary revitalization of the witchcraft pattern in *The Scarlet Letter* must be evaluated in light of all these mirroring effects. While the conventional witchcraft narratives only reverse the ambivalent cathexis of the witch stereo-type, *The Scarlet Letter* uses the same ambivalence as a field of tension. While Hester emancipates herself from the stigma that the community has imposed on her, she at the same time reveals that the cultural witchcraft pattern is re-stricted neither to historical witches nor to the romanticized witches in literary witchcraft narratives. Precisely because she is never explicitly accused of being a witch, it becomes all the more clear how the pattern has been culturally in-teriorized, surviving in displaced forms as part of the political unconscious, manifested in the social stigmatization of certain types of women whose bod-ies and behavior might nourish male phantasms of the witch.

The different modes of treating the witch stereotype in *The Scarlet Letter* with respect to the different female characters—Hester, Pearl, Ann Hutchin-son, and Ann Hibbins—produce a common effect: the witch has lost her onto-logical status and is, instead, seen as a cultural symbol. At this point, the reality status of the witch gains a new and fundamental ambiguity. The question of whether the allusions to witchcraft in Hawthorne's text are staged as fictional reality or as the parabolic evocation of a past witchcraft craze ultimately misses the point. The text focuses instead on the more important dimension of the flexibility and hence the continuous psychosocial efficacy of the witchcraft pattern, which reaches far beyond the historical context in which the existence of witches was to be "empirically" tested. Hawthorne's romance exposes the roots of the historical ambivalence underlying the witch stereotype that even-tually led to its reevaluation, to the disappearance of the witchcraft pattern from public social practice and discourse, but at the same time also to its con-tinuing phantasmatic effects.

There is one further device which Hawthorne uses to account for the chang-ing status in which the witchcraft pattern is effective: the polarization between Hester and the narrator.[11] Even though the latter clearly exposes the cruelty and destructiveness of the Puritan moral law, and even though his allusions to witchcraft are mediated by ironic distance, he nevertheless constantly chastises Hester's development, and especially her own emancipation from the witch-craft pattern, as a deviation from her womanhood.

> There seemed to be no longer any thing in Hester's face for Love to dwell upon; nothing in Hester's form, though majestic and statue-like, that Passion would ever dream of clasping in its embrace; nothing in Hester's bosom, to make it ever again the pillow of Affection. Some attribute had departed from her, the

permanence of which had been essential to keep her a woman. Such is frequently the fate, and such the stern development, of the feminine character and person, when the woman has encountered, and lived through, an experience of peculiar severity. (182)

There is a significant ambivalence in the narrator's romantic imagination of women that leads him to describe Hester's emancipation as a loss of femininity. "She who has once been woman, and ceased to be so" (182) is supposed to have lost her womanhood because "her life had turned, in a great measure, from passion and feeling, to thought" (182). The seventeenth-century Puritans persecuted women for passion as well as for thought. (Reading, for example, was brought up in several of the Salem trials as an indication that a woman stood under the influence of the devil.) The nineteenth-century Puritan narrator frowns upon woman's thought while romanticizing her passion. And yet, even with respect to the latter, he retains some ambivalence. When Hester manages to win over the community "with a woman's strength" (180), the narrator comments, "society was inclined to show its former victim a more benign countenance than she cared to be favored with, or, perchance, than she deserved" (180–81).

The reason why she does not deserve, in the narrator's eyes, the benevolent gaze of the community is Hester's secretly developed anti-Puritan intellect, which, as he rightly thinks, his Puritan forefathers "would have held to be a deadlier crime than that stigmatized by the scarlet letter" (183). Thus the narrator himself pays his own tribute to the split language game of the Puritan code. This narrator, with his unconcealed hatred of the rigidity of Puritanism, but with his unresolved ambivalence toward Puritan norms, suggests that Hester's secret affinities with witches or heretics like Ann Hutchinson are a deviation not only from Puritan belief but also from the "nature of womankind."

Yet it is precisely those attributes condemned by the narrator that make for the strength of Hester as a literary character. The latter by far outweighs whatever weight the narrator's morality can gain in guiding the readers' responses. Thus Hester's portrayal as a literary character reenacts a pattern of seduction for the community of readers very similar to the one Hester herself uses to change the attitude of the Puritan community toward her. As she seduces the community into a reevaluation of her social role, so the reader is seduced into siding with her against the morality of the narrator. Hester challenges not only the image of the Puritan woman, both of the seventeenth and the nineteenth centuries, but also the norms of a romantic imagination of femininity.

The aesthetic ambiguity that arises from the polarization of an unconventional female character portrayed and judged by a conventional narrator is clearly resolved in Hester's favor—all the more so since the narrator's very moralizations can hardly conceal his secret sympathy and fascination. Thus the text works against the norms its narrator explicitly professes. This does not mean, however, that Hester is no longer figured as a victim of the Puritan norms and of the social environment in which she lives, but only that she is shown as surviving her victimization as a person—a decisive fact in determining the overall textual perspective and the status of the narrator's voice. Hester's decision not to flee the community that has stigmatized her makes her victimization, from a reader's point of view, fall back all the more vehemently on the violence and destructiveness inherent in the Puritan norms of femininity and female deviancy.

Thus Hester's tacit language game not only changes the community's attitude toward her but also asserts itself aesthetically against the official language game of the narrator. Just as Hester could use the scarlet *A* against the grain of its codified cultural reading according to Puritan norms, so the reader can read the text against the grain of those very norms embodied by the narrator. Letter and text, as emblematic as they might originally have been conceived to be, thus open themselves up for historically changing readings. Instead of attempting to refer to a historical reality of the witch, *The Scarlet Letter*, as sign and as text, plays its game with the flexibility of the witch stereotype and the phantasms it nourishes. Thus it becomes a "purloined letter," purloined from its cultural codification as much as from its fixation to a referent. This is why Hawthorne's novel reveals more of the witch than those texts that conventionalize the historical witches by turning them into a literary monument or a romantic myth. While conventional witchcraft romances cannot afford to portray the reality of witches and therefore depend on reviving mere phantasms of the witch, Hawthorne uses these phantasms to demonstrate how to make a witch or how to avoid becoming one.

# 5

# CARNIVAL AND ABJECTION

The Mother's Dead Body in *As I Lay Dying*

> I could just remember how my father used to say that the reason for
> living was to get ready to stay dead a long time.
>
> —Addie, in *As I Lay Dying*

## 1. The Grotesque Body in Carnivalesque Literature

WILLIAM FAULKNER'S *As I Lay Dying* is, on one of its multiple levels, a novel about the grotesque life of a dead body. It is not so much, as the title might suggest, about the process of Addie Bundren's dying but about the bizarre extension of her life beyond death. Just as Addie's corpse figures as the protagonist of the Bundrens' carnivalesque funeral procession, so her sons' phantasmatic distortion of this corpse[1] reflects the ambivalent drama of their mourning.

On the surface, both the plot and imagery of Faulkner's novel, and especially its portrayal of the grotesque body of the dead mother and the offensive transgressions of cultural taboos during her funeral procession, are indebted to the carnivalesque tradition. According to Bakhtin,[2] carnivalesque literature creates its grotesque bodies as universal and cosmic bodies. In this context, the grotesque body of the dead mother evokes the archaic fear of the mother with her overwhelming powers and the mysteries of her reproductive functions. On a more general level, the carnival of the dead body of the "great mother" (see Neumann) reveals a dark form of dealing culturally with fears of the female body and with the threatening aspects of femininity.

Faulkner's spectacle of the dead mother's grotesque body pushes beyond the boundaries of pure carnival and exposes such fears through a poetic language designed to externalize internal images of the mother and the maternal body. While the figurative bodies in *As I Lay Dying* resemble the grotesque bodies in carnivalesque literature, Faulkner does establish a crucial difference in perspective. Bakhtin emphasizes an external view of a spectator who beholds a grotesque body in its deviations from the cultural norm. By contrast, the characters in *As I Lay Dying* create the deviations and distortions of bodily images as internal images of the body, thus obliterating the otherness of the grotesque body. This phantasmatic distortion becomes especially meaningful where it expresses the characters' respective internal images of the mother.

There is a whole range of literature that presents the grotesque female body as the other of male desire. The abject *dead* body of the *mother* can be understood as one of the most radical cases of this cultural symbolization of the female body. In twentieth-century literature, grotesque figurations of the dead maternal body invoke the cultural coding of a phantasmatic body whose opposite is represented by the "exquisite cadaver"[3] of young girls or brides. Their dead bodies function as symbolic objects for a necrophilic male economy displayed in a whole canon of romanticizing literary forms, the most radical of which is the Gothic novel. In contrast to this romanticization of the dead body of the young heroine, the carnivalization of the dead body of the mother can be read as a cultural abjection of the maternal body. Following Bakhtin, one would be inclined to see this carnivalization as a subversion of the official cultural coding of the maternal body. But this relationship to the cultural code is ambivalent: while the carnivalesque maternal corpse violates the dignity of the dead, it nonetheless affirms the pervasive cultural abjection of the maternal body. The carnivalesque figuration thus retains the marginal, deviant, and transgressive status of the mother's dead body.

Faulkner enfolds this figuration in a series of highly stylized inner voices of different characters that incorporate diverse and often conflictive perspectives. This "polyphony of voices"[4] conveys the abjection of the maternal corpse from the perspective of the members of a family belonging to the culture of the impoverished white farmers of Mississippi. But on a different level of abstraction, this literary figuration of a maternal body is also a product of the early twentieth-century literary culture that experiments with the inner speech of literary characters in order to explore the boundaries of a fictional mind. *As I Lay Dying* radicalizes such experiments by extending Addie Bundren's, that is, a dead character's, mind beyond her death, and by filtering her voice through a multiplicity of voices that speak her mind within their own.

This exploration of inner speech in the experimental literature of the time is accompanied by an intense interest in figurations of the female body, and particularly in literary transgressions of its boundaries or violations of cultural taboos associated with it. The characters in *As I Lay Dying* perceive the dead body of Addie Bundren as a transgressive body. Very much like the grotesque bodies in carnivalesque literature, the mother's dead body is presented in multiple forms of dissolution, fragmentation, mutilation, metamorphosis, decay, and putrefaction. The fact, however, that these figurations appear in interior monologues transcends the generic form of pure carnivalization and parody. Carnival rather turns into a verbal equivalent of what Artaud termed "theater of cruelty."

The grotesque body in this theater of cruelty reveals a striking resemblance to the raw phantasms of an uncoded or unsublimated body. Faulkner's creation of a poetic language capable of evoking images of the unsublimated body constitutes an aesthetic paradox of sorts, because any literary or dramatic figuration of the unsublimated body—be it theatrical performance as in the case of Artaud's theater of cruelty or a speech performance as in the case of Faulkner's novel—necessarily entails the sublimation inherent in any artistic presentation. The aesthetic paradox of sublimating the unsublimated body forms one of the major achievements of Faulkner's use of poetic language in *As I Lay Dying*. His verbal theater of cruelty collapses the distance of an outside perspective on the grotesque body of the dead mother because this body is created by inner voices that give expression to a "grotesque soul,"[5] which, in turn, is the creator and beholder of the grotesque body. Instead of portraying the grotesque body and the grotesque soul in isolation from each other, *As I Lay Dying* grasps them in their interaction and reveals how they engender each other. As readers we are never granted the distance of spectators because Faulkner's inner voices assimilate us to the Bundrens' internal drama, exposing their grotesque souls in their phantasmatic abjection of the maternal corpse. Addie's death has unleashed a process of desublimation that affects the boundaries of the body as much as the boundaries of the mind, perception, and speech.[6]

## 2. The Carnivalesque Funeral Procession

Addie's corpse is the main protagonist of a plot centered around the Bundrens' carnivalesque funeral procession to Jefferson. The longer Addie is dead, the more active her corpse becomes—not only through the purely biological process of decomposition but also through an increasing power of the dead body over the other protagonists. The longer this body is dead, the more difficult it becomes to bury it, to simply get rid of it, or even to destroy it. The longer it is dead, the more it affects the bodies of the other characters, melting them into a collective body that begins to inhabit a closed entropic system with its own order of space and time. And the further this corpse decays, the more it changes into a macabre transitional object used by the members of the family to act out a black symbiosis in death, the regressive dynamic of which expresses itself in a somatic grief and prepares the final separation from the mother. What seems like a carnivalization from the distance of characters outside the family or from the distance of the overall textual perspective, corresponds, in the internal dynamic of the Bundrens, to a process in which, for the family, the biological body of the mother disappears to the extent to which its decomposition requires an obsessive if not obscene presence. Unable to bury it, the characters let it disappear behind the diverse phantasmatic bodies which they create, or else they allow its very existence to be swallowed up by actions which are aimed at preparing the funeral while, in fact, they delay it endlessly. Like prisoners of a collective system of madness, the Bundrens become blind to the reality of the decomposing body of the mother.

At the beginning of the novel, Addie Bundren is seen dying, her head bedded on a pile of pillows from which she can survey her eldest son Cash working on her coffin. The whole family awaits the death of the mother in a kind of suspense, each of them mistrusting the others. Anse Bundren, the father, cherishes the fantasy of using the funeral trip to the city to buy himself new teeth after fifteen years of a toothless existence. Dewey Dell, the daughter who is pregnant from a secret love affair, waits for her mother's death in order to "buy" an abortion in the city. She is so absorbed by her unwanted pregnancy that she can experience the grief for her mother only in a hysterical fit "beside herself," throwing herself onto her mother's emaciated body, which is said to resemble "a bundle of rotten sticks" (37). In fact, Dewey Dell literally buries Addie's body under her own sensual corporeality. In this image mother and daughter melt into a dark version of a grotesque "pregnant death," with the only difference being that this image does not, like the carnivalesque "pregnant death," exhibit life in death but instead inverts the process by drawing the unborn life into death. Thus, the image even mirrors Addie's philosophy, according to which life itself is only a preparation for a long death. The daughter and the father, however, are more successful than the sons in escaping the swallowing presence of the dead body—Dewey Dell, because she is more obsessed with getting rid of the living body of her unborn child than with burying Addie's dead body, and Anse, because he has already displaced the minimal amount of libidinal energy he is capable of mobilizing onto the acquisition of new teeth and a new wife.

The sons' phantasmatic cathexis of the mother's dead body turns the cultural abjection of the maternal body into a grotesque and obscene spectacle. Cash, the pragmatist in the family, loses himself in his maniacal hammering on his mother's coffin. The obsessive concentration with which he works toward its absolute perfection reveals his tendency to fetishize the coffin—a cathexis which, during the process of events, the other characters begin to share when they experience the coffin as intermingled with the body of the mother. Darl and Jewel, the two antagonistic brothers, steal away from their dying mother for a three-dollar business—only to return after a fateful delay which generates the carnivalesque spectacle of an endlessly delayed funeral. Thus begin the grotesque lives of Addie's dying, dead, and finally decomposing body, and the catastrophic odyssey to Jefferson with the coffin in a wagon, followed by an increasing number of buzzards.

Addie herself has prepared the staging of the carnivalesque funeral procession in an act of aggressive distancing from her family, following her unwanted pregnancy with Darl. Thus the journey to Jefferson becomes a last manifestation of Addie's power over the family beyond death.

> Then I found that I had Darl. At first I would not believe it. Then I believed that I would kill Anse. It was as though he had tricked me, hidden within a word like within a paper screen and struck me in the back through it. But then I realized that I had been tricked by words older than Anse or love, and that the same word had tricked Anse too, and that my revenge would be that he would never know I was taking revenge. And when Darl was born I asked Anse to promise to take me back to Jefferson when I died. (136–37)

This motif of an aggressive maternal power is the driving force behind the obscene activities that stage Addie's corpse as the main protagonist of the Bundrens' odyssey to Jefferson. Addie's dead body is turned into a symbol of the negative, overpowering, and devouring mother. It seems as if her body grows into the bodies of her family in order to work on their endangerment or mutilation from the inside. On the concrete level of plot, Addie's body affects the others through body experiences and mutilations which afflict them under the extreme conditions of the journey, especially during the various adventurous attempts to save the coffin from water or fire. Cash, for example, who nearly dies after recovering the coffin from the violent river, is finally bedded with a broken leg on his mother's coffin in the wagon. This spectacle is all the more grotesque as Cash has turned the coffin into a fetish of the dead mother. Lying on it in his fever, his leg rotting in the concrete cast devised for him, he now tries to spare Addie's coffin from every stain by compulsively polishing it over and over again, displaying his futile desire to impose his order on the overwhelming chaos that threatens to devour all of them. Jewel, who recovers the coffin from the river and also, after Darl's arson, from the burning barn, continues the journey covered with blisters and open wounds. They recall those other wounds, which Addie had earlier inflicted on him during the cruel ritualistic whippings with which she wanted to tie him back to her own body, acting upon the magic fantasy "that only through the blows of the switch could my blood and their blood flow as one stream" (136). Darl and Vardaman, the two sons who share Addie's oversensitive state of mind, are so haunted by their phantasms of Addie's dead body that they begin to live on the verge of psychotic breakdown.

This carnivalesque spectacle of the characters' bodies is grounded in different textual strategies, all of which place the grotesque body in relation to the grotesque soul. There is no real outside perspective of a narrator but a kaleidoscope of inner perspectives that continually shift between closeness and distance, and coalesce in what could be described as a strategy of wandering gazes. The voices of characters outside the family incorporate a more distanced gaze —one which, as in the case of Samson or Armstid, represents the external perspective of the community on the obscene, insane, and grotesque spectacle of the funeral procession. More importantly, shifts within the characters' perspectives reveal how actions are driven by grief or, conversely, represent a defense against grief and denial of emotion, or even a breakdown of the boundaries of the self. The spectrum of those shifting perspectives ranges from a decidedly distanced spectatorship, a kind of "interior outside perspective," to an absolute loss of distance or even to the breakdown of semiotic articulation. Especially Darl, whose voice occupies by far the most sections, juggles artistically with shifting perspectives—all the more so as his capacity for extrasensory perception allows him even to describe events which take place in his absence.

This orchestration of distances both draws and transgresses the boundaries of the novel's own process of textual carnivalization. The more distanced the perspective, the more space is granted for a carnivalization that shows the spectacles of body and soul in a grotesque light. Yet the breakdown of distance in the characters' voices simultaneously crumbles all those comic or grotesque effects which stem from the inadequacy of the Bundrens' social behavior. Carnivalization in fact fulfills a distancing function in Faulkner's text, and whenever the characters obliterate that distance through the effects of their inner voices, they also overstep the bounds of a carnivalesque presentation, pulling the reader into an obscenely displayed and terrifying interiority. Functioning as an aesthetic equivalent of a displaced, denied, or temporarily suspended grief, the carnivalizing strategies then further enhance the spectacle of the grotesque soul. This, however, does not preclude the possibility that even the carnivalization of death itself achieves a specific work of mourning. But in the latter case it would be a form of sublimation which turns the actual emotion into its opposite. Darl's fit of laughter at the foot of the coffin, for example, emerges on the boundary between a hysterical dissolution of the self and a reflective carnivalesque mocking of death.

The carnivalization of bodies, mainly achieved through that distancing perspective which I have called an "interior outside perspective," belongs to a more general textual strategy which mediates outer and inner events through a precise description of bodily expressions. This way of representing the body can still be understood in the tradition of an "unconscious realism."[7] If Faulkner's bodies appear fantastic or overdimensional, it is not because a parodic gaze exposes their weaknesses in grotesque distortions, but because a relentless naturalism approaches the characters through their bodies and reads all deviations from the norm as inscriptions of the grotesque soul. When Darl says about Peabody, "He has pussel-gutted himself eating cold greens. With the rope they will haul him up the path, balloon-like up the sulphurous air" (34), his dissecting observation sees Peabody's bloated body as more than merely a sign of a deformed personality; through the lens of this deformity he also grasps the deformed culture which has produced this body. Mediated through Darl's gaze, the textual perspective thus pierces through the surface of codified bodies. Or, more precisely, the gaze that is stylized in the text observes what a culturally coded gaze on the body normally excludes: the uncodifiable, the bizarre, the eccentric, or obscene, in short, all those dimensions which transgress the social body. Concrete bodies are seen with their deformations, exuberances, or mutilations, as, for example, Anse's missing toenails or his toothless face, which is explicitly described as a carnivalesque farce: " 'Why don't you go on to the house, out of the rain?' Cash says. Pa looks at him, his face streaming slowly. It is as though upon a face carved by a savage caricaturist a monstrous burlesque of all bereavement flowed" (63).

Darl's description of his father's face reveals a more general feature of the ways in which Darl grasps the world. His observations of the body have become so hypersensitive, obsessive, or even fantastic, that all bodies appear to him as grotesque bodies. In addition, Darl's observation contains a textual self-reflection, indicating that the text's "savage caricatures and monstrous burlesques" themselves focus primarily upon those aspects of the body which escape social codification. The paradox of a carnivalesque sublimation of the unsublimated body is based on this very device. Darl's gaze tears off the conventional veils that cover bodies in order to read these bodies as signs in which the grotesque soul reflects itself in its "abject nakedness." In this respect Darl turns, in fact, into an opponent of Addie by revealing precisely what she tried to conceal with her relentless pride, her "furious desire to hide that abject nakedness" (39).

The nakedness of the unsublimated body in Faulkner's text exposes the abjection of the human condition with a gaze that seems all the more compelling because it is itself implied in the abjection, is itself naked and unprotected. It is not the cold exterior gaze, but the passionate interior gaze that exposes the abject not as other but as the innermost core of the self. The grotesque side of Faulkner's abjection is, at the same time, the most human because his grotesque bodies emerge in a domain where the archaic life of the biological body maintains itself against all helpless attempts to conceal or sublimate it.

From the perspective of the community, the Bundrens gradually lose all sense of reality and piety conventionally required when dealing with the dead body of a close person. In the experience of the characters, however, the mother's body in the coffin loses its organic reality to the extent to which they either abstract from it pragmatically or transform it phantasmatically. It is true that throughout the trip the family continues to pursue the aim of burying Addie's body in Jefferson. However, this aim becomes an empty telos in a system of action governed by different laws. To the extent to which the characters deny the organic reality of the dead body, that is, its decomposition, the body itself turns into the obscene protagonist of an insane odyssey. With its bulkiness, its chemical processes of decomposition, its stench, its obstinate burdensome presence, and the necessity of getting it under ground, it ultimately asserts itself against all attempts to ignore it. At the same time, however, the family can only get through all the catastrophes if it succeeds in at least partially denying the penetrating reality of Addie's corpse, thus defying all rules that prohibit public offense. This denial enables the family to continue the journey, unperturbed by the ordeals of nature or the disapproving gaze of the townspeople, who see in the funeral procession an undignified and obscene spectacle and try to flee the smell of the corpse.

This collision of the Bundrens' temporarily autonomous system of order with the social order of the community not only contributes to the carnivalization of the text, but also to the psychological portrayal of the characters. The psychosocial economy of the family[8] is mediated by a system of signs that constitutes itself on the cutting line between two contrary systems of order and continually transgresses that line on one or the other side: the Bundrens act temporarily from inside a closed system of madness in which the habitual orders and behaviors fall prey to increasing entropy. Even the notion and experience of time is affected. While the decay of the corpse is tied to historical time or, as one might say, to the Bakhtinian "little time," the characters seem to act in an arrested "here and now" which denies the "little time" along with the temporality of the mother's dead body. This denial, however, which, on a practical level, allows for the endless delay of the funeral, reveals, on a psychological level, the insistent but ambivalent tie of the Bundrens to the mother. The sheer incapacity to separate the dead body of the mother from the familial body makes it appear as if an unacknowledged mourning with all its ambivalences has been displaced onto the body. The characters' emotions remain bound to the life of their bodies and can be read as signs of a somatic mourning which replaces the emotional mourning and practices rather the denial of death than a carnivalesque laughter at death. Thus the Bundrens' grim adventures during the journey, as well as Vardaman's and Jewel's flight into the imaginary life with a phantasmatic maternal body, reveal a spectacle of unachieved or displaced mourning in which the mother is incorporated in fantastic shapes.

The end of the text, on the other hand, stages the externalization of the mother from the family. When, after an eight-day-long journey, the Bundrens' outrageous parade arrives in town, their funeral wagon has a macabre resemblance to a circus wagon—with the only difference being that the coffin is not the prop of a spectacle but carries the mother's corpse.

> It was Albert told me about the rest of it. He said the wagon stopped in front of Grummet's hardware store, with the ladies all scattering up and down the street with handkerchiefs to their noses. . . . It must have been like a piece of rotten cheese coming to an ant-hill, in that ramshackle wagon that Albert said folks were scared would fall all to pieces before they could get it out of town, with that homemade box and another fellow with a broken leg lying on a quilt on top of it, and the father and a little boy sitting on the seat and the marshal trying to make them get out of town. (161)

The parade with the coffin reveals the abject dimension of Faulkner's carnivalization. Different from Bakhtin's grotesque bodies which celebrate their corporeality in lustful excesses, Faulkner's bodies are grotesque because life has turned them into grotesque forms or mutilated them. Similarly, Addie Bundren's corpse is grotesque because the decay of the body, death, and decomposition seem obscene to those who do not—like the members of the family—

avert or censor their gaze. In fact, the Bundrens become increasingly distracted from the apparent aim of their journey, the mother's funeral, so that her actual burial finally appears like an anticlimactic coda. The funeral procession has been overgrown with such bizarre events that the Bundrens become not only oblivious of the time constraints regarding the burial of a dead body but hardly even think any more of mentioning the mother's funeral in their exchanges: " 'Let's take Cash to the doctor first,' Darl said. 'She'll wait. She's already waited nine days' " (186). All cultural or ritual significance of a funeral ceremony has vanished. The actual burial is reduced to the raw act of putting Addie's body under the earth. By the end it is mentioned only in a subclause in Cash's report about the actual event, Darl's arrest: "But when we got it filled and covered and drove out the gate and turned into the lane where them fellows was waiting, when they came out and come on him, and he jerked back, it was Dewey Dell that was on him before even Jewel could get at him" (188).

The desacrilization of the mother's funeral which follows the nine days of humiliating treatment of her corpse reveals how the Bundrens have literally and figuratively done away with the body of the mother. From this perspective their odyssey resembles a macabre ritual of liberation. At the end, after the mother's image is repressed along with her body and her death, the terror is contained and everyday life can return—if only on a brittle surface level. Cash is treated by a doctor, Dewey Dell fails in getting an abortion, and Anse buys new teeth with the money for the abortion, stolen from Dewey Dell. This elimination of the mother seems complete when, instead of Addie, Anse takes a new Mrs. Bundren back home.

Even this lamentable spectacle of a return to a fragile "normality" is mediated through images of the grotesque body. Cash describes the appearance of the new couple as a carnivalesque parade. Anse, with a guilty "hangdog face" appears with his new teeth in grotesque metamorphosis while his new bride follows him, "a duck-shaped woman all dressed up, with them kind of hard-looking pop eyes" (208), with her "graphophone," the technological object of desire from the big world, which Cash will henceforth invest with nearly the same intense interest he had invested in his mother's coffin.

Pa was coming along with that kind of daresome and hangdog look all at once like when he has been up to something he knows ma ain't going to like, carrying a grip in his hand and Jewel says,
    "Who's that?"
    Then we see it wasn't the grip that made him look different; it was his face, and Jewel says, "He got them teeth." It was a fact. It made him look a foot taller,

kind of holding his head up, hangdog and proud too, and then we see her behind him, carrying the other grip—a kind of duck-shaped woman all dressed
up, with them kind of hard-looking pop eyes like she was daring ere a man to
say nothing. (207–208)

This condensed final image in *As I Lay Dying* is paradigmatic for the way in
which Faulkner links the spectacle of the grotesque body with that of the grotesque soul. The parade of grotesque bodies and the phantasmatic cathexis of
objects like the new teeth or gramophone reveal not only what the characters
observe but also what they try to hide from themselves and others. This image
shows the new normality of the Bundrens to be a spectacle of repressions and
displacements, of guilt and hypocrisy. At the same time it renders a grim expression of a familial economy, in which women are as exchangeable as other
fetish objects that can be invested with fantasies and desires.

## 3. The Phantasmatic Body

The strongest expression of the spectacle of the grotesque soul on the familial stage of the Bundrens is found in the fantasies which transform the body
of the mother. They belong to the spectacle of the grotesque body, too, with
the difference that they do not stage the living body but the internalized body.
The latter, in turn, not only founds the internal image of the maternal body,
but also the characters' own body image that helps to mark the boundaries of
the self.

Jewel's and Vardaman's phantasmatic representations of the mother as horse
or fish are the best examples. Faulkner uses Darl's voice to tell us that Jewel's
mother is a horse in order to mark the fact that Jewel's phantasmatic displacement of the mother is unconscious. Darl, who not only has access to the events
which take place in his absence but also to the inner dramas which remain
hidden to the protagonists themselves, tries obstinately, and not without ambivalence, to confront Jewel with their mother's death. Jewel refuses to answer
the reiterated question "Do you know she is going to die, Jewel?" (34). But when
Darl insists, "It's not your horse that's dead, Jewel," he hurls a desperately an-
gered "Goddam you" (75) at him. When Darl ends this exchange by simply
stating with absolute certitude his inner perception that "Jewel's mother is a
horse" (75), the reader's attention is drawn to the phantasmatic aspects of
Jewel's obsessive fixation on his horse, a detail which retrospectively overdetermines the meaning of all scenes with Jewel's horse. The most compelling image
in this context is again attributed to Darl's perception when he describes how

Jewel rides through the flames on the coffin of his mother. "This time Jewel is riding upon it, clinging to it, until it crashes down and flings him forward and clear and Mack leaps forward into a thin smell of scorching meat and slaps at widening crimson-edged holes that bloom like flowers in his undershirt" (176).

On a psychological level, all these scenes enact displaced oedipal desires. Instead of being made explicit, the oedipal connection is grasped in the way it is unconsciously acted out: through the displaced images and objects of an inner drama. This process overdetermines the imagery of the whole text. The visuality of the interior voices exceeds the functionality of a purely poetic device. Visual metaphors invoke concrete fantasies, thus allowing for the poetic stylization of a character's unconscious.

In addition, the phantasms of the body are integral to Faulkner's textual carnivalization. Apart from resembling images of the carnivalesque body, the phantasms of the maternal body also determine the characters' actions in their social world. The Bundrens' social behavior during their funeral trip to Jefferson draws its carnivalesque effects from a collision of the social order with the order of the unconscious. Vardaman's dealing with the body of the fish shows the uncannily grotesque dimensions of this collision because it results in the actual mutilation of the dead body of the mother. Faulkner shows how, in his mind, Vardaman condenses the dead maternal body with the body of a fish, which he cuts up and carries, full of blood, into the house in order to have Dewey Dell cook and serve it to the whole family. Thus Vardaman takes part in a totemic familial meal at which the dead body of the mother, which he has himself cut up, is devoured. Regarding the distribution of power in the family, it is relevant that the totemistic meal is not a patriarchal but a matriarchal one where the body of the archaic "great mother" is incorporated. This matriarchal totemistic meal, too, performs an excess, staging archaic guilt while affirming immortality.[9] One could even say that on the unconscious scene of the phantasmatic body, Vardaman stages the archaic maternal variation of the Freudian totemic meal.

In his dispersed and fragmented monologues, Vardaman dissolves the boundaries of Addie's body in order to recreate it in a world in which "I" and "Not-I," inner and outer space, human and animal body are melted together to form an undifferentiated whole. At times, Vardaman's fantasized mother leaves her dying body and reemerges in new bodies like that of a rabbit, a horse, or a fish. At one time, Vardaman sees the old shell of her body inhabited by another, strange woman. Then he can conclude that it is not the mother who is nailed into Cash's coffin but the other woman. The feverishly shifting transformations of the moldable body of the mother ward off the terror of her death:

> It was not her. I was there, looking. I saw. I thought it was her, but it was not. It was not my mother. She went away when the other one laid down in her bed and drew the quilt up. (54)

> And so if Cash nails the box up, she is not a rabbit. And so if she is not a rabbit I couldn't breathe in the crib and Cash is going to nail it up. And so if she lets him it is not her. I know. I was there. I saw it when it did not be her. I saw. They think it is and Cash is going to nail it up.

> It was not her because it was lying right yonder in the dirt. And now it's all chopped up. I chopped it up. It's lying in the kitchen in the bleeding pan, waiting to be cooked and et. Then it wasn't and she was, and now it is and she wasn't. And tomorrow it will be cooked and et and she will be him and pa and Cash and Dewey Dell and there won't be anything in the box and so she can breathe. (55)

Vardaman's fantastic metamorphosis of his mother's dead body aims at preserving her internal image. However, the freeing of the mother from her bodily existence, symbolized in the cutting up of the fish body, is only partially successful. Fantasies that Addie slips into other bodies, including the bodies of her own family, cannot totally repress the obstinate presence of the real dead body in Cash's coffin. While, from an outside perspective, the phantasmatic bodies create a conflictive polarity with the "real" dead body, on a textual level and, correspondingly, on the level of the fictional world of the characters, this polarity is effaced along with the boundaries between their conscious social and their unconscious phantasmatic perceptions. Even the fact that after the totemic fish meal Vardaman believes the mother to be in the bodies of the other family members does not prevent him from poking holes into the lid of the coffin and thereby mutilating his dead mother's face. This desperate act reveals the complex contradictions of Vardaman's imaginary world along with a subliminal aggressivity toward the dead mother. Yet, he fantasizes this act as liberation. Similar to the cutting up of the fish, the poking of holes into the coffin releases the mother from her dead body into other bodies:

> But Jewel's mother is a horse. My mother is a fish. Darl says that when we come to the water again I might see her and Dewey Dell said, She's in the box; how could she have got out? She got through the holes I bored, into the water I said, and when we come to the water again I am going to see her. My mother is not in the box. My mother does not smell like that. My mother is a fish. (155)

At a symbolic level, the very same act can thus achieve both a liberation from death and a mutilation. The mutilation, however, can take place only in conjunction with a fantasy of liberation. By cutting up the fish as well as by boring holes into the coffin Vardaman acts out phantasms of the fragmented body.[10] Both actions show how Vardaman attempts to ground his threatened sense of self in a phantasmatic attachment to the dead body of the mother. By condensing it with other bodies, by transforming and mutilating it, or by having it devoured, Vardaman turns the body of the mother into the space where he enacts the drama of his own internalized mother.

## 4. The Phantasmatic Body as Stage for the Grotesque Soul

Faulkner's phantasmatic bodies gain a specific relevance as carnivalesque figurations because they stage the spectacle of the grotesque soul. On the one hand, the *grotesque* bodies in Faulkner's text are used to express psychic or social deformations of the characters. On the other hand, however, the *phantasmatic* bodies can be read as the unconscious subtext of the familial drama. The characters expose their inner drama not only in their grotesque bodies or exuberant body language, but also in the phantasms of the body which serve as the props for their fantastic actions.

Vardaman's phantasm of the mother as fish, for example, reveals the affinity of the grotesque body in carnivalesque literature to the psychological phantasms of the fragmented body. Since body phantasms are produced unconsciously, they can be understood as a special manifestation of the unsublimated body. Vardaman's unsublimated body phantasms reveal the abjection that underlies images of the grotesque body. But while the latter sublimate abjection by carnivalizing it, Vardaman's phantasms retain its latent horror. What appears as raw material in the phantasms of the fragmented body is formed and molded in the literary images of the grotesque body. These images are ambivalent: it is true that the grotesque body in carnivalesque literature exposes that which tries to transgress, protrude from, or destroy the boundaries of the body, including death as the most extreme case. But in emphasizing the grotesque body's comic dimension, carnivalesque figurations traditionally integrate and neutralize the abject on a formal level. The aesthetics of the "other body" is subversive only insofar as it opposes the official body images of a specific culture. This subversion, however, does not change the status of the grotesque body as the "other body" that deviates from the official coding of bodies.

Vardaman's raw phantasms of the fragmented body undermine this dynamic between a cultural norm and a deviant carnivalesque image. Instead of sublimating the terror of the other body in a carnivalesque figuration, Vardaman's phantasms bring the terror to the surface of the literary presentation. This device goes to the core of Faulkner's way of radicalizing grotesque images of the body. Though inspired by the literary tradition of grotesque realism and the carnivalization of the grotesque body, *As I Lay Dying* goes beyond the specific kind of aesthetic sublimation which founds that tradition. While carnivalesque literature in the narrow sense presents the grotesque body from an outside perspective, Faulkner shifts the presentation into the consciousness or even the unconscious of literary characters. For them, the dead body of the mother turns factually into a grotesque body because they can neither face the terror of the mother's death nor the reality of her decaying body. A defense against death is thus at work in both cases. But while the participants in carnival see the grotesque body (and, mediated through it, death) from the outside, and while they create distance with their laughter at death, the Bundrens produce the grotesque body themselves, be it through their endlessly delaying Addie's funeral or through Vardaman's performing his imaginary transformations of Addie's body, followed by its real mutilation. Instead of distancing the dead body in a carnivalesque ritual, the Bundrens are overpowered by the insistence of the dead body with its decay, its stench, or even the pure fact that it is always there because they are unable to bury it.

Darl's voice plays a special role in conveying how the phantasmatic body functions as a scene for the grotesque soul. Orchestrated by an artful shifting of distances, his interior monologue displays a high level of self-reflexivity. These features culminate at a breaking point when Darl splits into two personalities and talks in an interior monologue about the "other Darl" who has been taken to an insane asylum in Jackson. Darl's arrest is a consequence of his setting fire to the barn containing the mother's coffin. With this ambivalent act he not only wants to terminate the undignified situation with the rotting corpse but also to break out of the Bundrens' closed system of collective madness. Darl's desperate act fails because of Jewel's intervention, and the relative restabilization of the familial system is achieved at the price of Darl's exclusion. To confine Darl, whom Addie herself had never accepted and with whose birth she planned her dying, to an insane asylum is, within the familial system, supposed to guarantee the family's normality. At the same time, Darl's expulsion is like a belated affirmation of Addie's secret rejection. From the perspective of the familial system, however, both Darl and Addie are excluded at the end because the hospitalization of Darl is concomitant with Addie's burial. Just as

Addie increasingly exerts her power as a dead character and Darl gains more power as a dominant voice, they both become further removed from the family and ultimately forgotten. Darl's expulsion is thus a symbolic act which stands for and covers up the more important one: the final expulsion of Addie from the familial system and the liberation from the terror of her devouring dead body. From his outside perspective, Darl is now able to perceive the familial madness as a carnivalesque spectacle in which all the family members played their part. "Beside himself," he breaks into an unbounded archaic laughter which, as the only semiotic sign available to him, grasps the situation somatically. This laughter is comic and tragic at the same time, but it is not parodic because it includes Darl himself without any distance. Neither is it cathartic because it does not provide relief. The others misunderstand this archaic laughter in stupefied horror, whereas Darl finally smothers it in an animalistic foaming. In his last monologue, in which he sees and describes himself as other, he hurls an endlessly desperate "yes" against the system of denial and repression which founds the family's madness.

"What are you laughing at?" I said.
  "Yes yes yes yes yes." (202)

Our brother Darl in a cage in Jackson where, his grimed hands lying light in the quiet interstices, looking out he foams. "Yes yes yes yes yes yes yes yes." (202)

While Darl's actions fail in the social context of his fictional world, they become all the more effective in counterbalancing the other characters' perspectives. Cash voices a notion of the fragile boundaries between madness and sanity, a fragility which marks the whole text and gives the theme of the grotesque soul its sociocritical dimension: "But I ain't so sho that ere a man has the right to say what is crazy and what ain't. It's like there was a fellow in every man that's done a-past the sanity or insanity, that watches the sane and the insane doings of that man with the same horror and the same astonishment" (189).

In the splitting from himself through an outside perspective, Darl stages himself on the scene of the two colliding systems of order which mark the text and found its carnivalesque dimension. Darl's performance goes beyond a carnivalesque self-parody because it plays on different levels at once and synthesizes his capacity to dwell simultaneously in different places and in different minds. The ambivalence underlying his arson, for example, can be understood fully only when one considers it as an action on two levels simultaneously: on the level of a social order where Darl, recognizing the obsolescence of the funeral procession, wants to end it violently, and on the level of the temporarily effective inner order of the family's collective madness, where Darl sees the events according to the inner logic of the familial economy. On this level, the spectacle stages the Bundrens as "grotesque souls." Addie Bundren's dead body is phantasmatically invested or transformed according to each protagonist's position and status in the familial system. In this process her body assumes the quasi-mythical dimensions of the archetypal "great mother," in whose presence the protagonists of the familial drama regress to a level of archaic emotions.

On that level, Darl reacts with his arson against the devouring primordial mother who uses even her decaying body to assert her power beyond death. Intuitively Darl thus also grasps the motif of revenge with which Addie had planned her funeral in Jefferson long ago. Darl's arson was supposed to mark both the real and the imaginary mother's death as an annihilation, a transformation of her body into ashes, and an expulsion from the center of the family. At the same time, he takes revenge for Addie's refusal ever to admit him to that center. The fact that it is Jewel, Addie's favorite, who recovers the coffin from the flames, adds to the overdetermination of the whole scene.

It is important to understand why Darl acts directly and unmediatedly against the imaginary mother while the other sons transform her body phantasmatically: Cash by fetishizing the coffin, Jewel by shifting the inner representation of the mother onto a horse, and Vardaman by fantasizing a fish-mother. Darl is the only son who consciously renounces any phantasmatic representation of the mother. Her death is no more representable for him than its denial. With his radical insistence on the empirical dead body, however, he tries to abandon any image that could provide an inner representation of his mother. She is for him neither in a fantasized shape nor in her dead body. Darl literally obliterates her existence because he does not create any internal image of the dead mother.

> "Then what is your ma, Darl?" I said.
> "I haven't got ere one," Darl said. "Because if I had one, it is *was*. And if it was, it can't be *is*. Can it?"
> "No," I said.
> "Then I am not," Darl said. "Am I?" (79)

Vardaman's and Jewel's fantasies of the mother as horse and fish, as well as Darl's refusal to create an inner representation of the dead mother, all disconnect the internal mother from her dead body. As much as these attitudes differ otherwise, they all assert the radical otherness of the maternal corpse. But Darl's ambivalent game with the phrase "if I had one" and the surprising conclusion "Then I am not" reveals that his refusal to create an inner representation of the mother is itself overdetermined. If Darl "is not" because the mother is not, then this must not only be understood in the simple sense that *her* death annihilates *him*. On a more complex level, Darl also plays with the fact that his mother has never given birth to him completely in the sense of a psychological birth which presupposes the recognition and acceptance of a child. In that respect, his mother was a phantom for him even during her lifetime, an ever-present absence. In a way she only gains an uncanny presence through her death. The dead body stands for the mother who refuses him an existence. Like an uncanny transitional object which extorts a never-lived symbiosis in death, the dead body simultaneously is and is not the mother. To expose this body to the flames in order to free himself from its tyranny would seem like a cathartic self-creation from her ashes. When this fails, Darl splits himself into the one who, like a sacrificial victim, takes over the role of madness, and the one who now perceives himself from the outside with his old clairvoyance.

The privileging of Darl's perspective complicates the carnivalesque form of the text in multiple ways. For Darl, the spectacle of the grotesque body cannot be separated from the spectacle of the grotesque soul because he reads the others and speaks himself in the language of the body. He has developed his own "somatic semiotic" on the basis of which he not only understands and regulates "the exchanges between body and world, but also those between inner and outer world, I and we, identity and alterity."[11] Darl's "somatic semiotic," however, appears to be the inverse of Bakhtin's because it does not celebrate the joyful eccentricity of the body, which ecstatically overflows the world with its inside or with the ecstatic laughter of the grotesque soul. Darl's laughter is an act of destitution. Behind the carnivalesque masks of socially coded bodies it grasps the grotesque bodies and souls in their "abject nakedness." Darl's gaze desublimates the bodies for the gaze of the reader. Desublimated bodies, however, appear grotesque because they violate the internalized social gaze on the body. At the same time, and therein lies the paradox, desublimated bodies are, in the strict sense, not representable in a text without gaining a secondary form of sublimation. Addie Bundren's rotting corpse, for example, affects the reader always on two levels. Darl's perspective transmits the horror both of concrete organic decay and of the raw phantasms of the body which work in the characters' unconscious beyond sublimation. His perspective evokes thus the two different forms which the unsublimated body can assume: the organic and the phantasmatic embodiment. As a literary character who carries a specific textual perspective, Darl also creates an aesthetically sublimated body of the mother which can be situated on the boundary between the literary tradition of a carnivalesque presentation of the grotesque body and a verbal "theater of cruelty," which tries to evoke the horror of the unsublimated body within aesthetic sublimation.

## 5. Forms of Sublimation in the Carnivalesque Text

The paradox of an aesthetic presentation of the unsublimated body determines the status of the grotesque body in Faulkner's text. Instead of celebrating the deliberate distortions and exaggerations of universalized bodies in an archaic ritual of carnival, Faulkner's "realism" externalizes the bizarre performances of the unsublimated or desublimated body. In this context, it is decisive that the grotesque body in the center of the text is the body of the mother. This body of the mother is the cultural body which forms the basis not only for the body- and self-images of the children, but also for the first forms of symbolizing the female realm. The prohibitions and taboos, the mysteries and mythologies which turn the body of the mother into a symbolic object for the cultural formation of subjects require ever new forms of sublimation which control the archaic desire directed toward this body.

The mother's body is both the real and the imaginary object of that primal symbiotic stage which Addie, in her monologue, opposes to the empty world of false words. It is precisely because the maternal body dominates the primordial realm of archaic emotions that it has to be symbolized and acculturated in an endless chain of imaginary displacements and transformations. The culturally internalized maternal body which differs from, doubles, replaces, or obliterates the equally cultural body of the "real" mother is the phantasmatic body of the primordial mother. As an imaginary space where the most archaic desire coincides with the most abject horror, this imaginary body not only creates the Other of the real body of the mother but Otherness as such.

The rotting corpse of the mother radicalizes the horror of the phantasmatic great mother. As I Lay Dying sublimates this horror by exposing the old myth and making it the object of a potentially transforming aesthetic experience. Without the relieving function of a literary carnivalization, the rotting, smelling, and mutilated body of the dead mother in Faulkner's text would be the apotheosis of abject horror. It is significant for the economy of an oedipal family structure[12] that it is the sons who evoke the body of the mother in their monologues by describing how they exert real or fantasized violence toward it. In these monologues Addie's dead body is, for her sons, less a symbol of the death of the mother than an incorporation of the primordial mother as Other.

Here lies the deeper power of Addie Bundren's corpse. It is as if the power bestowed on it in the minds and emotions of her sons enabled Addie to use her own corpse in order to recreate her primordial attachment to the sons. This very corpse has the power to draw them into a regressive fusion, a moribund symbiosis in which a mother asserts her will to power beyond her own death. For the sons, the mother's dead body is replete with resonances of a devouring and overpowering symbiosis with, as well as violent separation from, the maternal body. It is the culturally "significant" body of the mother, the untouchable, impossible, absent, tabooed body that dies by giving birth in death to its negative Other: a raw, dead female body which, with the drama of its decomposition and the imaginary horror which it inspires, threatens the life, the body, and the self-boundaries of those to whom it has given birth. This is why the decomposing body of the mother eventually ceases to represent the dead mother and begins to represent instead the deadly female principle of the negative archaic mother, the mother who devours her children, or death that infects life.

By presenting a carnivalesque epos of this cultural body of the primordial mother, Faulkner's text performs a sublimation of the abject that reactualizes an archetypal fantasy of feminine abjection in modernist form. In the fight about and with the dead maternal body, in its imaginary transformations and its real mutilations, the sons react, among other things, against their fear of the archaic mother. The decidedly flat ending of the text shows the rotten corpse and along with it the dead mother finally defeated, neutralized, and buried. The abject is under control; everyday life regains its force. The weird normality of the Bundrens at the end of the novel, however, shows the inseparable link between that normality and the forceful expulsion of the abject from the social realm. From this perspective, the abject gains the status of a cultural unconscious which Faulkner's text enacts in the creation of a phantasmatically overdetermined functional world.

For the reader, of course, this control of the abject is effective from the very beginning and throughout the whole text, for the text as a whole sublimates the archaic mother as a grotesque character. We encounter a certain irony here: the carnivalesque figuration of the unsublimated body of the archaic mother generates an aesthetic sublimation which, while exposing this cultural abjection of the maternal body, also allows readers to act out their own ambivalence—if not hostility—toward the archaic mother. The text thus plays the role of a third party (usually occupied by the father) which, according to Kristeva, ultimately helps to carry through the fight against the archaic mother. "In such close combat, the symbolic light that a third party, eventually the father, can contribute helps the future subject, the more so if it happens to be endowed with a robust supply of drive energy, in pursuing a reluctant struggle against what, having been the mother, will turn into an abject" (*Powers* 13).

By carnivalizing Addie Bundren's grotesque corpse, Faulkner's text provides a cultural form of sublimating the dead maternal body. The archaic fight for and with that body recreates and exposes the taboos, fears, and ambivalences which form the basis of the mother's cultural and phantasmatic body. This recreation, in turn, mediates a specific cultural sublimation of the maternal body as an aesthetic experience which is open to interpretation and thus ultimately works toward a cultural change of the underlying patterns.

## 6. Carnivalesque Epos and Theater of Cruelty

Carnival and death, involuntary comedy and displaced mourning, the drama of the maternal corpse and the phantasmatic spectacle that doubles it— those are the emotional poles of tension which, through their interaction, guide our responses to Faulkner's text. The history of reception reveals a striking tendency to solve this tension by isolating the two conflicting tendencies from each other. The question of whether *As I Lay Dying* should be read as grotesque farce or as heroic epos misses the point because both tendencies are inseparable in the text and fulfill their function only in their fusion. This tension determines the atmosphere of the textual world as much as the status of the grotesque bodies.

The epic structure of the long funeral procession is as evident as its carnivalization. Since Valéry Larbaud, in his preface to the French edition of the novel, emphasized affinities with the funeral procession of the Homeric queen, critics have incessantly highlighted the epic character of the Bundrens' odyssey. The epos, more precisely the eleventh book of Homer's *Odyssey*, also provides the source for Faulkner's title: "As I lay dying the woman with the dog's eyes would not close my eyelids for me as I descended into Hades" (see Dickerson 189). But historically the novel gains its specific relevance as a narrative that articulates the specific in the general. The carnivalesque principle, on the other hand, is seen as dialogical, polyphonous, dionysian, and antirationalistic.[13] According to Kristeva, carnivalesque literature draws upon the language of the body and the language of dreams, creating homologies between linguistic structures and structures of desire.

If one assumes with Bakhtin and Kristeva that the epic and the carnivalesque are the two basic currents which form the tradition of narrative, then one would argue that Faulkner's text joins these two currents in one flow. The eruptive force of the carnivalesque explodes the epos from within, drawing it into an archaic swirl bordering on the fantastic and phantasmatic, and flooding the boundaries which ideally guarantee the identity, substance, causality, and definiteness of the epic. The voices of Faulkner's characters show all the basic features of the carnivalesque. The characters think analogically and inclusively, their perspectives relativize each other if not themselves, their fantasies and phantasmatic actions are excessive and transgressive. The epic structure remains there as a wrapping unable to contain what protrudes from inside—not unlike the grotesque bodies in carnivalesque literature, or Addie's dead body, which can or do no longer want to contain what protrudes from them.

The closeness of Faulkner's carnivalesque voices to the body and the dream, their primordiality and visuality, their performance as a glee of inner dialogues and monologues creates another closeness too, which is as important to the status of the text as the carnivalization itself. This is the closeness to the theater. It was again Larbaud who first stressed the affinities of *As I Lay Dying* to the theater. Carnival and theater both have their roots in the archaic forms of festival. The roots of representation itself reach back to an originary theater without representation from which the tradition of theater has inherited an insistent longing to efface the traces of representation. (See Derrida, "Theater"; Schwab, "Die Provokation.") A similar longing is voiced in Addie's monologue, both in her deep mistrust of language and in the theater of cruelty which she stages again and again in her violent rituals with the children.

Addie's monologue, inserted after two-thirds of the novel, polarizes the world of the text. Her voice provides a central perspective because it has a privileged position in the polyphony of voices. While the other monologues direct their perspective toward Addie's dying, her death, and the drama of her dead body, the focus of Addie's monologue lies on her life and the roots of her planned death in this life. Addie is the only one who projects her life as a story with a narrative structure. This is as important for the status of her monologue as for the image that one gains of Addie from the totality of monologues. While the other monologues complement, relativize, or contradict each other and add to an oscillatingly overdetermined and principally open, continuable whole, Addie's inner perspective reaches from a different level into the perspectives of the other characters. The latter carry strikingly few memories of Addie. The overwhelming reality of Addie's dead body overshadows the memories of her life. Instead of consciously controlled memories, the stream of consciousness brings rather unconscious representations and fantasies of the mother to the surface. These images, however, with their archaic shapes, their elementary passions, and their uncensored unconventionality, are, in a way, closer to Addie's self-image than conscious memories could ever be, closer even than the form of expression used in her own monologue, because they penetrate into those archaic domains which are more primary but also more abject than the world of verbal shapes which Addie rejects as false and alien.

The world which Addie opposes to the world of verbal shapes is characterized by an archaic solitude and by the desire for a symbiotic primordial unity in which the sheer separation of bodies is already a torture. In violent rituals she injures the children's bodies in order to recreate forcibly an aggressive form of primary undifferentiation. Her passionate rejection of the empty speech of coded words makes her regress to a form of body language which does not express itself through gestures but instead marks the body of the other directly. Addie rejects language in its function of separation and differentiation because she sees it as founding the separation of bodies. This attitude is rooted in a romantic idealization of the archaic and the primordial. For Addie, language founds the death of body and soul by substituting actions with empty sounds and by turning people like Anse into echoes of their words. The sadistic rituals with the children are Addie's privately staged "theater of cruelty" in the strong Artaudian sense of a theater which rebels against representation. As the simple act of naming is already too much for Addie, she tries in the dark of the night to regain the lost unity with her children by a repudiation of their names: "And then I would think *Cash* and *Darl* that way until their names would die and solidify into a shape and then fade away, I would say, All right. It doesn't matter. It doesn't matter what they call them" (137). With the same passion with which Addie dreams of abandoning herself to the wordlessness of nature and the body, she refuses herself the symbolic order of the world with its words, separate bodies, sublimated socialities, and intimacies.

And yet, in her social world, Addie, the former schoolteacher, is far from living the form of archaic femininity which she cherishes in her fantasies. Her monologue, self-reflexive and self-confident, reveals a relatively high rhetorical articulation. Her cutting criticism of the mindless empty world of Anses and Tulls is a cogent social criticism, voiced in "inner words" which cannot live the primordial dream but only conjure it verbally. Yet it is precisely in the face of this inner contradiction in Addie, which she herself consciously lives and articulates, that the funeral procession gains its deeper significance not only for the psychology of the Bundrens but also for the aesthetic status of Faulkner's text.

The seemingly contradictory form in which Addie voices her passionate desire for the archaic and primordial—namely, a highly self-reflexive and sharply articulated verbal criticism of language—actually provides a valuable insight into the two polar forms of expression which Faulkner's text constantly plays off against each other: the empty speech of characters like Anse Bundren, Cora Tull, or the minister Whitfield on the one hand, and the archaic language of the body or of phantasms which expresses itself in Addie's whippings of the children, Vardaman's phantasmatic fragmentation of the body of the fish/mother, or even in Cash's and Jewel's forgetfulness of the body in pain. These forms of bodily expression are, of course, themselves voiced verbally and thematized on the abstract level of literary articulation. The text itself as a form of literary speech stages these forms of bodily expression in the polyphony of different voices as a performance on the boundaries of carnival and verbal theater of cruelty.

The resonance of Artaud's "theater of cruelty" in Faulkner's text has not remained unnoticed in its history of reception. Five years after the publication of the novel, none other than Jean-Louis Barrault, who celebrated Faulkner as one of the writers with the greatest influence on his generation, staged the text's first theatrical adaptation inspired by Artaud. Based on the language of the body, *Autour d'une mère* unfolds itself as a drama in its primitive stage, as a form of pantomime around the grotesque body of the dead and totemic mother, who, with a mask and an oversized black wig, owns the only voice in the text and speaks two lyrical monologues. Artaud himself, fascinated by Faulkner's text and Barrault's adaptation, mentions them in his writings as attempts to revitalize drama in its magic and ritual forms.

The question is, then, what the metaphor of a "theater of cruelty" or, more precisely, a carnivalesque theater of cruelty means when used to characterize a narrative text—a text which has only language available as a means of expression, while Artaud has conceived his "theater of cruelty" against the "tyranny of the word." "The signifier is the death of the festival," writes Derrida in his analysis of Rousseau in *Of Grammatology* (306). The word sublimates the greed for living, the cosmic relentlessness, the utter necessity, and the painful corporeality for which Artaud chooses the metaphor of cruelty. Artaud problematizes the relationship of language to the body, or, more precisely, the separation of language from the body, with the aim of subverting the power of language on the theatrical stage. Faulkner, on the other hand, stages the language of the body within poetic language and on the basis of a narrative structure. The language of the characters is centered in the body and expresses itself over and again as a breakdown of the semiotic. The characters read themselves and their world because they know how to read bodies—their own, the bodies of others, and the bodies of the objects in their world.

This is also the context in which I understand a problem that has been discussed so insistently in Faulkner criticism, namely, that the verbal articulateness of the characters by far exceeds the likely capacity of articulation in persons of a similar social background. This is only a problem if one reads the monologues as realistic inner monologues. It seems more appropriate, however, to read the monologues partly as poetic abstractions of inner experiences. The monologues are understood, then, as the linguistic equivalents of something that is usually not articulated or cannot be articulated in a social context but which expresses itself socially in the drama of the body, especially the drama of the unsublimated and uncivilized, the undomesticated and uncodable body which violates the boundaries of social conventions and taboos. Like Artaud in his "theater of cruelty," Faulkner, too, grasps the body in extreme situations such as death or decay, in situations, that is, in which bodies are threatened by desublimation and which release unconscious energies and fantasies in those who assist the drama of those bodies. This is why the carnivalesque spectacle in Faulkner unfolds itself toward its vanishing point in a theater of cruelty. The carnivalesque in Faulkner's text is more archaic, undomesticated, and cruel than the sublimated carnival of parodic or satirical carnival rituals or, for that matter, of carnivalesque language games. Like Darl's laughter, the laughter provoked by Faulkner's text is not parodic but archaic, murderous, and deadly serious. Rather than using parodic exaggerations to ridicule the civilized and coded body, Faulkner's carnivalesque figurations evoke the unsublimated, abject body in the face of death. Faulkner stages this theater of cruelty as a purely verbal theater of interior voices and thus forgoes the antagonistic polarization of language and archaic desire or abjection which Artaud presupposes. The grotesque body in Faulkner's text, and particularly the abject body of the dead mother, already bears the traces of unconscious phantasms. The phantasmatic theater of cruelty which Addie Bundren's husband and sons perform with her dead body thus invokes the abjection of the maternal body in the cultural unconscious. On this stage, the drama of the grotesque body forms an indivisible unity with the drama of the grotesque soul.

# TRAUMA, TRANSGRESSION, AND TRANSFERENCE: THE OTHERNESS OF GENDER

## ❖ 6 ❖

# THE JUNGLE AND THE DRAWING ROOM
## Urban Nomads in *Nightwood*

The woman who presents herself to the spectator as a "picture" forever arranged is, for the contemplative mind, the chiefest danger. Sometimes one meets a woman who is beast turning human. Such a person's every movement will reduce to an image of a forgotten experience; a mirage of an eternal wedding cast on the racial memory; as insupportable a joy as would be the vision of an eland coming down an aisle of trees, chapleted with orange blossoms and bridal veil, a hoof raised in the economy of fear. (37)

THE WOMAN WHO thus presents herself is Robin Vote, an enigmatic character in Djuna Barnes's *Nightwood,* "the born somnambule, who lives in two worlds—meet of child and desperado" (35). The "picture" she evokes is Rousseau's *The Dream,* showing a woman who "seemed to lie in a jungle trapped in a drawing room . . . ; the set, the property of an unseen *dompteur,* half lord, half promoter, over which one expects to hear the strains of an orchestra of wood-winds render a serenade which will popularize the wilderness" (35). Barnes's fascination with the *douanier* Rousseau—which she shares with numerous other modernists and surrealists—may highlight one of the most central spatiotemporal configurations of her work, namely, a highly stylized "primitivism" enfolded into a self-reflexive artistic space. Barnes's "jungle" is an urban jungle replete with the decadent aesthetics of the cosmopolitan underworld and its nightlife as well as the sublimated wilderness of the circus. The "drawing room" in which Robin Vote seems trapped is reminiscent of the dreamlike pictogrammatic narratives produced by all those who attempt to trace Robin or track her down with words.

Robin Vote inhabits a paradoxical space, if any space at all. While presenting herself as a " 'picture' forever arranged," she refuses to remain within its suggestive frame. She traverses every space, from the unconscious traces of an archaic "racial memory" to its extensions into an unpredictable future. Created during the height of modernism, she appears strangely contemporaneous, a postmodern nomad whose aura is permeated by the life of plants and animals as much as by the nocturnal life of cities, coffeehouses, bars, and back alleys. There is a decisive streak of archaic primitivism in her portrayal, combined with the abject eroticism of urban destitutes. It appears to be more sinister than the primitivism we know from modernist art, resulting less from a cultural appropriation of so-called primitive art than from an artistic translation of archaic drives and phantasms. For the reader, the exotic urbanity of Barnes's uprooted and marginal figures might appear as a form of modernist primitivism; but it is one generated from within rather than through appropriation of an exotic other.

The characters in *Nightwood* belong to a new type of city nomad: eternal wanderers, traversing the boundaries of cities, countries, continents, gender, age, and time as well as genus and species, whether human, animal, or plant. Their internal nomadology is the motive signature of the time, with Robin Vote being its most extreme incorporation. "[A] tall girl with the body of a boy" (46) who carries the name of a bird and wears trousers, Robin Vote is bisexual but with a clearly lesbian desire. Her narrators portray her as a "dog" who "strays" in the streets (46), a woman with the "iris of wild beasts" (37) whose body exhales the perfume of earth and fungi and whose "flesh was the texture of plant life" (34). Barnes's text explores this archetypal figure of "untamed" female desire in sequences of narrative loops which begin by portraying Robin as "beast turning human" and end with her figuration as "human turning beast." And yet, this archetype is invoked in the fantasies of those who try to "domesticate" Robin, while she herself remains intrinsically "void."

Torn between an inextinguishable passion, an instinctual desire to sustain her polymorphous multiplicity, and an unfulfilled dream of coming to rest, of rooting herself in one person, Robin Vote becomes "the eternal momentary" (127) who, living outside of time, is nonetheless captivated by the glamor of famous historical or fictional women—Louise de la Vallière, Catherine of Russia, Madame de Maintenon, Catherine de' Medici, Anna Karenina, and Catherine Heathcliff (47).

The invocation of these women within the aura of a decaying Old Europe evokes an inner archaeology of history, a site where the debris of historical memories is animated by an intense affective cathexis, a melancholic nostalgia for the past and a bittersweet indulgence in the decadence of a vanishing aristocracy or the morbid dream of orientalist splendor. Amidst the nightmare of history between the two world wars, Robin Vote becomes addicted to the narcotic life of the underworld, the streets and coffeehouses in Vienna and Paris or the " 'paupers' salon" in the American West, meeting place for "poets, radicals, beggars, artists, and people in love; for Catholics, Protestants, Brahmins, dabblers in black magic and medicine" (50). The aura of the underworld is one of exotic doom, abomination, and abjection, of secondhand emotions, turbulence, and catastrophe, of eroticism and death.

Following Robin Vote's somnambulistic traversals of exotic spaces, we encounter the cultural embodiment of a "new woman"—decidedly urban, cosmopolitan, and born within the economy of fear that governs her time—a woman who, never domesticated, abhors nothing more than the space of domesticity and the maternal (see Benstock). Yet she also remains a victim of her time whose contradictions she enacts, a "figure of doom" with "the face of an incurable yet to be stricken with its malady" (41). Her malady is what Marguerite Duras later terms "the malady of death," a confinement to melancholy and narcissism, to emotionless passion in the absence of love.

The notion of an "emotionless passion" refers to the territorial economy[1] of those who are eternally driven but never moved. Robin's emotional state is one of a "cataleptic calm" (45), while her motive state is one of frantic movement. At the heart of this psychological condition of turbulence we do not find the peace of meditative silence, but the *horror vacui* of an empty space.

Djuna Barnes portrays her characters in terms of motion, of traversals of outer and inner spaces. Felix, for example, whom Robin marries and whom she leaves after the birth of their son, is cast as the eternally wandering Jew, a vagrant figure who shares with Robin a "laborious melancholy" and a fundamental uprootedness in time and space:

> What had formed Felix from the date of his birth to his coming to thirty was unknown to the world, for the step of the wandering Jew is in every son. No matter where and when you meet him you feel that he has come from some place—no matter from what place he has come—some country that he has devoured rather than resided in, some secret land that he has been nourished on but cannot inherit, for the Jew seems to be everywhere from nowhere. When Felix's name was mentioned, three or more persons would swear to having seen him the week before in three different countries simultaneously. (7)

Felix's oral if not cannibalistic relationship to space and his mythical "omnipresence" in the world are enforced by his parents' Gentile "family romance." Felix is the son of Hedvig Volkbein—a Viennese woman who claims descendance from the "House of Hapsburg"—and Guido Volkbein, a Jew of Italian descent with the public manners of a late-nineteenth-century dandy. Both

Guido and his son Felix are "heavy with impermissible blood" (3), haunted by the ghost of nobility and the futile pretense to a barony. Obsessed with the irretrievable past of what he terms "Old Europe," Felix seeks out the mock barons and mock queens of the circus because they satisfy his hunger for real kings and queens. Merged with the circus's simulations of aristocratic splendor, his carnivalized nobility crumbles into the "humble hysteria" of a pathetic mock pageantry. Through a trapeze artist, Frau Mann, who calls herself the "Duchess of Broadback," Felix meets Matthew O'Connor, a melancholic Irish lay philosopher and illegal abortionist "whose interest in gynecology had driven him half around the world" (14). O'Connor is also figured as a transvestite who likes to refer to himself as "the bearded lady" or "the last woman left in this world" (100). The doctor's discourse forms a connective tissue between the characters and their inner spaces. He has brought Robin's lover Nora Flood into the world, the American whose "salon" draws together the "wandering people" from all over the globe. He befriends Felix, extracting his fantasies and stories about Robin and their son Guido, who, being mentally deficient, embodies the curse of a decadent nobility. And finally, he introduces Robin to her lover Jenny, a "collector of destiny" (98) and hysteric whose inability to connect translates spatially into a lifelong "feeling of being removed" (98). All these characters traverse the same spaces, wandering across cities and continents, pursuing each other, hungry for fleeting points of contact in some interior space. The notion of "interior space" pertains to both a psychic interiority and a textual effect. Insisting on a convergence between exterior and interior, Barnes's imaginary ethnography of cities is the effect of a poetic discourse that traces the imprints of inner spaces onto outer landscapes and objects, just as Nora, during her nocturnal wanderings, no longer looks for Robin but learns to read the traces she has left on buildings, streets, and other people.

*Nightwood* develops a poetics of the city nomad as a new figure of modernity. Its language is attuned to the movements of uprooted figures through unterritorialized spaces, to their inner exile, the broken dreams and fake emblems of a lost aristocracy, the frivolous *flânerie* of outlived dandies and the plush simulations of glorious historical styles. Barnes's modern nomads, in fact, are in many ways reminiscent of one of their most prominent precursors: the *flâneur* as Walter Benjamin describes him in his essays on Charles Baudelaire. Both inhabit the decadent and pretentious underworld of dandies, bohemians, asocials, prostitutes, and gamblers, of erotomania and noctambulism, or of what figures in Benjamin as the "erotology of the condemned" (see Buck-Morss 722).

Being an eternal wanderer, addicted to exotic spaces and a noncommittal eroticism, haunted by solitude, narcissism, and self-absorption, Robin Vote, for one, could well be perceived as a female counterpart of the *flâneur*. Like him, she is drawn to outcasts, artists, and the world of "paupers and bums." But while the *flâneur* pursues the fetishistic pleasures of a noncommittal gaze, Robin, the "somnambule," radicalizes the abjection of the *flâneur*, walking blindly, her eyes turned inward. She becomes his "other," not ambulating but driven and dominated by a different territorial politics. Susan Buck-Morss argues that "sexual difference complicates the politics of loitering" (118) and defines prostitution as the female version of *flânerie*. When Robin roams through the streets and coffeehouses of Paris, the narrator compares her to "a practised whore who turns away from no one but the one who loves her" (57).

Robin's "prostitution" is an internal affliction that compels her to "throw herself away" rather than to "sell herself." She marries Felix, for example, because her "life held no volition for refusal" (43). It is this disposition, paired with the paradoxical desire of a narcissistic woman who wants "to make everyone happy" (155), which locates her on the trajectory of the prostitute. Her inability to refuse only covers up a deeper incapacity to give or to do "anything in relation to anyone but herself" (146). Robin thus suffers from the paradoxical economy of one who never refuses because she has nothing to give.

Barnes's text, in fact, carefully exempts Robin from any rhetoric of commodification, fetishization, or exchange value—be it capitalist or psychological. Instead, her figuration rather pertains to a spatiotemporal politics, locating her through terms like appropriation or disappropriation, foreignness, otherness, uprootedness, or degradation. When the doctor and Felix first find her unconscious in a Parisian hotel, "in white flannel trousers, heavy and dishevelled" (34), Felix "felt that he was looking upon a figurehead in a museum" (38), while the narrator describes her as "the infected carrier of the past" (37). Her attractiveness for Felix, in fact, stems from his fantasy of making her participate in his own phantasmatic reenactment of European aristocracy. Just like his house, his mind seems a mere extension of the European museums through which he begins to drag her and later their son Guido.

Felix, who has inherited from his father the disposition of the *flâneur* and sightseer, tries to restore the lost splendor of aristocratic life by gazing at its remainders: old buildings and furniture, museums and galleries. Robin, by contrast, wanders through these museum spaces without "seeing," her perception replaced by touch. When Felix marvels that "[s]he has the touch of the blind who, because they see more with their fingers, forget more in their minds" (42), he also realizes that they will never belong to the same time because he lives in the past, while she knows only the present, which, however, contains an "alchemy" of the future.

Robin's different spatiotemporal location or locomotion leads to the dramatic rupture with Felix after the birth of their son. Conceiving herself pregnant before she is, Robin prepares herself for her child with a "stubborn cataleptic calm" (45). "[S]trangely aware of some lost land in herself" (45), her pregnancy becomes an exercise in territorial survival: "she took to going out; wandering the countryside; to train travel, to other cities, alone and engrossed" (45), often not returning for days. On the day before she gives birth, the aura of the whore temporarily merges with that of a destitute madonna who roams the churches for salvation and talks to the nuns, only to return home and read the memoirs of the Marquis de Sade. She is drunk when she gives birth in fury and horror to a son who is mentally impaired and a melancholic from birth. Fiercely rejecting her child and her motherhood, she takes to wandering again and to intermittent travel from which she comes back in utter disinterest. Felix looks for her in the cafes—as Nora will later—and often finds her drunk and surrounded by "people of every sort" (49).

*Nightwood* is set in the twenties in Europe, about a hundred years after the culture of the *flâneur* analyzed by Benjamin. The "politics of loitering" is undergoing drastic changes by this time. The *flâneur* and his leisure culture give way to a new type of "urban destitute," outcasts from different social groups and classes, from the run-down or would-be nobility to impoverished artists and bohemians, gamblers, and prostitutes. As Buck-Morss has shown, by the Depression in the thirties, this group of urban destitutes will mainly be formed by the *Lumpenprotelariat*, by vagabonds, ragpickers, cab-drivers, and bag ladies (110).

Robin Vote appears as a transitional figure between the two cultures, strangely suspended in time and bent upon a future that has not yet happened—her attention taken, as Felix feels, "by something not yet in history" (44). After she leaves Felix in an outburst of rage against her unwanted son, she takes up with Nora Flood who inhabits a different future, that of America poised against a Europe that is "going down." While the mood of her relationship with Felix was one of indifference and unconnectedness, her mood with Nora is one of frantic passion, despair, and imprisonment. Nora's " 'paupers' salon" is a strange blend of the old Gentile European salons and the Western cowboy saloon: "She was known instantly as a Westerner. Looking at her, foreigners remembered stories they had heard of covered wagons; animals going down to drink; children's heads, just as far as the eyes, looking in fright out of small windows, where in the dark another race crouched in ambush" (51).

This merging of urban space with wilderness or jungle in Barnes's invocation of the Wild West recalls Baudelaire's "poetics of the Apache" (*Poesie des Apachentums*), a myth of the Indian which, according to Benjamin, plays such a prominent role for the *flâneur* (see Buck-Morss 583). The Indian, Mohican or Apache, incorporated the myth of the urban adventurer (see Benjamin, "Das Paris" 543; 582ff). Dumas's *Mohicans de Paris*, for example, promises the reader a jungle and a prairie amid the urban landscape of Paris. Baudelaire's "poetics of the Apache" stylizes the Parisian Apache as the supreme adventurer who abjures all virtue and law. A similar merging of urban space with wilderness or jungle also generates the interior landscape of *Nightwood*. If Robin Vote can be seen as a female counterpart to the *flâneur*, then Nora Flood is that of the Apache. Just as the latter had never been an ethnic character but a figure who stood for the dandy's appropriation of the exotic and the outlaw, so Nora, the Western woman, becomes a figuration of the exoticism of the new world and the Wild West. But while the *flâneur* and the dandy reduce the exotic wilderness to a merely ornamental function, Barnes's characters generate it from within. While the *flâneur* paraded exotic animals such as turtles on a leash through the Parisian arcades, Robin Vote possesses a magical power over wild animals and, in the end, undergoes a metamorphosis that resembles the very condition which Deleuze and Guattari have termed "becoming-animal."

This is important if we want to determine the status of what I have termed the "primitivism" of Barnes's textual world. In the culture of the *flâneur*, the primitive, the archaic, and the exotic are on display, exposed to the gaze of an urban dandy who appropriates them as commodities from a supposedly superior position. In this sense, the *flâneur* is entangled in the urban effects of cultural colonialism and imperialism which make the primitive, the oriental, and the native available as consumer goods and exotic objects. By contrast, the "exoticism" of Barnes's characters is that of natives of the city whose otherness stems from their being foreign to themselves and the spaces they temporarily inhabit.

Only Nora Flood's nomadic life is not imposed from within but from without. She would rather create a "salon" for other wandering people or a home for her lover Robin Vote than wander herself. And yet with Robin she travels to all the old European cities and becomes a true collector, filling their house with mnemonic objects of their restless life: circus chairs, wooden horses, venetian chandeliers, stage props, wooden boxes, and ecclesiastical hangings (55). But Nora's being a collector of objects is a very different condition from the one described by Benjamin. Very much like the *flâneur*, Benjamin's collector expresses the logic of a capitalist economy. Nora Flood, by contrast, expresses the inner economy of one who must collect her life in order to prevent it from falling apart. In her collected objects she encrypts the memory of her life with Robin just as, when their love falls apart, she encrypts Robin herself, keeping her inside like a corpse:

> Love becomes the deposit of the heart, analogous in all degrees to the "findings" in a tomb. . . . In Nora's heart lay the fossil of Robin, intaglio of her identity, and about it for its maintenance ran Nora's blood. Thus the body of Robin could never be unloved, corrupt or put away. Robin was now beyond timely changes, except in the blood that animated her. (56)

This melancholic encryptment of the Other will take the form of a self-effacing mimicry; Nora, who is unable to "mirror" others, her eyes having the "mirrorless look of polished metals which report not so much the object as the movement of the object" (52), now mimics Robin in her absence: "I said to myself, I will do what she has done, I will love what she has loved, then I will find her again" (136). This turns Nora into a ghost of Robin, the simulacrum of a shadow in the face of a shadowless object. Within this dynamic of a mirrorless gaze, the registered movement of the object must be halted, since movement is linked to loss and only death may convey a sense of permanence and belonging: "To keep her (in Robin there was this tragic longing to be kept, knowing herself astray) Nora knew that there was no way but death. In death Robin would belong to her" (58). This link between love and death, played out on every scale of Robin's and Nora's turbulent encounters with each other, reveals that Nora's encryption of Robin had already begun even before she lost her. As the doctor says about their relationship, "[D]eath is intimacy walking backward. We are crazed with grief when she, who once permitted us, leaves to us the only recollection" (128).

The mimetic desire in Nora's mimicry of the encrypted lost object, combined with the negative intimacy produced by the fantasy of possessing her in death, is complicated by the fact that Robin and Nora also figure as hieroglyphics of lesbian desire. Benjamin called the lesbian the "heroine of modernity" ("Das Paris" 594), and one could hardly imagine a more complex figuration of this heroine than Robin Vote. In nineteenth-century literature and art, the lesbian often appears as an androgynous figure frequently intertwined with a male fantasy of a femme fatale. Robin, too, is portrayed as androgynous and might have appeared as a "femme fatale" to the male characters in the novel, but the text certainly does not present her *as* a male fantasy. The love between Robin and Nora is doomed not because they are lesbians or because Robin is a "femme fatale," but rather because Robin suffers from a contagious "malady of death." This most insidious link between love and death in Barnes's novel stigmatizes not only lesbian desire but desire in general. As there is no leisure in Robin's and Nora's wandering, there is no *jouissance* in their love; rather the turbulence and despair of a desire that lives in anticipation of a catastrophe.

Memory, pain, and desire generate the motive power of *Nightwood*, and the three are inseparably linked to each other, to the body and the poetics of the text. One reason why all of Barnes's characters are constantly driven from one space or person to another is that they fail to inhabit not only their homes, their cities, or their countries, but also their "official" bodies. It is as if they had to parade one body for the world while living in another, so that in actual fact they become suspended in the space between two incompatible bodies, namely, the coded body and the tacit body. O'Connor calls himself an "uninhabited angel," and Nora muses that "the devil has set foot in the uninhabited" (148). The "uninhabited body" appears as a problem of gender or, more specifically, the lack of a culturally accepted gender or of unequivocal gender boundaries. O'Connor, the man who is gendered as a woman and likes to masquerade as one, defines himself as belonging to "the third sex":

> The last doll, given to age, is the girl who should have been a boy, and the boy who should have been a girl! The love of that last doll was foreshadowed in that love of the first. The doll and the immature have something right about them, the doll because it resembles but does not contain life, and the third sex because it contains life but resembles the doll. (148)

The doctor discloses his "third sex" in the masquerades that reveal his true gender—be it his cross-dressing or the performative masquerade of his speeches. During the night, O'Connor lives as an "old woman in the closet," giving birth to his discourse, while during the day he is "driven around the world" as an unlicensed gynecologist who performs illegal abortions, helping women to evacuate their wombs of the children he craves and will never have. O'Connor's male hysteria recalls, in fact, the old definition of hysteria as a symptom of the "wandering womb." Endowed with "a mother's reverence for childhood," the doctor likes to confess his "maternal" instincts: "no matter what I may be doing, in my heart is the wish for children and knitting. God, I never asked better than to boil some good man's potatoes and toss up a child for him every nine months by the calendar" (91).

By contrast, Robin, the girl who should have been a boy, violently rejects her child, leaving the mothering functions to Felix, while her relationship with Nora is haunted by the figure of a doll in whom the two women have encrypted the wish for the child they can never have. Given his own obsession with the womb, the doctor explicitly links their lesbian desire to a phantom of motherhood: "Love of woman for woman, what insane passion for unmitigated anguish and motherhood brought that into the mind?" (75). But such a perspective is too confining for the desire between Robin and Nora, whose unboundedness transgresses the boundaries of gender and age. Nora loves in Robin not only the woman or the girl, but also the child and the boy and even her grandmother who herself appears in the clothes of man. Yet even though their desire retains the traces of children's polymorphous perversity, their *jouissance* is drowned in a sense of doom which by far surpasses the aestheticized "erotology of the condemned" described in Benjamin's analysis of Baudelaire. It is ultimately the incestuous quality of their love which destroys them, and Robin seems to physically enact and externalize a tacit knowledge of this when she plays her seductive games with the little girl, Sylvia.

In its figuration of the womb as a harbinger of death (in the case of Hedvig Volkbein), a cursed container for a rejected and mentally impaired child (Robin) or a barren and empty void (Matthew O'Connor), the text also enacts what Edward Said claims to be one of the most persistent themes in high modernism, namely, the "impossibility of natural filiation":

> Childless couples, orphaned children, aborted childbirths, and unregenerately celibate men and women populate the world of high modernism with remarkable insistence, all of them suggesting the difficulties of filiation. But no less important in my opinion is the second part of the pattern, which is immediately consequent upon the first, the pressure to produce new and different ways of conceiving human relationships. ("Secular" 614)

*Nightwood* enacts the difficulties of filiation in its figuration of social outcasts, tying it to the decay of Old Europe, the aristocracy, and the old filiative structures of the family. While, according to Said, the pressure to produce new human relationships is answered by communities whose social existence is guaranteed by affiliation, the characters in *Nightwood* are excluded from established communal affiliations, and the inoperative communities of urban destitutes fail to provide a ground for rootedness in space, time, or even in one's body.

Failing to confine desire into the boundaries of culturally sanctioned gender norms, the "uninhabited bodies" of Barnes's characters appear "indecent" (156), because their desire is unbounded, fluctuating, and incestuous. As Nora confesses to the doctor, "Robin is incest too; that is one of her powers" (156). Paradoxically however, being too close, they can share neither a space nor a time. Nora says about Robin:

> Yet not being the family she is more present than the family. A relative is in the foreground only when it is born, when it suffers and when it dies, unless it becomes one's lover, then it must be everything, as Robin was; yet not as much as she, for she was like a relative found in another generation. (157)

This asynchronic quality marks the relationships of Barnes's characters as much as their inability to inhabit a space. It also marks the "spatial form" (see Frank) of the novel, a form in which time and space no longer function as separate categories but merge and generate each other. Being no longer poised in "still motion" (see Krieger, *Ekphrasis*), this "spatial form" contains turbulence in all its recursive loops. Even though it enfolds the narratives of its characters' lives, the poetic language of *Nightwood* develops in continual tension with narrative and storytelling. At the heart of narrative is the lie, since narratives simulate a synchronicity which is never lived. Even Matthew, the would-be storyteller, maintains, "Life is not to be told, call it as loud as you like, it will not tell itself" (129).

In Barnes, narratives interfere with the dynamic of remembering and forgetting; they create a spatiotemporal order of their own, halting motion by establishing the fixity of a "still life" of loss, mourning, and encryptment. From this perspective, narrative mainly appears as a function of nostalgia. But, as Marshall Berman has reminded us in "Hitting the Street," "The biggest trouble with the politics of nostalgia is that it forces us to lie to each other and to ourselves about who we were and who we are" (11). In *Nightwood,* the relationship of narrative to memory is established as a function not only of time, but also of inhabiting and filling a space. Those who remember become tied to space, while those who forget are condemned to wander eternally. Or, as Nora says, "Robin can go anywhere, do anything . . . because she forgets, and I nowhere because I remember" (152). Through space, memory is intrinsically linked to the motive power of the body. The memory of a *flâneur* or of a dandy—like Felix's father Guido Volkbein—is very different from the memory of Barnes's nomadic destitutes. Marked by his leisurely pace and freely floating attention, the *flâneur*'s memory is shaped like a museum or a display of merchandise or collected objects, while the memory of Barnes's nomads—like her textual memory—is eternally wandering, syncretistic, and unfocused, yet "anchored in anticipation and regret" (60).

This memory then is itself "a form of locomotion" (59), covering distances that can never be spread out into a story. O'Connor, who says of himself, "my mind is so rich that it is always wandering" (105), is not a storyteller but a mock philosopher who shores up the fragments of old philosophical wisdom against the pain of those like Nora who come to listen to him. Whenever he gives in to storytelling, his stories are lies, cynical mock resonances of a family romance he has never attempted to live, or a synchronicity he will, as he says, never have: "Matthew, you have never been in time with any man's life and you'll never be remembered at all, God save the vacancy" (159). And yet, his discourse creates a different synchronicity of the incompatible, the contradictory, and the un-censored flow of conflicting images. Instead of producing a narrative, he re-leases a torrent of thoughts, his mind fueled by a passionate anger and the void of his unlivable desire.

It is as if instead of containing pain like a narrative, this torrent of thought serves rather to flush it out of the system. In this sense, the doctor is also a lay psychoanalyst who inverts the principles of transference and the direction of the talking cure. The others come to him in order to tell him their lives, but instead of the analyst's silence, the doctor offers them a torrential discourse of madness. It is he rather than his patients who produces the free associations, thus turning the psychoanalytic situation around, converting it into a pseudo-philosophical performance. He plays the role of a most ingenious nonsense philosopher, mocking the coherence of philosophical narratives and the reli-ability of the word with his drunkard's babble, heavy with the wisdom of the charlatan. (In this respect, his speech already contains the seeds of one of his most prominent descendants—Lucky, in Samuel Beckett's *Waiting for Godot*.)

O'Connor's posture in these performances is deeply anti-Cartesian, for he doubts the word, celebrates his own artifice of lying, and defines thinking as an effect of the body. "I think, therefore I am," for him, means "I think, there-fore I am sick" (158), for "we who are full to the gorge with misery should look well around, doubting everything seen, done, spoken, precisely because we have a word for it, and not its alchemy" (83). Instead of the Cartesian movement of systematic separation and isolation of spheres, O'Connor celebrates a holistic alchemy, forcing his thoughts back into the crucible of desire, thinking with the body—or "the eye that you fear" (83)—rather than with a rational mind.

In this respect, his thought becomes "primary process" in the very specific and volitional sense that it defies the law and censorship of the symbolic order and the soothing rhythm of a story line. It deliberately retains the turbulence of primary experience, exploring the abjection of the unconscious through a delirious speech which flows across the boundaries of his own discourse, infecting the speech of the other characters and the whole text like a "virus from outer space."[2]

It is no exaggeration to say that the doctor's speech performances enact a verbal "theater of cruelty" which pursues the Artaudian project of reuniting language and the body, speaking the body and its confinement to desire and death. This is why the doctor's speech does not really "represent" the turbulence of desire—his own as well as the other characters'—but rather enacts desire in a psychodrama that is always threatened by paralysis and death. Instead of a linear narrative, this speech generates sequences and networks of free associations, ripe with the visuality and intense emotional cathexis of the dream. Like the dream it is alogical, inclusive of oppositions and contradictions—as if it ran at a deep level at which opposites have not yet been categorically separated by the logical mind (see Freud, "Über den Gegensinn"). Rhetorically, these turbulent tensions are evoked and contained in a flood of paradoxical metaphors—highly suggestive and compelling metaphors which often recall spatial and emotional impasses and yet, at the same time, generate the motility and drivenness peculiar to both characters and text: "moving toward him in recoil" (3); "to be everywhere from nowhere" (7); "living statues" (13); "recoil and advance" (65); or "the child, sitting still and running" (106); "[o]ut looking for what she is afraid to find" (61); and many more. Critics like to describe Barnes's tropes as self-canceling metaphors (see Kaviola). But rather than self-canceling, these metaphors are self-mobilizing, introducing movement into the sculpted word—just as Nora's gaze introduces movement into the statue that reminds her of Robin.

Toward the end of *Nightwood*, O'Connor disrupts Nora's endless stories: "can't you rest now, put down the pen?" (126). In one of its last recursive loops, the text becomes self-reflexive: just as Robin circles around Nora's house in ever narrowing loops, so the text circles around the loop of writing. Writing, as the doctor's words imply, resides not only in the act of putting down words on a page. O'Connor exposes writing as the internal condition of the storyteller who encrypts her life by retelling it endlessly—like Nora who "believes the word" and turns her life with Robin into stories. For the doctor, this type of "writing" functions very much like the mirrorless gaze that reflects the motion of the object rather than the object itself. Writing follows only the traces of the lost object while the doctor envisions an aura—an "alchemy of the word"—in which the anthropomorphic word becomes flesh so that the object may grasp us.[3] Exploring the notion of an inverted *Sprachmagie*, the doctor envisions himself "eating the bitter book of his life" (127): "The archives of my case against the law, snatched up and out of the tale-telling files. . . . And didn't I eat a page and tear a page and stamp on others and toss some into the toilet for relief's sake" (127). This feasting on the word and its aggressive ejection are the inverse of Nora's encryptment. They give language back to the archaic dynamic of devouring the good and ejecting the bad.

Nora, by contrast, remains bound to a melancholic reading of traces. Abandoned by Robin, Nora needs to "go down" herself, become Robin in order to recreate Robin's ghostly presence within herself. Wandering the streets of Marseilles, the ports of Tangier and Naples, haunting the cafés where Robin had lived her nightlife, drinking with men and dancing with women, Nora looks for the traces of Robin in those who have slept with her and in the places which she had traversed. And yet, as Benjamin reminds us, "The trace is the apparition of a presence, as far as the object might be that has left the trace. The aura is the apparition of an absence, as close as the object might be that has evoked the aura. In the trace we grasp the object, in the aura the object grasps us" (*Das Passagenwerk* 560; my translation). Nora fails to find the traces she looks for because she cannot make Robin appear as a presence. Instead she remains in "the shadow of the object" at "the centre of eroticism and death" (158; see also Bollas).

It seems to be this aura that pervades their final encounter. Robin's wandering finally comes to an end in an archaic inner metamorphosis, a "becoming-plant and -animal."[4] She merges with the woods in which she sleeps and plunges into a "fixed stillness, obliterating her as a drop of water is made anonymous by the pond into which it has fallen" (168), all the while blindly heading up toward Nora's house, circling it closer and closer, entering a "sensuous communion" with Nora's dog who rushes toward her, followed by Nora. A mutual "call of the wild" brings them together in a chapel where, in front of Nora's eyes, Robin "goes down," becoming-dog: "And down she went, until her head swung against his; on all fours now, dragging her knees" (169).

The scene is both possession and exorcism at once: "Then she began to bark also, crawling after him—barking in a fit of laughter, obscene and touching" (170). The obscene spectacle of the body explodes in a hysterical catharsis, both the dog and Robin crying, until they give in and come to rest: "crying in shorter and shorter spaces, moving head to head, until she gave up, lying out, her hands beside her, her face turned and weeping; and the dog too gave up then, and lay down, his eyes bloodshot, his head flat along her knees" (170). This is the very end of Barnes's *Nightwood*, a closure of movements and migration, an uncanny "coming home" to an archaic space. This space is no longer "other" or exotic but a space of mutual assimilation. By "becoming-animal," Robin, about whom the doctor said that she was "outside the 'human type' " (146), mirrors and is mirrored in a dog. By making the dog cry she makes it become "human." We are left with this ambiguous and uncanny vision of a catharsis. This is no longer the exotic world of the circus with which the text began. Instead, we witness a haunting transformation that effaces otherness, one in which humans, dogs, saints, whores are reduced to sameness, afflicted by an incurable malady yet to be contracted.

Returning to a more integrated perspective of the novel as a whole, one could also say that Barnes's fierce critique of the various cultures through which her characters move might be linked to the trope of an incurable malady yet to be contracted. If we look closely, we might see that this malady not only afflicts Robin but forms a deadly chain of contagion that links all the characters. In this sense we may say that Barnes's critique of culture is located in her diagnosis of a disease that spreads across cities and continents, disregarding the boundaries of race and gender. The malady is, however, intimately linked to such boundaries since it is an expression of what Jane Marcus calls "the modern failure to understand or assimilate the difference of race, class, and gender" (qtd. in Broe 22). Mary Lynn Broe argues that it took Marcus's "radical feminist reclaiming of *Nightwood*'s 'political unconscious' " (22) to disrupt the critical reception of Barnes's text, which was established along the lines of a canonized male modernism. But then this reception also reveals that ironically Barnes's critics have perpetuated the very failure to deal with difference manifested by her own textual practice. When Marcus highlights *Nightwood*'s insistence on non-Aryan, non-heterosexual bodies, she links Barnes's "political unconscious" with fictional bodies that transgress the boundaries of the codified body. The latter, in turn, are embedded in what I have called a "geopolitical unconscious," generated by the ways in which Barnes moves these fictional bodies through space and has them transgress cultural and national boundaries. Spatial dislocations reveal the links between the politics of bodies and emotions. Nora Flood, for example, infuses the decadent and exotic, yet nonetheless racist and homophobic, politics of European metropolitan culture with a dose of American Puritanism. When Shari Benstock stresses Nora Flood's role as "representative of American culture—a woman puritanized and purified," she does so in order to explain why this character rejects her own lesbianism, or why she is "caught in an interpretive act that forces her to read perversion in her own actions, to interpret herself as a pervert" (261). Nora's failure to understand or assimilate her own sexual orientation, then, appears as a cultural malady that displays symptoms similar to those of other characters' failure to deal with racial or class difference. We are, for example, never to forget that, despite his own ostracism and marginalization, the doctor is a ranting racist who also indulges in Felix's aristocratic aspirations.

Ultimately it is this cultural disease that links *Nightwood*'s multiple trajectories and establishes a connection between its different layers of meaning. It is as if the "malady" ravages what one could call the "unconscious spaces" of *Nightwood*—dream and desire, nightmare and fear, spaces of transference in which the dialogues resonate in a void. At a conceptual level, this "malady" must then also be understood from within what I would call Djuna Barnes's "aesthetics of unconscious space." This term, in fact, may bring together the different strands of our theoretical traversal of *Nightwood*: namely, the archaic dream space and the space of passions, the cosmopolitan city-space, the territorial politics of and the culture contact between different countries and continents, the modernist "multiculturalism" of its characters, and finally the eclectic modernism and the "spatial form" of the novel which enfolds all these strands into a fractal space.

Within this perspective, "spatial form" is conceptualized in a fashion completely different from that proposed by Joseph Frank. Rather than being simply produced by disruptions of linear narrative or juxtapositions that evoke simultaneity, "spatial form" in Barnes also performs a condensation of cultural and interior spaces. The latter are less "translated" than "enfolded" into each other. The characters' "eternal wanderings," their traversals of multiple spaces and boundaries, in other words, are not—like hieroglyphics of a dream—"translations" of inner spaces or unconscious desires. Rather, they are a condensed simultaneous apparition and experience of both inseparably.

From a slightly different perspective, one could also say that the characters' movements through spaces *are* exteriorizations of interiorized cultural spaces and (e)motions. This "transcoding" between space, motion, and emotion is crucial. *Nightwood* visualizes the politics of emotions as a territorial politics, showing that space is never simply "outside"—not even in the distant gaze of the *flâneur*.[5] We may now better understand why oral metaphors play such a crucial role in Barnes's text and why its characters "devour" rather than reside in countries or are "nourished" by a space rather than inhabiting it (7). Barnes's "geopolitical unconscious" reminds us that spaces and their cultures are interiorized in rather archaic ways. They mold our unconscious in such a way that what we see when we wander through the streets, cities, or museums of the world already contains the condensed traces of individual and cultural memory—including the effects of encrypted memories.

In this sense, Barnes, like her characters, is a true melancholic. Her nostalgia, however, is not that of the *flâneur* who ambulates through the Parisian Arcades. It rather inverts that of the surrealist who explores the *Ideal Palace*. One of the sacred places of the surrealist world, the *Ideal Palace* was constructed by the famous "Facteur" Cheval (in whose honor Max Ernst made a collage and Breton wrote a poem). By his own account, Cheval was bored with "walking forever in the same decor" and constructed his sublime palace in order "to bring to a new birth all the ancient architectures of primitive times" (Hughes 229). Cheval adapts "Greek, Assyrian, and Egyptian architecture, with side-glances at the Taj Mahal, the Maison Carrée of Algiers, the mosques of Cairo, the White House, and the Amazon Jungle" (229). The fractal facade of this palace is not made up of straight lines and angles but contains innumerable miniature palaces full of resonances and symmetries across different scales. And, most importantly, the interior of this palace replicates this pattern in a minute architecture of catacombs—which the Facteur called "Hecatombs."

The narrative strands of *Nightwood* reassemble the shards of a decaying aristocracy—the broken dream of the "ideal palace" in an old aristocratic Europe. But the text inverts the characters' nostalgia by exposing the dark grottoes and catacombs of this palace—its encrypted cultural memories. The aesthetic of encrypted memories at the core of *Nightwood*'s textual turbulence determines the dynamic spatial form of Barnes's novel, leaving its readers the task of absorbing the characters' melancholy into a mournful reading process. Within this dynamic, the crypt loses its petrifying grip and is reinserted into the mobility of a living space.

# "WHILE SHE LIVES SHE INVITES MURDER"
## The Malady of Death

ON THE SURFACE, the narrative of Marguerite Duras's *The Malady of Death* (*La maladie de la mort*), a short prose piece published in French in 1982, is simple enough: a man hires a woman to spend an indeterminate amount of time with him during which he wants—as he confesses to her—to "try loving" and to find out "how loving can happen—the emotion of loving" (49).[1] This curious encounter unfolds its dramatic tensions and ends when the woman leaves after the termination of the contract.

The simplicity of this setting, however, is deceptive. Woven through the text's sixty-odd pages in poetic prose is a postmodern incantation of archetypal fears and desires and their epistemological resonances: the vicissitudes of the gaze, the intricate ties between love and death, desire and its impossible enactments, engulfment and aggression or the threats of the Other, and the instabilities of gender. The piece is masterfully orchestrated by a melancholic drama of narrative voices, intertwined around abysses of silence that are rendered graphically in the abundance of blank spaces and margins in the text. Everything in Duras's piece depends on this narrative framing established with the very first sentence:

> You wouldn't have known her, you'd have seen her everywhere at once, in a hotel, in a street, in a train, in a bar, in a book, in a film, in yourself, your inmost self, when your sex grew erect in the night, seeking somewhere to put itself, somewhere to shed its load of tears. (1)

We pass over the threshold of the text with a narrator directly addressing the male protagonist in a conditional tense that opens up the abstract time of an imaginary space and marks its tentative, dreamlike quality. Like a stage director, this narrator who is identified as male only in an appendix,[2] envisions the speech performances of the two protagonists, simultaneously playing with the ambiguity that accompanies his abstract, general, yet direct address "vous." While it signals a direct address to the male protagonist, this "vous" also extends an invitation to the male reader to partake in a "fantasy" scripted by a woman author and mediated by an abstract narrative voice—a fantasy about a man's intimate encounter with a woman who is "everywhere at once," everywoman, anonymous, yet pertaining to everyman's "inmost self."

From the outset, this rhetorical strategy places the female reader in a paradoxical space where she is at the same time "inside" the narrative (through grammatical association and narrative perspective) and "outside" (through gender affiliation). Moreover, the man whose perspective she is compelled to assume casts the woman in the text as the absolute Other, a stranger, an object—"*la chose*"[3]—a "dark shape on the bed" (28).

The second passage introduces the "economical" terms of the contract: "You may have paid her."[4] We may suspect a familiar framework—the woman as prostitute, one who sells her services to a man and whose power and weakness consists in the fact that she is merchandise and saleswoman in one and can negotiate her price: "in that case it'd be expensive" (2).[5] Yet as it turns out, the woman is not a prostitute, and the social contract is a paradoxical one. When the woman asks, "What is it you want?" (2),[6] he answers that he wants to try to know and love a woman. The man's project runs counter to some of our deepest cultural assumptions, namely, that "you cannot buy love" and, as the woman asserts, that "you can never love through an act of will" (50). The tour de force performed in Duras's text lies precisely in how she works through this cliché.

If what a man wants in our culture—in terms of desire and lack—is love or, more generally, "emotion," then Duras plays with and overturns all familiar resonances of this assumption. If someone desires love who has, as we are led to believe, never experienced love, then his desire is entangled in paradox: only someone for whom love is radically "other" can embrace the impossible project of wanting an emotion that cannot be willed and entails, in Lacan's words, "the effusion of the subject towards an object without alterity" ("Aggressivity" 24).

The contract entails yet another paradox—love is incompatible with a structure of complete domination, but the male protagonist makes his role as absolute master part of the contract: "You say she mustn't speak, like the women of her ancestors, must yield completely to you and to your will, be entirely submissive like peasant women . . . at your mercy as nuns are at God's" (4–5).[7]

Based on an absolute submission of the woman, the contract entangles the protagonists in the Hegelian dialectic of master and slave: if the man's project were to succeed, the woman would have to cease being a slave, thereby breaching the contract. Moreover, the assumed role of an absolute master who refuses so much as a voice to the woman is but a desperate pose. The master's voice is continually disrupted by this other voice, whose paradoxical desire moves through stammered helpless words which, in turn, move us when we read:

> You say you want to try, try it, try to know, to get used to that body, those breasts, that scent. To beauty, to the risk of having children in that body, to that hairless unmuscular body, that face, that naked skin, to the identity between the skin and the life it contains. (2)[8]

There is an ineradicable tenderness in this calculated desperation. Rather than remaining the mere object of a cold and distant gaze, the woman's body becomes animated by a phantasmatic desire that wants to use the carnal knowledge of the skin in order to know the life it contains. The imaginary body of this woman is fecund, pregnant with life and potential children, a body and a life which the man wants to try loving—"perhaps even for [his] whole life" (3).[9] Is this a "male fantasy"? Or a "female fantasy" about a man who suffers from the malady of death? Or are we moved by this fantasy precisely because it may be both?

There is an archaic appeal, something decidedly erotic, in this fantasy of an affair between these two strangers at a remote place near the ocean, an affair in which a woman becomes the object of a man's attempt to love. Immediately responsive to this erotic appeal, the woman counters the man's confession that he wants to "weep" in that particular place with her by smilingly teasing him with the question "Do you want me, too?" "Yes," he says and clumsily imagines the technicality of penetration, speculating that, as "they" say, it "offers more resistance, it's smooth but it offers more resistance than emptiness does" (4).[10] At this point we are only four pages into the text, and yet the words "resistance" and "emptiness" have a decidedly emotional ring—*despite* the fact that the man utters them in a crude technical image. We have, in other words, already begun to fill his words with a life of their own, a life that has as much to do with our fantasies as it has with his.

This emotional cathexis will undergo deep alterations and modulations according to the dramatic changes of moods in the protagonists' encounters. The first day she strips, lies down, and lets him watch her all night, and the next night, and the night after. Soon they begin to engage in what Lacan once called "the rituals of everyday intimacy" ("Aggressivity" 26). She asks him about the time of year or the sound of the sea, he learns to identify and name her smell— small interstices between her extended periods of sleep. The whole text begins to live through this aura of intimacy, frailty, and suspense. When he approaches her sexually—"as arranged"—it nonetheless happens in this intimate space: instead of penetrating her aggressively, he sleeps with his face between her parted legs. "She offers no resistance" (9).

This intimate space, however, is threatened by the irruption of a cry, signaling the pleasure which he gives her "inadvertently" (9). This cry fills the empty space of intimacy with a spontaneous presence, an utterance of *jouissance* intolerable to him. The cry also signals that intimacy has turned bad, become threatening, Other. Herman Rapaport has analyzed this threatening otherness of intimacy in *The Malady of Death* as a manifestation of the paradoxical condition that Lacan calls extimacy (*extimité*) (257–63). Extimacy as the otherness of that which is given in intimacy pertains to the fragile boundaries, the fundamental ambivalence of intimate spaces: what is closest is, at the same time, that which is radically Other. What Rapaport says about *Savannah Bay* is also true for *The Malady of Death*: "The dialogue between the two figures on stage, then, has to traverse a fairly diverse field of subject positions that are at once too intimate and too distant" (262–63). This paradoxical coupling of closeness and distance, or intimacy and extimacy, is but another face of the male protagonist's malady of death. It also becomes a symptom of the very contract which he designs in order to *contain* intimacy.

The intrusion of the woman's cry violates the terms of their contract, which has a decidedly therapeutic side: she must remain an embodiment of extimacy, an "empty screen," and keep the ordained silence in order to grant the man the "protected space" of a transference based on the ideal of her impassibility. This is the only form under which intimacy may be tolerable: when it appears as the radical extimacy of transference. Similar to the rules of transference, the contract requires the woman to efface herself and refrain from all those expressions of interest, sympathy, or rejection which would invade the man with her own subjectivity. Thus depersonalized, however, she cannot fail to release in him the aggressive impulses that are commonly directed against an inanimate object of desire and equally mobilized by negative transference.

Within the woman's therapeutic "depersonalization," love may only occur as an imaginary projection—"transference love." The success of the project would, however, require that the protagonists transcend the paradox of transference—which would in turn breach the contract.

Clinging to the contractual terms, the man orders the woman to forsake any utterance of pleasure. His reaction—"No woman will ever cry out because of you now" (9)—reconfirms her as everywoman occupying every space and all time, past, present, and future. As such she must remain eternally undifferentiated, any trace of individuation arousing hostility. The contract for which he pays her thus appears to be less a sign of her "prostitution" than his "protection." This protection, moreover, functions simultaneously on two different levels whose interplay sustains a paradox. At one level, the woman's silence "protects" the man from the success of his project, namely, the experience of love, which at a deep level he still perceives as a deadly threat. On the other hand, her silence provides the artificiality of a protected therapeutic space and holds out the promise of success, that is, a cure from what the woman will term his "malady of death."

Significantly, however, his "therapy" is not a "talking cure" but a "weeping cure." Instead of talking to her, he watches her silently and weeps. His project is rooted in a language of the body that fears the intrusion of words. He would like to traverse her body in order to get back to the body of others and to his own body, and yet, this very necessity makes him weep. His gaze on her body and his weeping begin to interact with each other in complicated ways. His is decidedly not the male gaze we know from feminist theories, nor the persecuting gaze of the other theorized by Sartre and then adapted by Lacan and some versions of French feminism. Driven by a desperate search for attunement, this gaze does not create an object of pleasure but one of grief. And even though the "tears" are first introduced by a phallic image—"his sex shedding its load of tears"—they are not phallic tears but melancholic tears, bodily symptoms of his "malady of death."

How are we to understand these tears, the bodily manifestation of emotion, in relation to the "malady of death" which results from a lack of emotion? We have become used to reading "tears" as an expression of emotion and begun to endow masculine tears with a symbolic exchange value. They ostensibly bear witness to the fact that men do not *lack* emotion. And yet, the woman in Duras's text understands that the man's tears speak his malady of death. The "weeping cure" betrays as many semiotic vicissitudes as the "talking cure." The man's tears can, in fact, be seen as a bodily equivalent of Lacan's "empty speech" in that they form, on the level of a somatic semiotics, an insurmountable barrier between the subject and its forms of expression. These tears do not "express" him, they sensationalize an effect which is void of "reality" in order to give him a sense of being alive. But, at the same time, these melancholic tears also signal his grief about being unable to "take" the life of others. This, too, the woman pronounces: "You herald the reign of death. Death can't be loved if it's imposed from the outside. You think you weep because you can't love. You weep because you can't impose death" (46).[11]

Death and love, for this protagonist, are so intricately woven together that their modes of expression collapse into each other: paradoxically, both love and its absence threaten him with death. Fantasizing that "he can dispose of her in whatever way he wishes" (35),[12] he instead strokes her body "as gently as if it run the risk of happiness" (35). Can one learn to love through "mimetic gestures"?[13] Can one escape the malady of death by performing a mimicry of love? Can the empty sign engender the effects of "full speech"? These, too, are questions explored in Duras's text.

In this sense—but only in this very *precise* sense—it is true that the body of the woman becomes a text, read by a blind man, who has to "feel" its inscriptions as if they were in braille. This is a man who, in turn, inscribes the empty "technical" signs and gestures of making love onto her body in order to explore how they produce reality-effects. For this man, who knows only "the grace of the bodies of the dead," this "sexual performance" has the effects of bestowing life to a machine: "This fleshly machine is marvelously precise" (35).[14] Watching her having an orgasm as one would watch the precise functioning of a bodily machine, he can "animate" her yet keep her dead at the same time.

As she points out to him, his desire to reduce her to a machine or his fantasies of "killing" her are the effect of a cold rage bestowed on everything that is alive. They reflect a cultural "death drive," a desire to return to the inanimate or to embrace the constancy and controllability of the petrified rather than the quite different desire which the woman invokes, namely, the passionate desire of a lover to possess his object completely—even if this means that he can only possess it in death: "The wish to be about to kill a lover, to keep him for yourself, yourself alone, to take him, steal him in defiance of every law, every moral authority—you don't know what that is" (42).[15]

Duras's male protagonist ignores this desire for archaic incorporation of the object and for the complete effacement of its alterity that forms the paradox of love. In this sense, the man has never been completely born. And it is this lack of "an object" which the woman perceives in him as his "malady."

Her most crucial intervention, which also provides the title for Duras's text, reads, "As soon as you spoke to me I saw that you were suffering from the malady of death" (18).[16] She comes to this pronouncement gradually, proceeding from allusions to the symptoms without naming the illness:

> The malady is getting more and more of a hold on you. It's reached your eyes, your voice.
> You ask: What malady?
> She says she can't say, yet. (13)[17]

What she still suspends here is the literal pronouncement of the "death sentence." Suspense, however, is a common part of the torture inflicted by a death sentence. And yet, in this case the death sentence establishes a "future anterior" (*futur antérieur*); the death has already happened and the suspense refers to that future moment when she names the malady and pronounces the sentence of death, insisting on the recognition of death as a life form: "She smiles, says this is the first time, that until she met you she didn't know death could be lived" (45).[18]

The woman's allusion to this malady engenders a passionate desperation in his actions that forms a striking tension with the malady of death. Night after night he sleeps with her, stays inside her, while she becomes more and more impenetrable: "She's more mysterious than any other external thing you've ever known" (14).[19] Even the most subtle knowledge of her body leaves her outside, an "external thing."[20]

She fails him precisely by playing the role he imposes on her. The desired impassibility of her body unleashes the murderous aggressivity of a negative transference, and the body becomes a site on which to confer death: "The body's completely defenseless, smooth from face to feet. It invites strangulation, rape, ill usage, insult, shouts of hatred, the unleashing of deadly and un-mitigated passions" (16).[21]

His gaze, like his pleasure always blinded by tears, begins to fragment her body, to take her apart: "Her legs have a beauty distinct from that of the body. They don't really belong to the rest of the body" (16).[22] Fragmented, however, her body mirrors his blindness: "Until that night you hadn't realized how ig-norant one might be of what the eyes see, the hands and the body touch" (17).[23] Precisely in its semiotic inaccessibility her body begins to mirror *him* while he grants her to be the carrier of a knowledge about himself that he will never possess. Inadvertently, the terms of the contract have become inverted. While his gaze remains blind, he nonetheless realizes that he has exposed himself to her look: "You realize she is looking at you. You cry out" (20).[24]

Her look, however, forms an "insurmountable barrier" (20)[25] that holds him paralyzed, in suspense. Only when her sleep protects him from her look does her body come together to form a holograph of her spirit:

> You go on looking. Her face is given over to sleep, it's silent, asleep, like her hands. But all the time the spirit shows through the surface of the body, all over, so that each part bears witness in itself to the whole—the hands and the eyes, the curve of the belly and the face, the breasts and the sex, the legs and the arms, the breath, the heart, the temples, the temples and time. (22)[26]

His gaze on her body has acquired a new intimacy and attunement to de-tails. As the first yearning for recognition begins to stir in him, a timid fear arises that her "invulnerability" might be based on indifference. She has finally "conquered" him in the simple sense that, as he says, "she fills the whole world" (24) and halts the flow of time with her eternal presence, one that is "more present than the presence of death" (26), leaving his room unrecognizable, "occupied only by the long, lithe streak of the alien form on the bed" (30). The image of death, her death, begins to haunt him, subtly at first, then with increasing vehemence: "You tell yourself it would be best for her to die" (25–6).[27] She who has pronounced the death sentence on him has also committed the crime of being alive.

Sharon A. Willis highlights the inextricable link between death and difference in Duras's piece: "While death might be constructed as what is most alien to, most utterly, radically different from life, it is also bound to the indifferentiation of death and life—too much or too little difference" (117). When the man says, "You don't love anything or anyone, you don't even love the difference you think you embody" (32–3), he alludes to a stage of undifferentiation that forms the extreme opposite of symbiotic union, namely, the undifferentiation where life itself has become equal to death. In this stage it is his gaze that imposes death—even before it translates into his murderous fantasies. Any sign of life in her, any familiarity or intimacy that would bespeak a bond with this Other, becomes threatening, obtrusive.

In order to destroy the familiarity with her body and the intimacy of their nightly rituals, his gaze turns cold, converts her into a "stranger," a "shape" that holds him with a paradoxical power: "the unconquerable strength of its incomparable weakness" (27).[28] Her smell becomes oppressive, bespeaking her organic life, which he wants to make "disappear off the face of the earth."[29] Invaded by fantasies of murdering her, or of simply watching her die, he turns the death sentence back onto her and makes us fear for her life. We begin to live in the suspense of that shrinking space between the real and the imaginary which opens over the abyss of a "controlled paranoia."[30]

She has committed yet another crime: she has refused to become complicit in his malady. Had she fallen prey to the temptation he has laid out for her—to be the first woman able to win the love of a man who has never loved before—then he might have led her into the trap of his paradoxical project. Then he would *have* to have killed her. Instead, she simply "mirrors him"—she acknowledges *her* knowledge of his illness with a nearly serene "indifference" which nonetheless is grounded in wisdom and requires her utmost strength.

This performative indifference makes him "give up" (32).[31] Finally he looks at himself, at his "malady of death," consumed by a desire to convey it to her like a contagious illness or to project it back onto her: "She's still alive. While she lives she invites murder. You wonder how to kill her and who will. You don't love anything or anyone, you don't even love the difference you think you embody" (33).[32] "You realize it's here, in her, that the malady of death is fomenting, that it's this shape stretched out before you that decrees the malady of death" (34).[33]

This is how he comes to see her as the carrier of the death sentence: not only does she pronounce it, name it, and thus endow it with symbolic shape and reality; she mirrors a death sentence to him at the very deep level of a melancholic mood; she takes that "insurmountable weariness"[34] over from him and reflects it back to him as an unformulated "knowledge" that he carries within himself without being aware of it.[35] As long as this mood remained unidentified, that is, as long as she had not yet "symbolized" it by pronouncing the death sentence, it did not have a real "object." Seen in this way, we could say that, rather than becoming the object of his love, the woman becomes the object of his mood: she makes him see this mood "from the outside," fomenting in *her* but creating in him the wish to make it/her disappear from the face of the earth.

This, in fact, becomes one of her most crucial functions: she mirrors and pronounces what he knows without knowing. When he repeatedly asks her his final and most crucial question, if anyone could love him (43–44), the one who answers no is the woman about whom the narrator said at the beginning that he would find her in his "inmost self." Throwing him back onto himself, she forces him to see that she is giving him what he has always wanted: "You go on talking, all alone in the world, just as you wish. You say that love has always struck you as out of place. . . . She's not listening, she's asleep" (47).[36]

Afraid now of her silence, he frantically tells the story of his childhood, crying out loud. "She opens her eyes, says: Stop lying" (48). Like his tears, his attempt to perform a "talking cure" is a lie, empty speech, an overused convention and mechanical narrative gesture, much like the mimetic gestures of his lovemaking: "She smiles, says she's heard and read it too, often, everywhere, in a number of books" (49).[37] What she finally teaches him is not love, but something about the paradox of love: that you can never gain it through an act of will, but that it can come from anything. And then *she* makes love to him, for the first and last time.

When he wakes up, she is not there anymore. No trace left but the cold mark of her body on the sheets. "The difference between her and you is confirmed by her sudden absence" (52). There is relief in this confirmation of difference;

she has become "safe" again, that is, "other." But indirectly this sentence also confirms that he had already lost himself in her, the bearer of his knowledge who had filled his whole world. Asserting this difference becomes a tricky matter of survival: the survival of his malady of death. But by asserting this difference he performs the cheapest stereotype of male denials, another "empty speech" like the story of his childhood: he tries to tell their story in a bar. But the very telling of the story becomes a performance of its "failure": "At first you tell it as if it were possible to do so, then you give it up. Then you tell it laughing, as if it were impossible for it to have happened or possible for you to have invented it" (53).[38]

And yet this is where the text reverts back onto *itself*. All of a sudden, his empty speech no longer finds any resonance in him, his words fall back on him as if they were still mirrored by her. The difference crumbles, but the fulfillment of his desire to see her again is precluded: he would never be able to recognize her if he saw her. Soon he gives up looking for her, remembering only certain words like "the malady of death."

Duras's text ends, however, with a provocative ambiguity. The male protagonist's final utterance leaves him suspended in a scene of recognition: "Even though you have managed to live that love in the only way possible for you. Losing it before it happened" (55).[39] Paradoxically, while he *misses* her in the traces that are left of his affair—the cold mark of her body on the sheets, the failure of his story in the bar, and the empty signifier of his illness—he *finds* her in the aura of her absence: "the crazy din of the ravenous gulls sounds as if he had never heard it before" (52).[40] We recall here how Walter Benjamin formulates the difference between a trace and an aura: "The trace is the apparition of a presence, as far as the object might be that has left the trace. The aura is the apparition of an absence, as close as the object might be that has evoked the aura. In the trace we grasp the object, in the aura the object grasps us" (*Passagenwerk* 560).

In the final passages, the protagonist of Duras's text is grasped by the woman's aura—despite his attempts to deny it. Only when he "gives up" can he allow for this "recognition" that this *is* a form of loving, that he has lived it in the only way possible for him: losing it before it happened. The lost object has cast a shadow. And this shadow is more than a mere trace: it evokes an aura that continues to inhabit his solitude. More than just a central theme, the experience of an aura becomes a crucial part of the aesthetic response to *The Malady of Death*. If we share Benjamin's assumption that cultural objects lose their aura in the age of mechanical reproduction, we might see Duras's piece as an attempt at nostalgic recuperation. Like Benjamin, but in more subliminal fashion, Duras connects the aura to memory, reproduction, and aesthetic reception. And indeed, a work's aura inextricably depends upon and emerges from a specific receptive disposition. In her appendix to *The Malady of Death*, Duras develops a series of reflections concerning a possible staging of her piece. She envisions a tension between drama and text, with the female actor speaking her lines from memory, as if she were reading, and a male narrator reading the text, including the lines of the male protagonist, who would never appear on stage. Acting is displaced by a reading that evokes the "effect of a text not memorized"[41]: "So the two actors should speak as if they were reading the text in separate rooms, isolated from one another. . . . The text would be completely nullified if it were spoken theatrically" (57).[42]

What do these imaginary stage directions tell us about what Duras envisions as the aura of her piece? I see them suggesting a link between the "effects of an unmemorized text" and an experience that is "recorded" but not "remembered" or—to use a key word from *The Malady of Death*—an "immemorial" experience.[43] Duras's male protagonist possesses two kinds of knowledge: an empty one that can be rendered in a story (his story about the child, which I compared to Lacan's "empty speech") and an immemorial knowledge of his own melancholic state of being, his "deadly routine of lovelessness."[44] When the woman tells him, "I don't want to know anything the way you do" (48),[45] she refers to this "split knowledge" which remains forever disconnected from the objects it apprehends, but nonetheless weighs on him through a subliminal experience that one could term, following Christopher Bollas, "the unthought known." In his seminal book *The Shadow of the Object*, Bollas develops a theory of an unconscious experience that does not result from the repression of unbearable thoughts but is instead formed by unconscious memories of very early stages of being and relating before the acquisition of language and object formation. Because they are formed during a preverbal phase of development, these early memories are not "symbolized" or represented in language. According to Bollas, these "non-symbolic self-states" are preserved in our *moods* and continue unconsciously to determine our most intimate and elusive relationships to others and the world, "perhaps awaiting the day when they can be understood and then either be transformed into symbolic derivatives or forgotten" (5).

The "malady of death" seems to me rooted in such a nonsymbolic self-state. A mood of hopeless monotony and weariness, combined with a fundamental lack of understanding and disconnectedness from his actions, weighs down Duras's male protagonist—and by extension grasps the woman. He turns her into the bearer of his knowledge, the one able to translate this nonsymbolic state into words, while he himself only "knows" at a level that cannot be "thought" or "spoken."

According to Bollas, any translation of nonsymbolic self-states or moods into a language that may convey their aura helps to make them accessible and thus transforms them. Literature may function subliminally in such a way as a "transformational object." An aesthetic experience in which—to use Murray Krieger's words—"a person feels uncannily embraced by an object" (qtd. in Bollas 4) may be grounded in unconscious memories of nonsymbolic self-states or the early transformational processes that accompany them. The formal qualities of a work and the "mood" they convey or the "aura" they create play a crucial role in the invocation of such memories. We recall that, according to Julia Kristeva, the presymbolic or "semiotic" dimension of poetic language carries the memory traces of our earliest experience of language as rhythms, sounds, and an entire range of tonal symbolism. One may assume that an unconscious aesthetic experience of this semiotic dimension shapes a crucial part of our attunement and emotional response to a text. Or, to reinvoke the Benjaminian distinction between the trace and the aura, we may say that when we consciously absorb the narrative or meaning of a text, we follow the traces of language and grasp the literary object, while when we unconsciously respond to its aura, the literary object grasps us and enables a transformational experience of the "unthought known."

Many narrative theories have emphasized the importance of "moods" in aesthetic experience (see, for example, Genette, Ricoeur, and Kristeva, *Séméiotiké*), but despite the tremendous impact of psychoanalysis on literary criticism, the scope and cultural function of unconscious aesthetic experiences remains largely undertheorized (see also Schwab, *Subjects*). Duras's *The Malady of Death*, and her imaginary stage directions, emphasize the experience of a very intense emotional aura that reaches beyond memory. I have viewed the artificial setting of the contract between the two protagonists as a configuration in which the woman functions as a transformational object for the man. I have further suggested that we read Duras's piece itself as a transformational literary object. In fact, Duras's whole work is concerned with this type of transformational aesthetic experience. In a short theoretical essay entitled "The Dark," Duras develops the concept of a "dark film" where a voice is reading a text—reminiscent of how she envisions the narrator of *The Malady of Death* reading the text for a theatrical performance. Distinguishing between the cognitive response of "deciphering" a text/film and the more subliminal and inte-

gral response of "allowing oneself to be acted upon" ("The Dark" 87), Duras
argues that this "dark film" becomes a space in which the explicit and the implicit meet in an interval of darkness. This encounter—which we may perceive
as an encounter between language and the unthought known—enables a
transformational experience in a viewer who must, according to Duras, create
within him/herself "the space for receiving the film without being aware of it":
"I am not only at the movies but suddenly somewhere else, somewhere else
again, in the undifferentiated zone of myself where I recognize without ever
having seen, where I know without understanding" (88). Duras envisions here
an aesthetic experience in which literature/film becomes a processing form for
the "unthought known," a "transformational object" which we allow to affect
and change us and which resonates with other transformational experiences
that may never have been symbolized but are nonetheless uncannily familiar.

In *The Malady of Death*, the narrator assumes a crucial role as mediator between language and the "unthought known." Every word in this text is mediated through an anonymous narrator who speaks in the conditional tense. This
performative triangulation is especially important since we indirectly bear witness to the most intimate encounter between a man and a woman who, se-
cluded in a room, display their sexual intimacies as well as their most intimate
emotions. The narrator not only exposes these intimate spaces, he also guarantees their protection. Preventing us from ever directly witnessing the scenes
between the two protagonists, he precludes an imaginary voyeuristic spectatorship that would reduce the piece to its action and keep the reader at the safe
distance of one who peeps through a keyhole.

Instead, this narrator draws us in, compelling us to witness a drama that
elicits attunement. As the narrator mirrors the imaginary scenes back to the
male protagonist, he also mediates them for us, the readers. The male protagonist is thus reflected in two complementary mirrors: while the woman is his
Other who mirrors his "malady of death," the male narrator is his double who
mirrors his attempt to cure his malady as well as his most intimate reactions
to the transformational processes engendered by their contract. The narrator,
in other words, mirrors him from inside; he speaks his unthought known for
him as well as for us. It is crucial to see that the man himself would not be able
to *think* what the narrator, his double, *says*, since it belongs to the sphere of the
"unthought known."

But the narrator also speaks from "inside" in yet another sense. His absolute
attunement to the other man makes him move so closely to the male protagonist that the narrative distance is effaced in an immediate presence in which

they seem to merge completely. This effect, too, is retained in Duras's vision of a theatrical performance: "the man reading the text should seem to be suffering from a fundamental and fatal weakness—the same as that of the other, the man we don't see" (59).

The intimate connection between the two men raises the question of desire in this triangular relationship. One of the most discrete details of the text is, in fact, the revelation of the man's homosexuality. It is referred to only in passing and matter-of-factly but nonetheless further complicates the issue of gender and its discontents in this text.[46] If critics have largely overlooked the issue of homosexuality in Duras's piece, it is certainly because at one level it hardly seems to matter: the man's homosexuality does not preclude his figuration as "everyman" nor his contractual engagement with "everywoman." And yet, on a different level, it affects the terms of this figuration and the status of the contract.

Why did Duras choose a homosexual man for her aesthetic reflection on the structural relationship between men and women? In one of her interviews she argues that male homosexuality is the latent ground for men's heterosexual relationships in our culture: "All men are potential homosexuals, they only don't know it, they lack the situation or evidence which reveals it to them. Homosexual men know this and say it, too. And the women who have known homosexuals and had physical relationships with them know and say it also."[47]

Yet the beginning of The Malady of Death also suggests that each man is inhabited by an imaginary woman from whom he remains eternally disconnected. The "malady of death" then appears as a cultural disease caused by the relegation of women to the status of a supplement and the simultaneous encryptment of the feminine as myth or fantasy. This perspective casts a new light on the piece's relational structure of triangulation. The narrator appears as the imaginary other man who makes every relationship to a woman triangular—and in this case again it does not make a great difference if the man is manifestly or latently homosexual. Moreover, since the narrator is the protagonist's double, their roles are potentially reversible: the narrator would need to envision another man trying to gain access to a woman in order to enact his own encrypted desire for the feminine.

Our culture has an astute awareness of the triangulation of desire and especially men's use of women as substitutes for a desired man. We are much less familiar with this impossible desire for the encrypted woman who, in Duras's words, haunts the man "everywhere at once." If we are willing to (at least provisionally) share Duras's perspective, we assume that this desire will most often go unrecognized, relegated to the cultural "unthought known," an invisible scar on the relationship between man and woman, or man and man alike.

In this respect, too, Duras's piece creates a stage of recognition rather than one of cure. The man is not cured from his malady, but he is transformed. The vehicle for this change is a peculiar sort of transference brought about not by words but by gestures or, more precisely, the simulation of gestures. Because he cannot feel desire or love for the woman, the man simulates the gestures of desire and love. He performs a willful spectacle of empty sexual encounters, a kind of empty speech of the body. And yet we must not mistake this for "deceit," since it is the most authentic act he can perform and the one that leaves him most vulnerable.

Rather than witnessing a postmodern simulacrum of emotions in which the man effaces the difference between an emotion and a performance, we then witness a transference of a very different kind, one that recalls the spirit of an Eastern mystic who enacts the state of being he wants to reach. In this transference, the man and the woman become complicit in an attempt to transcend their gender antagonisms. The woman attunes herself to the "mimetic gestures" of the man, but she also mirrors the lack that gapes behind the gesture. The "malady of death" appears then as a cultural disease which victimizes both man and woman, who, in this text, form an ecological unit of survival and/or death. And the reader of the text, male or female, becomes part of this ecology. We bear witness to a battle unto death between the man and the woman that is at the same time a struggle to survive the "malady of death." We witness how this struggle releases the most murderous instincts in the man, culminating in the desire to destroy the feminine, to make it disappear from the face of the earth.[48] But we also witness an aggressive "indifference" of the woman—moments when her therapeutic indifference turns bad and she pronounces the death sentence with a vengeance. Both man and woman, however, traverse these moments and come out not cured, but different, marked by a faint aura of recognition.

# NOTES

## Preface

1. The theoretical section of *The Mirror and the Killer-Queen* also contains a brief discussion of various theories that deal with the relationship between language and otherness and have inspired my own theory in different ways. I stage this critical debate less as a mere survey than as a contact between theories that draws out certain strengths and weaknesses and generates an interaction between theoretical perspectives that becomes productive for my own model. Asking what each theory may contribute to assessing the cultural function of literature and reading, I am in general more interested in the strengths than in the weaknesses of theories. I consider this approach to be not only a matter of temperament, but, more importantly, of relating to theoretical otherness. We will always perceive certain theories as closer to our own theoretical biases than others, and some will at first glance appear utterly "foreign." But I have always found theoretical polemics that mainly consist in exposing one's opponents' weaknesses utterly unsatisfying. I do enjoy certain theoretical polemics, but only under the condition that the "other" theory is taken at its highest level, thus avoiding dogmatic theoretical positions that gain their profile only through easy dismissals or caricatures of other theories.

2. See my discussion of these positions in chapter 1.

## 1. Reading, Otherness, and Cultural Contact

1. This chapter rethinks and expands a theoretical framework first sketched out in my 1984 essay, "Reader-Response and the Aesthetic Experience of Otherness."

2. I will not discuss here the specific problems inherent in this attitude, such as the problem of the anthropologist's interfering presence, of intercultural communication, or of translation and editing that will raise different issues of interpretation.

3. Recall, for example, Shoshana Felman's subtitle to her *Literature and Psychoanalysis*, "The Question of Reading: Otherwise."

4. I have demonstrated this at length in *Subjects without Selves*.

5. The latter has been analyzed in an exemplary way by Stephen Greenblatt in *Renaissance Self-Fashioning*.

6. For a more detailed discussion of Artaud's aesthetics, see Schwab, *Samuel Becketts*.

7. Such a culturally situated interactive model of reading presupposes a specific

textual agency. Being aware that metaphors of agency have been criticized for "anthropomorphizing" a text, I nonetheless find it useful to perceive a text as a depersonalized textual agency, such as a virtual life form (in the Wittgensteinian sense of a language game as a life form), or a play of signifiers that continually reshapes a cultural system. In assuming such a textual agency, one may analyze literary communication as a form of contact with the otherness of both poetic language itself and foreign, historically remote, or otherwise different cultural discourses. Literature would then assume a specific cultural function as a medium that facilitates, structures, or challenges certain experiences of otherness.

8. In talking about a text's otherness, we need, however, to avoid the trap of assuming that (its) meaning resides *in* the text. The recognition of textual otherness necessarily entails accepting certain constraints for interpretation as well as a basic openness to being affected if not changed by texts. Very few theories of reading are sensitive to the fact that not only the reading of other cultures, but reading in general entails appropriations of otherness that may potentially turn violent. To be sure, the violence toward other cultures is more insidious and also more obvious than the violence toward language, but I will argue that the ways in which we deal with the otherness of language reflect back on how we deal with otherness in general, including cultural otherness.

9. This is one of the reasons why psychoanalysis—or at least a dynamic concept of the unconscious—continues to play a crucial role in cultural theories and why, accordingly, a theory of reading needs to incorporate a concept of unconscious reception. It also explains why, in the context of my discussion of theories, psychoanalysis and French theories occupy a relatively large space.

10. However, as recent invocations of Gadamer's hermeneutics in postmodern anthropology show, his conceptual model as such allows one to consider cultural otherness and to differentiate between various modes of its appropriation. James Clifford, for example, emphasizes its "radical dialogism," while Michael M. J. Fisher names Gadamer's hermeneutics as one of the theories that exert a strong impact on the current mood in anthropological research. Here, interdisciplinarity becomes a form of contact with another discipline that may fill in its own gaps and blind spots.

11. See Iser's *The Implied Reader* and *The Act of Reading*. I will in the present context not deal with Iser's new work on literary anthropology, which I will discuss in detail in *Imaginary Ethnographies*.

12. My analysis of Bakhtin is in many ways indebted to Todorov's book on Bakhtin. Todorov has collected and systematically analyzed Bakhtin's writings on otherness and exotopy. Many of the passages are not yet available in translation and are therefore here directly quoted from Todorov.

13. We see here that Bakhtin's concept of the other has fewer affinities with Lacan than with Winnicott, who, in his critique of Lacan, points out that without the infant's prior mirroring in the mother's animated gaze, its own mirror image would remain completely void and meaningless.

14. I will not specifically discuss here the rich history of feminist reception of Bakhtin since it does not systematically impact my theory of reading as a form of cultural contact. I will, however, include a discussion of Julia Kristeva in my section on

French theory. Regarding feminist receptions of Bakhtin see, for example, Booth, Hermann, and Bauer.

15. For a detailed discussion of oral imagery in Hegel's work see Werner Hamacher's introduction to Hegel's *Der Geist des Christentums: Schriften 1796–1800.*

16. See also my extensive analysis of this function of literature as an "intermediate area" (Winnicott) in *Subjects*, ch. 2.

17. See a more detailed discussion of the phenomenon of inner boundaries and the formation of a tacit knowledge in Schwab, *Subjects*, ch. 2.

18. I omit here a discussion of Lévi-Strauss because I include a chapter on Lévi-Strauss in *Imaginary Ethnographies.*

19. See Hartman, *Saving*, 118–57.

20. See, for example, Lacan, "The object," where he asserts that he finds Sartre's analysis of the gaze "quite especially convincing" (215).

21. "a state of fusion (*un fusionnel*) which does not succeed in emerging as a subject." See Whitford, 112.

22. I would also like to emphasize the affinities of Kristeva's "thetic phase" with Winnicott's "transitional space."

23. See also the following quotes:

> In this realization of the signifier, particularly as it is seen in poetic texts, alterity is maintained within the pure signifier and/or in the simply syntactic element only with difficulty. For the Other has become heterogeneous and will not remain fixed in place: it negativizes all terms, all posited elements and thus syntax, threatening them with possible dissolution. (*Kristeva Reader* 108)

> Though absolutely necessary, the thetic is not exclusive: the semiotic which also precedes it, constantly tears it open, and this transgression brings about all the various transformations of the signifying practice that are called "creation." (113)

> Language thus tends to be drawn out of its symbolic function (sign-syntax) and is opened out within a semiotic articulation; with a material support such as the voice, this semiotic network gives "music" to literature. (113)

24. This definition opens up an interesting parallel to Bakhtin's notion of exotopy. Bakhtin's much more positive figuration of otherness posits a subject who finds herself outside. His concept of exotopy requires the other as one who completes the self in a positive and constructive sense. Alienation for Bakhtin would be nearly the inverse of Lacan's or Sartre's alienation: it would lie in the (always impossible) enterprise/fantasy to construct a self independent from the formative impact of the Other. From a Bakhtinian perspective one could read Sartre's and Lacan's texts as cultural symptoms and see this nostalgia for an independent and impermeable subject as an underlying narcissistic fantasy that informs their whole conceptual framework.

25. The discussion of cultural theories of reading will systematically highlight certain features that are relevant for my readings of literary texts. A more detailed discussion that deals with the intersections between literary criticism, anthropology, and cultural theory will be reserved for *Imaginary Ethnographies.*

26. In drawing so strongly on the negative predication of otherness on the persecuting gaze of the Other in French theory, some of the more recent theories of culture share their tendency to ontologize destructive historical patterns of cultural contact. And yet, as object relations theories have tried to emphasize against Lacanian psychoanalysis, the gaze of the other is not inherently destructive but becomes so only in an adverse cultural environment. If we essentialize difference (as in the inverse essentialism of some currents in French feminism), or if we ontologize the destruction of otherness in capitalism, colonialism, or even fascism (as in some trends in cultural criticism), then we remain negatively tied to the cultural paranoia that structures the political unconscious of such formations. Ultimately, they are all predicated on escalations of violence against others and on war as the supreme model of cultural relations. The harder it becomes historically to find nondestructive patterns of cultural contact, the more urgent it becomes to envision what such patterns might look like. Or, to formulate it in Maxine Hong Kingston's words, the more important it becomes to "think peace."

Because of the dangers of ontologizing negative cultural histories, we need critically to rethink the potential legacy of cultural paranoia inherited from French and German philosophy, particularly those strands of the tradition that predicate the formation of the subject on a negative, persecuting, and annihilating gaze of the other. The predication of cultural otherness on a persecuting gaze of the other continues to inform many cultural patterns of relating to otherness and perceptions of other cultures in general. The most prominent fantasies about other cultures, ranging from an exoticizing primitivism to a paranoid vilification of others, testify to this legacy.

27. See Luhmann's systems theory.

28. We recall here Foucault's theory of culture in which the subject's relation to the other is symbolized within each culture.

29. Regarding Joyce's critique of colonialism and imperialism see also Kuberski, 55.

30. Tropes of the frontier, the border and border crossings also pervade recent theories of reading. I will here merely point to their programmatic relevance for a model of reading as a form of cultural contact because their detailed analysis is part of my next project on imaginary ethnographies. In *Border Writing: The Multidimensional Text*, D. Emily Hicks propagates a "reading that is willing to engage in a kind of border crossing, that is, a critical consideration of the nonidentities between the referential codes of the writer, the reader, and the sociohistorical semiotic context." In Hicks's model, reading appears as a form of cultural contact across the different cultural borders of texts and their very diverse readers.

In all these models the reading process entails a mediation of cultural difference—even in cases where reader and text belong to the same culture and the differences are relatively minimal. In *Keeping Slug Woman Alive: A Holistic Approach to American Indian Texts*, Greg Sarris, for example, draws on my own model of reading as delineated in "Reader-Response and the Aesthetic Experience of Otherness" in order to analyze Native American storytelling as culture contact and cultural critique. Similarly, in "Ethnicity as Text and Model," Michael M. J. Fischer argues for a "reading of ethnographies as the juxtaposition of two or more cultural traditions."

Other authors and critics rewrite the many disjunctive histories of colonialism. In *Borderlands/La Frontera*, Chicana writer and critic Gloria Anzaldúa performs a switching of "codes," using English, Castilian Spanish, the North Mexican dialect, Tex-Mex, and the old native language Nahuatl to develop a hybrid mix of critical discourse and poetry. She chooses this experimental form in order to rewrite the history of colonialism in a way that reflects the new "language of the Borderlands." In doing so, she deliberately exposes readers unfamiliar with the borderlands to its "foreign" languages.

31. Another, more postmodern response may be seen in the deliberate "incorporation" and pastiche of media junk by authors such as Barthelme, Coover, or Pynchon.

32. See also the more detailed and extensive discussion of this type of response in Schwab, *Subjects*, ch. 2.

## 2. Nonsense and Metacommunication

1. I invoke this term in order to recall D. W. Winnicott's assumption that literature opens up a "potential space" between the social and the inner worlds of the reader (*Playing*).

2. I use this term in the broad sense defined by Bateson in *Steps to an Ecology of Mind*, where he argues that not only can the concrete encounter between different cultures be considered a form of culture contact, but also the contact of different systems within a specific culture (for example, the contact between nuclear family and school system).

3. See Bateson's "metalogues" at the beginning of *Steps*.

4. It is no coincidence that we can draw direct historical lines from Carroll's nonsense to certain forms of postmodern schizophrenia. See also Deleuze's analysis of Artaud and Carroll, particularly his distinction between "non-sens de profondeur" and "non-sens de surface" in Deleuze, *Logigue*, 111–124.

5. See Bateson's remarks on syllogism (*Schizophrenie* 274–75): "Men die, grass dies. Men are grass."

## 3. Joyce, Cage, and Chaos

1. See also the compelling analysis of Joyce's anticolonial transnationalism in Kuberski, ch. 2.

2. See also the extensive discussion and revision of Ehrenzweig's theory in Schwab, *Subjects*, chs. 1–2.

3. See Sobchack, 148–155.

4. I do not mean to conflate fractal geometry and chaos theory; however, what facilitated the application of Mandelbrot's mathematics in chaos theory was precisely that strange attractors and other forms of chaotic order display a fractal structure.

5. Hugh Kenner, "Self-Similarity, Fractals, Cantos," *ELH* 44 (1988): 721–30.

6. Regarding the relationship between fractal structures and time see also Harris, "Fractal."

7. "Theme" should be understood here in the sense in which Gerald Holton defines "themata," that is, as a set of organizing epistemological presuppositions. See Holton, 18.

8. See also Ermath's use of this phrase to link Lyotard's *différand* to chaos theory.

9. See Ehrenzweig and my revision of Ehrenzweig's theory in *Subjects*.

10. This perspective may reopen the discussion about 'repetition' in *Finnegans Wake* under new premises.

11. Regarding the larger cultural implications of Cage's project see also Paulson's analysis of noise and culture in *The Noise of Culture*.

12. This is the most typical reaction described by undergraduate students who had never listened to Cage. Many experience *Roaratorio* as painful and react with impatience or anger. But there are in each class a few students who hold out and experience a meditative calmness. My own most powerful experience of meditative detachment happened during a performance of Cage's music in a cathedral at Kassel during the *Documenta*.

13. See also Kuberski's analysis of the *Wake*'s affinities with Indian philosophy in *Chaosmos*.

14. In this sense Joyce has, in fact, found a way of aesthetically embodying infinity—a goal that Brian Rotman, in *Ad Infinitum*, has formulated as an exigency of postmodern thought.

15. Nonetheless, it is striking that so little attention has been given to experimental women modernists such as Djuna Barnes (who experiments with the fluidity of gender boundaries and whose paradoxical metaphors mobilize spatial metaphors), Virginia Woolf (who experiments with fluid boundaries between characters and voices), and Gertrude Stein (who experiments with recursive structures of speech and consciousness). While entire books and articles are devoted to Joyce and other male modernists, women modernists are only mentioned in passing.

16. More radically than any other text, *Finnegans Wake* transgresses the boundaries between writing and speech in a form of presentation which the text itself, emphasizing its tripartite focus, most adequately calls "verbivocovisual." This tripartite focus reactivates oral modes of using language that are deemphasized during the acquisition of language as a code and historically devalued with the acquisition of print culture. With the invention of writing and printing, cultures privilege the functions of sign and meaning among the different uses of language, and this dominance is reinforced psychogenetically by the cultural practices of language acquisition: "After sound, light and heat, memory, will and understanding" (266.18-19).

17. This assumption places Kristeva's theory of poetic language within the larger context of other French feminist theories that perceive the fluidity and openness of Joyce's texts as characteristic of their notion of an *écriture feminine*. See also Cixous, 245-64.

18. Interestingly, the term "fractal" is itself a kind of Joycean coining. Benoit B. Mandelbrot coined the term from the Latin adjective *fractus* and the corresponding verb *frangere* (to break, to create irregular fragments) and gains a truly Joycean conden-

sation of meanings: "It is therefore sensible—and how appropriate for our needs!—that, in addition to 'fragmented' (as in *fraction* or *refraction*), *fractus* should also mean 'irregular,' both meanings being preserved in *fragment*." See Mandelbrot, 4.

19. The perspectives developed in this paper reveal interesting connections to Deleuze and Guattari's theory of territorialization and deterritorialization, especially because Deleuze and Guattari, too, reflect the recent move in scientific theories toward fluid epistemologies and use the fractal model in their theory of "smooth space." The many readings of Joyce developed in recent years from the perspective of Deleuze and Guattari's theory would add another dimension to the discussion of French feminist and fractal Joyce.

## 4. Seduced by Witches

This chapter is dedicated to the memory of Carlos Dominguez.

1. With respect to the cultural formation of a witchcraft pattern, see Honegger.

2. I use the term "social semantics" in the sense of Niklas Luhmann.

3. Though I have developed my arguments by reading fictions which deal with the Salem events, these arguments could be generalized beyond this historical frame. The focus on seventeenth-century New England Puritanism as a narrower historical context is motivated by my choice of *The Scarlet Letter* as the central paradigm.

4. Apart from the ones mentioned below, the best known among them include Mary Lyford's *The Salem Belle: A Tale of Love and Witchcraft in 1692* (1842); John W. De Forest's *Witching Times* (1857); Caroline Derby's *Salem* (1874); Pauline B. Mackie's *Ye Lyttle Salem Maide: Story of Witchcraft* (1898); Amelia E. Barr's *The Black Shilling* (1903); Marvin Dana's *A Puritan Witch* (1903); L. F. Madison's *Maid of Salem Towne* (1906); and Henry Peterson's *Dulcible: A Tale of Old Salem* (1907).

5. For further references, see G. Harrison Orians. Orians discusses some of the above-mentioned texts in more detail.

6. With respect to a desymbolization of social patterns and their internalization as clichés, see Lorenzer.

7. This has even led to a recent dispute in a medical journal where a doctor argued that Chillingworth actually murdered Dimmesdale with these plants.

8. The reversibility of the letter has also been analyzed under a different perspective in Kamuf.

9. Hawthorne's notion has, in fact, certain affinities to Jean-Paul Sartre's idea of the "derealization" of an "imaginary personality."

10. For a more detailed analysis of the affinities between Hester and Ann Hutchinson, see Colacurcio.

11. This is one of the most controversial issues among the literary critics, and it is specifically related to the ending of the text, which many readers consider unsatisfying, if not disturbing. I will argue for a textual perspective that is critical of the narrator's moralistic point of view. For a recent discussion, see Leverenz.

## 5. Carnival and Abjection

An earlier version of this article appeared in German in Haug and Warning, 342–367.

1. I use the term "phantasmatic" in the psychoanalytic sense of an unconscious fantasy that underlies and partly determines the experience and actions of a person or, in this case, a literary character. The phantasmatic body is an internalized image of the body where the body is transformed according to the cathexis of the person in question. In extreme cases this phantasmatic body can be experienced as real and replace the image of the organic body.

2. For the reference to Bakhtin's theory of carnivalesque literature and his conception of the grotesque body see Bakhtin, *Dialogic, Rabelais,* and *Speech Genres.*

3. I owe the analysis of the "exquisite cadaver" to Pike.

4. For a more detailed analysis of intertextuality in Faulkner's novels, see Matthews; and Gresset and Polk.

5. On the concept of the "grotesque soul," see Lachmann, 322–25.

6. The history of the reception of Faulkner's *As I Lay Dying* shows how unsettling these shifting inner perspectives and the loss of distance are for critics who try to determine the presence of an authoritative perspective. An interesting example is Eric Sundquist's attempt to grasp Faulkner's own presence in the text which, ironically, he ends up locating in the hovering buzzards.

7. See Schwab, *Entgrenzungen,* 63–75, on the concept of "unconscious realism."

8. The term "economy" in this context condenses the Freudian notion of the economy of the psychic apparatus with the notion of a cultural economy of a system of signs with exchange value.

9. On the relevance of the totemic feast see Freud, *Totem.* See also Lachmann, as well as Bakhtin's introduction to *Rabelais.*

10. See Lacan, "The Mirror," 4–5, on the phantasm of the fragmented body. For a Lacanian analysis of *As I Lay Dying,* see also Morris. Morris, however, does not discuss Lacan's concept of phantasms of the body, but rather the relationship between the real, the symbolic, and the imaginary.

11. For a discussion of the "somatic semiotic," see Lachmann, and Bakhtin's introduction to *Rabelais.*

12. See Irwin for a psychoanalytic reading of oedipal motifs in Faulkner's work.

13. See Kristeva's comparison of the carnivalesque with the epic in *Séméiotiké,* 143–73.

## 6. The Jungle and the Drawing Room

1. Barnes's text indeed reveals an intrinsic affinity with the geopolitical reflections in Deleuze's and Guattari's *Mille Plateaux,* especially to the dynamic of deterritorialization, nomadology, and "becoming-animal."

2. In this respect, he anticipates the cut-up speech performances of a Burroughs, which Laurie Anderson invokes in her "Language is a Virus from Outer Space."

3. Regarding the difference between trace and aura see Benjamin, *Das Passagen-werk*.

4. In the sense of Deleuze and Guattari.

5. A notion of the "political unconscious" emerges here in which each space is doubly coded: the unconscious is a transcoding of the geopolitical and vice versa. As readers we may still "translate" one sphere into the other, but instead of a logic of substitution, the text compels us to use a logic of dynamic enfoldment.

## 7. "While she lives she invites murder"

1. comment le sentiment d'aimer pourrait survenir (52).

2. For a different reading see Retif, 15–22. Retif has developed an alternative reading of *The Malady of Death* in which she takes the narrator to be a female character. Even though I do not find this reading convincing, it is interesting because it underscores Duras's play with gender boundaries and her deliberate refusal to gender the narrator in any explicit way in the piece itself. Retif's reading is also interesting because it reveals how strongly the imagined gender of the narrator ultimately determines any perception of the dynamic between the two characters in the piece. Such divergent readings are possible because, as Liliane Papin has argued, in Duras's work in general, the third character or storyteller "opens up a 'blanc' in the fabric of Duras's narration, a blank which is the integration and embodiment of the process of writing" (134). I think that one of the most interesting aspects of this "blanc" is that it may function as a space of transference, inducing readers to enact their own gendering of the text. The following reading will therefore emphasize the status of transference in Duras's piece.

3. la chose; cette forme sombre dans le lit (32).

4. Vous pourriez l'avoir payée (7).

5. elle vous aurait dit que dans ce cas c'était cher (8).

6. Vous voulez quoi?

7. Vous dites qu'elle devrait se taire comme les femmes de ses ancêtres, se plier complètement à vous, à votre vouloir, vous être soumise entièrement comme les paysannes dans les granges après les moissons, lorsque éreintées elles laissaient venir à elles les hommes, en dormant—cela afin que vous puissiez vous habituer peu à peu à cette forme qui épouserait la vôtre, qui serait à votre merci comme les femmes de religion le sont à Dieu (10–11).

8. Vous dites que vous voulez essayer, tenter la chose, tenter connaître ça, vous habituer à ça, à ces seins, à ce parfum, à la beauté, à ce danger de mise au monde d'enfants qui représente ce corps, à cette forme imberbe sans accidents musculaires ni de force, à ce visage, à cette peau nue, à cette coincidence entre cette peau et la vie qu'elle recouvre (8).

9. [p]eut-être même pendant toute votre vie (9).

10. Je ne connais pas encore, je voudrais pénétrer là aussi. Et aussi violemment que j'ai l'habitude. On dit que ça résiste plus encore, que c'est un velours qui résiste plus encore que le vide (9–10).

11. Vous annoncez le règne de la mort. On ne peut pas aimer la mort si elle vous est

imposée du dehors. Vous croyez pleurer de ne pas aimer. Vous pleurez de ne pas imposer la mort (48).

12. Vous savez que vous pourriez disposer d'elle de la façon dont vous voulez, la plus dangereuse. . . . Au contraire vous caressez le corps avec autant de douceur que s'il encourait le danger du bonheur (38–39).

13. See G. H. Mead on the performative quality of "mimetic gestures."

14. La machine de chair est prodigieusement exacte (38).

15. L'envie d'être au bord de tuer un amant, de le garder pour vous, pour vous seul, de le prendre, de le voler contre toutes les lois, contre tous les empires de la morale, vous ne la connaissez pas, vous ne l'avez jamais connue? (45).

16. Parce que dès que vous m'avez parlé j'ai vu que vous étiez atteint par la maladie de la mort (23).

17. La maladie vous gagne de plus en plus, elle a gagné vos yeux, votre voix.
Vous demandez: Quelle maladie?
Elle dit qu'elle ne sait pas encore le dire (18).

18. Elle sourit, elle dit que c'est la première fois, qu'elle ne savait pas avant de vous rencontrer que la mort pouvait se vivre (48).

19. Elle est plus mystérieuse que toutes les évidences extérieures connues jusque-là de vous (19).

20. évidence extérieure.

21. Le corps est sans défense aucune, il est lisse depuis le visage jusqu'aux pieds. Il appelle l'étranglement, le viol, les mauvais traitements, les insultes, les cris de haine, le dechaînement des passions entières, mortelles (21).

22. . . . ses jambes sont d'une beauté qui ne participe pas à celle du corps. Elles sont sans implantation véritable dans le reste du corps (21).

23. Jusqu'à cette nuit-là vous n'aviez pas compris comment on pouvait ignorer ce que voient les yeux, ce que touchent les mains, ce que touche le corps (22).

24. Vous découvrez qu'elle vous regarde.
Vous criez (25).

25. frontière infranchissable (25).

26. Le visage est laissé au sommeil, il est muet, il dort comme les mains. Mais toujours l'esprit affleure à la surface du corps, il le parcourt tout entier, et de telle sorte que chacune des parties de ce corps témoigne à elle seule de sa totalité, la main comme les yeux, le bombement du ventre comme le visage, les seins comme le sexe, les jambes comme les bras, la respiration, le coeur, les tempes, les tempes comme le temps (26–27).

27. Vous vous dites qu'elle devrait mourir (30).

28. la puissance infernale, l'abominable fragilité, la faiblesse, la force invincible de la faiblesse sans égale (31).

29. la faire disparaitre de la face du monde (32).

30. The notion of a "controlled paranoia," of course, recalls once more the affinities of their contract with a therapeutic transference.

31. Vous abandonnez (36).

32. Elle appelle le meurtre cependant qu'elle vit. Vous vous demandez comment la

tuer et qui la tuera. Vous n'aimez rien, personne, même cette différence que vous croyez vivre vous ne l'aimez pas (37).

33. Vous découvrez que c'est là, en elle, que se formente la maladie de la mort, que c'est cette forme devant vous déployée qui décrète la maladie de la mort (38).

34. fatigue immémoriale (24).

35. See the status of moods as a form of unconscious, nonsymbolic self-state in Bollas 110.

36. Vous continuez à parler, seul au monde comme vous le désirez. Vous dites que l'amour vous a toujours paru déplacé, que vous n'avez jamais compris, que vous avez toujours évité d'aimer . . .

Elle n'écoute pas, elle dort (49–50).

37. Elle sourit, elle dit qu'elle a entendu et lu aussi beaucoup de fois cette histoire, partout, dans beaucoup de livres (51–52).

38. Le soir de son départ, dans un bar, vous racontez l'histoire. D'abord vous la racontez comme s'il était possible de le faire, et puis vous abandonnez. Ensuite vous la racontez en riant comme s'il était impossible qu'elle ait eu lieu ou comme s'il était possible que vous l'ayez inventée (54–55).

39. Ainsi cependant vous avez pu vivre cet amour de la seule façon qui puisse se faire pour vous, en le perdant avant qu'il soit advenu (57).

40. Dans le noir, le cri fou des mouettes affamées, il vous semble tout à coup ne l'avoir jamais entendu (54).

41. rien ne remplace le manque de mémoire du texte (59).

42. Les deux acteurs devraient donc parler comme s'ils étaient en train d'écrire le texte dans des chambres séparées, isolés l'un de l'autre.

Le texte serait annulé s'il était dit théâtralement (60).

43. immémoriale.

44. fonction mortelle du manque d'aimer (50).

45. Je ne voudrais rien savoir de la façon dont vous, vous savez, avec cette certitude issue de la mort (50).

46. Ironically, the indication of the man's homosexuality all but disappears in the English translation because of the "indifference" of the English pronoun "their."

47. See the *Programmheft* for Robert Wilson's staging of Handke's translation at the *Schaubühne* in Berlin (3). See also the following remark in the same context: "If you are a man your favorite company in life as far as your heart, your body, your race, your gender is concerned is the company of men. This is the condition in which you receive women. It is the other man, the man number two in you who lives with your wife. . . . Yet the great man in you, the man number one enters decisive relationships only with his brothers, the men" (3; my translation).

Apart from its problematic universalizing gesture, this perspective opens up more questions than it answers. Most pointedly, it completely suspends the question of female desire within this triangulation as well as that of the lesbian desire that is prominent in other texts by Duras. I have myself chosen to suspend this perspective until the very end of my reading in order to focus on the dynamic encounter between the man and the woman. Most critics have chosen to do the same—as did Peter Handke, the German translator, and Wilson, who staged Handke's translation for the *Schaubühne* in Berlin. But perhaps I have chosen to forgo the profound challenge of Duras's statements about male homosexuality in our culture and given in to my own resistance against her universalizing claim.

On the other hand, Duras's statement might itself reduce the challenge of her piece in the sense that "homosexuality"—manifest or latent—might not be the main cause for the deep cultural division along gender lines enacted by the two protagonists. What troubles me with the figuration of the male protagonist as homosexual is the metonymic link between homosexuality and the malady of death it establishes. I rather see the latter as resulting from a specific male defense against the feminine.

Another problem is that in the text homosexuality is figured as manifest homosexuality—which would seem to undermine the figuration of the man as "everyman." I would find it very problematic to reduce "the malady of death" to a problem of male homosexuality.

48. See, for example, the following passages: "While she breathes she invites murder"; "The body's completely defenseless, smooth from face to feet. It invites strangulation, rape, ill usage, insults, shouts of hatred, the unleashing of deadly and unmitigated passion" (16); "You tell yourself it would be best for her to die" (25–26); "You tell yourself that if now, at this hour of the night, she died, it would be easier for you to make her disappear off the face of the earth, to throw her into the black water, it would only take a few minutes to throw a body as light as that into the rising tide, and free the bed of the stench of heliotrope and citron" (28).

# WORKS CITED

Adams, Hazard, and Leroy Searle, eds. *Critical Theory Since 1965*. Tallahassee: Florida State UP, 1986.

Adams, Henry. *The Education of Henry Adams*. Ed. Ernest Samuels. Boston: Houghton, 1973.

Anzaldúa, Gloria. *Borderlands/La Frontera: The New Mestiza*. San Francisco: Aunt Lute, 1987.

Artaud, Antonin. *The Theater and Its Double*. Trans. Mary Caroline Richards. New York: Grove, 1958.

Bakhtin, Mikhail. *The Dialogic Imagination*. Ed. Michael Holquist. Trans. Caryl Emerson and Michael Holquist. Austin: U of Texas P, 1981.

———. *Rabelais and His World*. Trans. Helene Iswolsky. Bloomington: Indiana UP, 1984.

———. *Speech Genres and Other Late Essays*. Ed. Caryl Emerson and Michael Holquist. Trans. Vern W. McGee. Austin: U of Texas P, 1986.

———. "Toward a Reworking of the Dostoevsky Book." *Problems of Dostoevsky's Poetics*. Ed. and trans. Caryl Emerson. Minneapolis: U of Minnesota P, 1984. 283–302.

Barnes, Djuna. *Nightwood*. New York: New Directions, 1961.

Barrault, Jean-Louis. *Reflections on the Theatre*. Trans. Barbara Wall. London: Rockliff, 1951.

Bateson, Gregory. "Culture Contact and Schismogenesis." *Steps to an Ecology of Mind*. New York: Ballantine/Random, 1972. 61–72.

Bateson, Gregory, et al., eds. *Schizophrenie und Familie: Beiträge zu einer neuen Theorie*. Frankfurt: Suhrkamp, 1975.

Bauer, Dale, ed. *Toward a Feminist Dialogics: A Theory of Failed Community*. Albany: SUNY P, 1988.

Benjamin, Walter. *Charles Baudelaire: Ein Lyriker im Zeitalter des Hochkapitalismus*. Vol. 1.2 of *Gesammelte Schriften*. Ed. Rolf Tiedemann and Hermann Schweppenhaeuser. Frankfurt: Suhrkamp, 1974. 509–690.

———. "Das Paris des Second Empire bei Baudelaire." *Charles Baudelaire* 511–604.

———. *Das Passagenwerk*. Vol. 1. Frankfurt: Suhrkamp, 1982.

Benstock, Shari. *Women of the Left Bank: Paris, 1900–1940*. Austin: U of Texas P, 1986.

Berman, Marshall. "Hitting the Streets." Rev. of *Variations on a Theme Park: The New American City and the End of Public Space*, ed. Michael Sorkin. *LA Times Book Review* 29 Mar. 1992: 11.

Blau, Herbert. "The Remission of Play." Hassan and Hassan 161–88.

Bleich, David. "Epistemological Assumptions in the Study of Response." Tompkins 134–63.

Blumenberg, Hans. *Die Lesbarkeit der Welt.* Frankfurt: Suhrkamp, 1981.

Bohannan, Laura. "Shakespeare in the Bush." *Natural History* 75.7 (1966): 28–33.

Bollas, Christopher. *The Shadow of the Object: Psychoanalysis of the Unthought Known.* New York: Columbia UP, 1987.

Booth, Wayne. "Freedom of Interpretation: Bakhtin and the Challenge of Feminist Criticism." Mitchell 51–82.

Borradori, Giovanna, ed. *Recording Metaphysics: The New Italian Philosophy.* Evanston: Northwestern UP, 1988.

Broe, Mary Lynn. "Introduction to Djuna Barnes." *The Gender of Modernism: A Critical Anthology.* Ed. Bonnie Kime Scott. Bloomington: Indiana UP, 1990. 19–20.

Bruns, Gerald. "Poethics." Perloff and Junkerman 206–25.

Buck-Morss, Susan. "The Flâneur, the Sandwichman and the Whore: The Politics of Loitering." *New German Critique* 39 (1986): 99–140.

Cage, John. *Roaratorio: Ein irischer Circus über "Finnegans Wake."* Königstein/Ts: Athenäum, 1982.

Calvino, Italo. *If on a winter's night a traveler.* Trans. William Weaver. New York: Harcourt, 1981.

Carroll, David. *Paraesthetics: Foucault, Lyotard, Derrida.* New York: Routledge, 1989.

Carroll, Lewis. *Alice's Adventures in Wonderland: Through the Looking Glass and Other Writings.* London: Collins, 1954.

Cixous, Hélène. "The Laugh of the Medusa." Marks and Courtivron 245–64.

Clarke, Bruce. "Resistance in Theory and the Physics of the Text." *New Orleans Review* 18.1: Spring 1991 86–93.

Clifford, James, and George E. Marcus, eds. *Writing Culture: The Poetics and Politics of Ethnography.* Berkeley: U of California P, 1986.

Colacurcio, Michael J. "Footsteps of Ann Hutchinson: The Context of *The Scarlet Letter.*" *English Literary History* 39 (1972): 459–94.

Culler, Jonathan. *The Pursuit of Signs: Semiotics, Literature, Deconstruction.* Ithaca: Cornell UP, 1981.

Deleuze, Gilles. *Logique du Sens.* Paris: Minuit, 1969.

Deleuze, Gilles, and Félix Guattari. *Mille Plateaux.* Paris: Minuit, 1980.

Derrida, Jacques. "Guter Wille zur Macht (I), Drei Fragen an Hans-Georg Gadamer." Forget, *Text und Interpretation.* 56–61.

———. *Of Grammatology.* Trans. Gayatri Chakravorty Spivak. Baltimore: Johns Hopkins UP, 1976.

———. "The Theater of Cruelty and the Closure of Representation." *Writing and Difference.* Trans. Alan Bass. Chicago: U of Chicago P, 1978. 232–50.

Dickerson, Mary Jane. "*As I Lay Dying* and *The Waste Land*: Some Relationships." *William Faulkner's "As I Lay Dying": A Critical Casebook.* Ed. Diane L. Cox. New York: Garland, 1985. 189–197.

Duras, Marguerite. "The Dark." *Green Eyes.* Trans. Carlo Barko. New York: Columbia UP, 1990. 87–88.

———. *The Malady of Death.* Trans. Barbara Bray. New York: Grove, 1986.

Eagleton, Terry. *Walter Benjamin: Towards a Revolutionary Criticism.* London: Verso, 1981.

Ehrenzweig, Anton. *The Hidden Order of Art: A Study in the Psychology of Artistic Imagination.* Berkeley: U of California P, 1967.

Elias, Norbert. *Über den Prozess der Zivilisation: Soziogentische und Psychogenetische Untersuchungen.* Bern: Francke AG, 1969.

Empson, William. "The Child as Swain." *Lewis Carroll, Alice in Wonderland.* Ed. Donald J. Gray. New York: Norton, 1971. 400–33.

Fanon, Frantz. *The Wretched of the Earth.* Trans. Constance Farrington. New York: Grove, 1968.

Faulkner, William. *As I Lay Dying.* Harmondsworth: Penguin, 1963.

Felman, Shoshana, ed. *Literature and Psychoanalysis, The Question of Reading: Otherwise.* Baltimore: Johns Hopkins UP, 1977.

Fischer, Michael M. J. "Ethnicity as Text and Model." George E. Marcus and Michael M. J. Fischer, eds. *Anthropology as Cultural Critique: An Experimental Moment in the Human Sciences,* Chicago: U of Chicago P, 1986. 173–177.

Forget, Philippe, ed. *Text und Interpretation.* Munich: Wilhelm Fink Verlag, 1984.

Foucault, Michel. "La folie, l'absence d'oeuvre." *Histoire de la folie à l'âge classique.* Rev. ed. Paris: Gallimard, 1972. 573–82.

———. *Madness and Civilization: A History of Insanity in the Age of Reason.* Trans. Richard Howard. New York: Pantheon, 1965.

———. *The Order of Things: An Archeology of the Human Sciences.* New York: Vintage, 1973.

Frank, Joseph. *The Widening Eyre: Crisis and Mystery in Modern Literature.* New Brunswick: Rutgers UP, 1963.

Freud, Sigmund. *Beyond the Pleasure Principle.* Trans. and ed. James Strachey. New York: Norton, 1961.

———. *Totem and Taboo.* Trans. A. A. Brill. New York: Vintage, 1918.

———. "Über den Gegensinn der Urworte." *Gesammelte Werke* Bd. VIII. London: Imago Publishing Company, 1940–52. 214–21.

———. "Der Witz und seine Beziehung zum Unbewussten." *Studienausgabe.* Bd. IV. Frankfurt am Main: Fischer, 1970. 9–220.

Gadamer, Hans-Georg. "Text und Interpretation." Forget 24–55.

Gardner, Martin, ed. *The Annotated Alice: Alice's Adventures in Wonderland and Through the Looking Glass.* Harmondsworth: Penguin 1965.

Gauthier, Xavière. "Oscillation du 'pouvoir,' au 'refus.' " Interview with Julia Kristeva. *Tel Quel* Summer 1974. Excerpted in Marks and Courtivron. Trans. Marilyn A. August. 165–67.

Gleick, James. *Chaos: Making a New Science.* New York: Viking, 1982.

Greenblatt, Stephen. *Renaissance Self-Fashioning: From More to Shakespeare.* Chicago: U of Chicago P, 1980.

Gresset, Michael, and Noel Polk. *Intertextuality in Faulkner.* Jackson: U of Mississippi P, 1985.

Hamacher, Werner. Introduction. *Der Geist des Christentums: Schriften 1796–1800.* By Georg Wilhelm Friedrich Hegel. Frankfurt: Ullstein, 1978.

Harris, Paul. "Fractal Faulkner: Scaling Time in *Go Down Moses.*" *Poetics Today* 14.4 (Winter 1993): 625–651.

Hartman, Geoffrey H. "Literary Commentary as Literature." *Criticism in the Wilderness.* New Haven: Yale UP, 1980. 189–213.

———. "The New Wilderness: Critics as Connoisseurs of Chaos." Hassan and Hassan 87–110.

———. *Saving the Text: Literature, Derrida, Philosophy.* Baltimore: Johns Hopkins UP, 1981.

Hassan, Ihab, and Sally Hassan, eds. *Innovation/Renovation: New Perspectives on the Humanities.* Madison: U of Wisconsin P, 1983.

Haug, Walter, and Rainer Warning, eds. *Das Fest in der Literatur.* Poetik und Hermeneutik XIV. Munich: Fink, 1989.

Hawthorne, Nathaniel. *The Scarlet Letter.* New York: Penguin, 1970.

Hayles, N. Katherine. "Chance Operations: Cagean Paradox and Contemporary Science." Perloff and Junkerman 226–41.

———. *Chaos Bound: Orderly Disorder in Contemporary Literature and Science.* Ithaca: Cornell UP, 1990.

Heidegger, Martin. "The Origin of the Work of Art." *Poetry, Language, Thought.* Trans. Albert Hofstadter. New York: Harper, 1971. 15–87.

Hermann, Anne. *The Dialogic and Difference.* New York: Columbia UP, 1989.

Hicks, D. Emily. *Border Writing: The Multidimensional Text.* Minneapolis: U of Minnesota P, 1991.

Holland, Norman N. "Re-Covering 'The Purloined Letter': Reading as a Personal Transaction." Suleiman and Crosman 350–70.

———. "Unity Identity Text Self." Tompkins 118–33.

Holton, Gerald. *The Advancement of Science, and Its Burdens.* New York: Cambridge UP, 1986.

Honegger, Claudia. Introduction. *Die Hexen der Neuzeit: Studien zur Sozialgeschichte eines kulturellen Deutungsmusters.* Ed. Claudia Honegger. Frankfurt: Suhrkamp, 1978.

Horkheimer, Max, and Theodor W. Adorno. *Dialektik der Aufklärung.* Frankfurt: Fischer, 1969. Rpt. as *Dialectics of Enlightenment.* Trans. John Cumming. New York: Herder, 1972.

Hughes, Robert. *The Shock of the New.* New York: Knopf, 1981.

Huizinga, Johan. *Homo Ludens: A Study of the Play Element in Culture.* London: Maurice Temple Smith, 1970.

Irigaray, Luce. *Speculum of the Other Woman.* Trans. Gillian C. Gill. Ithaca: Cornell UP, 1985.

———. *This Sex Which Is Not One.* Trans. Catherine Porter with Carolyn Burke. Ithaca: Cornell UP, 1985.

Irwin, John T. *Doubling and Incest/Repetition and Revenge: A Speculative Reading of Faulkner.* Baltimore: Johns Hopkins UP, 1975.

Iser, Wolfgang. *The Act of Reading: A Theory of Aesthetic Response.* Baltimore: Johns Hopkins UP, 1978.

# Works Cited

———. *The Implied Reader: Patterns of Communicating in Prose Fiction from Bunyan to Beckett.* Baltimore: Johns Hopkins UP, 1974.

———. "The Interaction between Reader and Text." Suleiman and Crosman 106–19.

Jauss, Hans Robert. "Anmerkungen zum idealen Gespräch." *Das Gespräch.* Poetik und Hermeneutik XI. Ed. Karlheinz Stierle/Rainer Warning. Munich: Fink, 1984. 467–72.

———. "Literary History as a Challenge to Literary Theory." *Toward an Aesthetic of Reception.* Trans. Timothy Bahti. Minneapolis: U of Minnesota P, 1982. 3–45.

Joyce, James. *Finnegans Wake.* London: Faber, 1939.

Kamuf, Peggy. "Hawthorne's Genres: The Letter of the Law Appliquée." *After Strange Texts: The Role of Theory in the Study of Literature.* Ed. Gregory S. Jay and David L. Miller. University, Alabama: U of Alabama P, 1985. 69–84.

Kaviola, Karen. *All Contraries Confounded: The Lyrical Fiction of Virginia Woolf, Djuna Barnes and Marguerite Duras.* Iowa City: U of Iowa P, 1991.

Kenner, Hugh. "Self-Similarity, Fractals, Cantos." *ELH* 44 (1988): 721–30.

Knapp, Stephen, and Walter Benn Michaels. "A Reply to Our Critics." *Critical Inquiry* 9.4 (1983): 790–800.

Krieger, Murray. *Ekphrasis: The Illusion of the Natural Sign.* Baltimore: Johns Hopkins UP, 1992.

———. *Poetic Presence and Illusion: Essays in Critical History and Theory.* Baltimore: Johns Hopkins UP, 1979.

Kristeva, Julia. *The Kristeva Reader.* Ed. Toril Moi. Trans. Léon S. Roudiez and Seán Hand. New York: Columbia UP, 1986.

———. *Powers of Horror: An Essay on Abjection.* Trans. Léon S. Roudiez. New York: Columbia UP, 1982.

———. *Revolution of Poetic Language.* Trans. Margaret Waller. New York: Columbia UP, 1984.

———. *Séméiotikè: Recherches pour une sémanalyse.* Paris: Seuil, 1969.

Krupat, Arnold. *Ethnocriticism: Ethnography, History, Literature.* Berkeley: U of California P, 1992.

Kuberski, Philip. *Chaosmos: Literature, Science, and Theory.* New York: SUNY P, 1994.

Lacan, Jacques. "The Agency of the Letter in the Unconscious or Reason since Freud." *Écrits: A Selection* 146–78.

———. "Aggressivity in Psychoanalysis." *Écrits: A Selection* 8–29.

———. "Desire and the Interpretation of Desire in *Hamlet.*" Felman 11–52.

———. "Desire, Life and Death." *The Seminar of Jacques Lacan.* Book II: *The Ego in Freud's Theory and in the Technique of Psychoanalysis 1954–1955.* Ed. Jacques Alain Miller. Trans. Sylvana Tomaselli. New York: Norton, 1988, 221–234.

———. *Écrits.* Paris: Seuil, 1966.

———. *Écrits: A Selection.* Trans. Alan Sheridan. New York: Norton, 1977.

———. "The ego and the other." *The Seminar of Jacques Lacan.* Book I. 38–51.

———. "The Freudian Thing or the Meaning of the Return to Freud in Psychoanalysis." *Écrits: A Selection* 114–45.

———. "L'instance de la lettre dans l'inconscient ou la raison depuis Freud." *Écrits* 249–89.

———. "The Mirror Stage." *Écrits: A Selection* 1–7.

———. "The object relation and the intersubjective relation." *Seminar.* Book I. 209–19.

———. *The Seminar of Jacques Lacan.* Book 1: *Freud's Papers on Technique, 1953–1954.* Ed. Jacques Alain Miller. Trans. Sylvana Tomaselli and John Forrester. New York: Norton, 1988.

———. "Seminar on 'The Purloined Letter.'" Trans. Jeffrey Mehlman. *Yale French Studies* 48 (1972): 38–72.

Lachmann, Renate. "Die Schwellensituation: Skandal und Fest bei Dostoevskij." Ed. Walter Haug and Rainer Warning, *Das Fest*, Munich: Fink Verlag, 1989. 307–325.

Lait, Matt. "Youth Gets Life Term in Honor Student's Death," *Los Angeles Times*, 9 Aug. 1994. A I (Front Page) and A 20.

Larbaud, Valéry. Preface. *Tandis que j'agonise.* By William Faulkner. Trans. Maurice E. Coindreau. Paris: Gallimard, 1934. 9–14.

Lecercle, Jean-Jacques. *Philosophy through the Looking Glass: Language, Nonsense, Desire.* La Salle, Illinois: Open Court, 1985.

Leverenz, David. "Mrs. Hawthorne's Headache: Reading *The Scarlet Letter.*" *The (M)other Tongue: Essays in Feminist Psychoanalytic Interpretation.* Ed. S. N. Garner, C. Kahane, and M. Sprengnether. Ithaca: Cornell UP, 1985. 194–216.

Levinas, Emmanuel. *En découvrant l'existence avec Husserl et Heidegger.* 1949. Paris: Vrin, 1949; 1967.

———. *Die Spur des Anderen: Untersuchungen zur Phänomenologie und Sozialphilosophie.* Trans. and ed. Nikolaus Krewani. Freiburg and Munich: Alber, 1983.

Lloyd, David. *Anomalous States: Irish Writing and the Post-Colonial Moment*, Durham: Duke UP, 1993.

Lorenzer, Alfred. *Sprachzerstörung und Rekonstruktion: Vorarbeiten zu einer Metatheorie der Psychoanalyse.* Frankfurt: Suhrkamp, 1970.

Luhmann, Niklas. *The Differentiation of Society.* Trans. Stephen Holmes and Charles Larmore. New York: Columbia UP, 1982.

———. *Gesellschaftsstruktur und Semantik: Studien zur Wissenssoziologie der modernen Gesellschaft.* Frankfurt: Suhrkamp, 1980.

Mandelbrot, Benoit. *The Fractal Geometry of Nature.* New York: Freeman, 1977.

Maranda, Pierre. "The Dialectic of Metaphor: The Anthropological Essay on Hermeneutics." Suleiman and Crosman 183–204.

Marks, Elaine, and Isabelle de Courtivron, eds. *New French Feminisms: An Anthology.* Amherst: U Massachusetts P, 1979.

Matthews, John T. *The Play of Faulkner's Language.* Ithaca: Cornell UP, 1982.

McHugh, Roland. *Annotations to "Finnegans Wake."* Baltimore: Johns Hopkins UP, 1980.

McLean, Clara. "Wasted Words: The Body Language of Joyce's 'Nausicaa.'" Ed. Margot Norris, Vincent Cheng, and Kimberly Devlin. *Joycean Cultures: Culturing Joyces.* Under consideration with Cambridge UP.

Mead, George Herbert. *Mind, Self, and Society from the Standpoint of a Social Behaviorist.* Chicago: U of Chicago P, 1970 (17th edition; ed. Charles W. Morris. 1st edition: 1934).

## Works Cited

Miller, Perry. *The New England Mind: The Seventeenth Century.* Cambridge: Harvard UP, 1963.

Mitchell, W. J. T., ed. *The Politics of Interpretation.* Chicago: U of Chicago P, 1983.

Morris, Wesley. "The Irrepressible Real: Jacques Lacan and Poststructuralism." *American Criticism in the Poststructuralist Age.* Ed. Ira Konigsberg. Ann Arbor: U of Michigan P, 1981. 116–34.

Neumann, Erich. *The Great Mother: An Analysis of the Archetype.* Trans. Ralph Manheim. Princeton: Princeton UP, 1970.

Nietzsche, Friedrich. *The Birth of Tragedy.* 1872. Trans. Walter Kaufmann. New York: Vintage, 1966.

Orians, G. Harrison. "New England Witchcraft in Fiction." *American Literature Two* (1930–31): 54–71.

Papin, Liliane. "Staging Writing or the Ceremony of Text in Marguerite Duras." *Modern Drama* 34.1 (1991): 128–137.

Paulson, William. *The Noise of Culture: Literary Texts in a World of Information.* Ithaca: Cornell UP, 1988.

Perloff, Marjorie, and Charles Junkerman, eds. *John Cage: Composed in America.* Chicago: U of Chicago P, 1994.

Pike, Judith. "The Spectacle of the Heroine's Death." Diss., U of California-Irvine, 1988.

Poulet, Georges. "Criticism and the Experience of Interiority." Tompkins 41–49.

Pratt, Mary Louise. *Imperial Eyes: Travel Writing and Transculturation.* New York: Routledge, 1992.

*Programmheft zu Robert Wilsons's deutschen Inszenierung von "La Maladie de la Mort" (Übersetzung Peter Handke).*

Rabinow, Paul. "Representations Are Social Facts: Modernity and Post-Modernity in Anthropology." Clifford and Marcus 234–61.

Rapaport, Herman. *Between the Sign and the Gaze.* Ithaca: Cornell UP, 1994.

Reichert, Klaus. *Lewis Carroll: Studien zum literarischen Unsinn.* Munich: Hanser, 1974.

Retallack, Joan. "Poethics of a Complex Realism." Perloff and Junkerman 242–73.

Retif, Françoise. "Maurice Blanchot et *La Maladie de la Mort.*" *Francofonia-Studie-Ricerche-sulle Letterature di Lingua Francese* 10.19 (1990): 15–22.

Ricoeur, Paul. "The Metaphorical Process as Cognition, Imagination, and Feeling." Adams and Searle 424–34.

Rochefort, Christiane. "Are Women Writers Still Monsters?" Marks and Courtivron 183–86.

Rotman, Brian. *Ad Infinitum: The Ghost in Turing's Machine.* Stanford: Stanford UP, 1993.

Said, Edward. "Secular Criticism." *Critical Theory since 1965.* Adams and Searle 605–22.

———. *The World, the Text, and the Critic.* Cambridge: Harvard UP, 1983.

Sarris, Greg. *Keeping Slug Woman Alive: A Holistic Approach to American Indian Texts.* Berkeley: U of California P, 1993.

Sartre, Jean-Paul. *Anti-Semite and Jew.* Trans. George I. Becker. New York: Schocken, 1948.

———. *The Family Idiot: Gustave Flaubert 1821–1857*. Trans. Carol Cosman. Chicago: U of Chicago P, 1981.

———. *The Words*. Trans. Bernard Frechtman. New York: Braziller, 1964.

Schwab, Gabriele. "The Dialectic of Closing and Opening in Samuel Beckett's *Endgame*." *Yale French Studies* 67 (1984): 191–202.

———. *Entgrenzungen und Entgrenzungsmythen: Zur Subjektivität im modernen Roman*. Stuttgart: Steiner, 1987.

———. "Genesis of the Subject, Imaginary Functions, and Poetic Language." *New Literary History* 15.3 (1984): 453–74.

———. "Die Provokation Artauds oder Grenze der Repräsentation und Sprachkrise im modernen Theater." *Samuel Becketts "Endspiel"* 14–35.

———. "Reader-Response and the Aesthetic Experience of Otherness." *Stanford Literature Review* 3.1 (Spring 1986): 107–36.

———. "Samuel Beckett's *Endgame* with Subjectivity: Towards a Psychoaesthetic Theory of Modern Drama." *English and American Studies in German: Summaries of Theses and Monographs*. Supplement to Anglia. Tübingen: Max Niemeyer Verlag, 1981. 106–108.

———. *Samuel Becketts "Endspiel" mit der Subjektivität: Entwurf einer Psychoästhetik des modernen Theaters*. Stuttgart: Metzler, 1981.

———. *Subjects without Selves: Transitional Texts in Modern Fiction*. Cambridge: Harvard UP, 1994.

Serres, Michel. *Hermes: Literature, Science, Philosophy*. Ed. Josué V. Harari and David F. Bell. Baltimore: Johns Hopkins UP, 1982.

Sewell, Elizabeth. *The Field of Nonsense*. London: Chatto, 1952.

Sexton, Anne. *Transformations*. Boston: Houghton, 1971.

Sobchack, Vivian. "A Theory of Everything: Meditations on Total Chaos." *Artforum* (October 1990): 148–155.

Sollers, Philippe. "Joyce and Co." *TriQuarterly* 38 (Winter 1977): 67–121.

Stallybrass, Peter, and Allon White. *The Politics and Poetics of Transgression*. Ithaca: Cornell UP, 1986.

Stewart, Ian. *Does God Play Dice?: The Mathematics of Chaos*. Oxford: Blackwell, 1989.

Suleiman, Susan R., and Inge Crosman, eds. *The Reader in the Text: Essays on Audience and Interpretation*. Princeton: Princeton UP, 1980.

Sundquist, Eric J. *Faulkner: The House Divided*. Baltimore: Johns Hopkins UP, 1983.

Theweleit, Klaus. *Männerphantasien*. Frankfurt: Stern, 1978. Rpt. *Male Fantasies*. Trans. Stephen Conway (in collaboration with Erica Carter and Chris Turner). Minneapolis: U of Minnesota P, 1987.

Todorov, Tzvetan. *Mikhail Bakhtin: The Dialogical Principle*. Trans. Wlad Godzich. Minneapolis: U of Minnesota P, 1984.

Tompkins, Jane P., ed. *Reader-Response Criticism: From Formalism to Post-Structuralism*. Baltimore: Johns Hopkins UP, 1980.

Whitford, Margaret. "Rereading Irigaray." Ed. Teresa Brennan. *Between Feminism and Psychoanalysis*. New York: Routledge, 1989. 106–26.

Wilden, Anthony. *System and Structure: Essays in Communication and Exchange.* New York: Tavistock, 1977.

Willis, Sharon A. "Staging Sexual Difference: Reading, Recitation, and Repetition in Duras' *Malady of Death.*" *Feminine Focus: The New Women Playwrights.* Ed. Enoch Brater. Oxford: Oxford UP, 1989. 109–25.

Winnicott, D. W. *The Maturational Processes and the Facilitating Environment: Studies in the Theory of Emotional Development.* New York: International UP, 1965.

———. *Playing and Reality.* London: Tavistock, 1971.

Wittgenstein, Ludwig. *Philosophical Investigations.* Trans. G. E. M. Anscomb. New York: Macmillan, 1968.

# INDEX

Adams, Henry: *The Education of Henry Adams* as a prototype, 72–73

Adorno, Theodor: influence from experimental modernist literature, 16; *Dialektik der Aufklärung,* 39–40; and anti-Semitism, 40; and "incommunication," 43

*Alice in Wonderland. See* Carroll, Lewis

Alterity: and Hans-Georg Gadamer, 10, 18; in modern and postmodern texts, 16; and Hans Robert Jauss, 18; of *Finnegans Wake* and *Roaratorio,* 84

Anzaldúa, Gloria: border languages, 188–89n30

Arnheim, Rudolf: origins of disorder, 51

Artaud, Antonin: "theater of cruelty," 14, 126, 147–48; and aesthetics, 44; on Lewis Carroll's *Jabberwocky,* 61–62; read by Gilles Deleuze, 189n4

*As I Lay Dying. See* Faulkner, William

*Asterix and Cleopatra:* and Manuel Schwab, 25

Aura: in the age of technological reproduction, xvi; in Djuna Barnes's *Nightwood,* 166; in Marguerite Duras's *The Malady of Death,* 179–81

Bacon, Francis, 41

Bakhtin, Mikhail: and cultural psychology in literary theory, 10; and gaze, 20–24; and psychogenetic theory, 20–23; *vnenakhodimost* ("exotopy"), 21–22, 186nn12,13, 187n24; and the carnivalesque, 22–23, 124–25, 145, 192n2; "little time," 132; grotesque bodies, 132–33; and "somatic semiotic," 141–42; feminist reception of, 186–87n14

Barnes, Djuna: *Nightwood,* xiii–xiv, 15, 153–69; criticism of, 190n15

Barrault, Jean-Louis: on William Faulkner, 147

Bateson, Gregory: *Steps to an Ecology of Mind* and cultural contact, x, 9–17, 45–46, 50, 63–64, 189nn2,3

Baudelaire, Charles: critiqued by Walter Benjamin, 150, 156–57, 162; *Poetics of the Apache,* 159

Beauvoir, Simone de: *The Second Sex* and otherness, 34, 90

Beckett, Samuel: aesthetics of, 44; *Waiting for Godot,* 164

Benjamin, Walter: on Charles Baudelaire and the *flâneur,* 150, 156–57, 162; on the collector, 160; *Das Passagenwerk* and trace and aura, 166–69, 179–81

Benstock, Shari, 168

Berman, Marshall: "Hitting the Street," 163

Blau, Herbert: on Jacques Derrida, 32; and the radical, 46; on *The Crucible,* 103

Blumenberg, Hans: nonsense and language, 68; death drive and entropy, 72

Bohannan, Laura: "Shakespeare in the Bush" and the Tiv, 1–33 *passim*

Bollas, Christopher: *The Shadow of the Object,* 180–81

Brecht, Bertoldt: aesthetics of, 14

Breton, André: and Cheval, 169

Broe, Mary Lynn: and reception of Djuna Barnes, 167

Bruns, Gerald L.: on John Cage, 87

Buck-Morss, Susan: on prostitution and the *flâneur,* 157–58

Burroughs, George: trial of, 106; in John Neal's *Rachel Dyer*, 110–11

Cage, John: *Roaratorio* and *Finnegans Wake*, xii, 73–74, 81–88, 99
Calvino, Italo: *If on a winter's night a traveler*, 13
Camus, Albert: *The Stranger*, 12–13
Carnival and carnivalesque: critiqued by Mikhail Bakhtin, 22–23, 124–25, 145, 192*n2;* in William Faulkner's *As I Lay Dying*, 124–49; and Artaud's "theater of cruelty," 126, 144–49; in Djuna Barnes's *Nightwood*, 156
Carroll, David: and Michel Foucault's "paraesthetic," 30–31
Carroll, Lewis: *Alice in Wonderland, Through the Looking Glass,* and literary nonsense, ix, xii, xvii, 8, 15, 49–70, 189*n4*
Cartesianism, 164–65
Cervantes Saavedra, Miguel de: *Don Quixote de la Mancha*, 12
Chan, Robert: and Albert Camus's *The Stranger*, 12–13
Chance Operations: and *Roaratorio*, 81–82
Chaos, xii–xiii, 71–99 *passim*
Cheval: as *Facteur*, 169
Child, Lydia Maria: *The Rebels: Or Boston before the Revolution*, 107
Cixous, Hélène: on James Joyce, 91–92, 97
Clarke, Bruce: and chaos, 95–97
Clifford, James: on Hans-Georg Gadamer's hermeneutics, 186*n10*
Constance School: and Wolfgang Iser and Hans-Georg Gadamer, 17
Culler, Jonathan, 7

Deleuze, Gilles: *Logique du Sens* and Lewis Carroll and Antonin Artaud, 61–62, 70, 189*n4;* territorialization and deterritorialization, 191*n19;* and Djuna Barnes's *Nightwood*, 192*n1*
DeLillo, Don: and *Imaginary Ethnographies*, xv

*Délire:* and Jean-Jacques Lecercle and Gilles Deleuze, 62–63; and Fredric Jameson's "surface intensities," 69
Derrida, Jacques: and experimental literature, 16; and Hans-Georg Gadamer's hermeneutics, 19; contrasted with Jacques Lacan, Michel Foucault, and French feminism, 28–34; and otherness and language, 45; *Of Grammatology* and Jean-Jacques Rousseau, 148
Dickens, Charles: *Great Expectations*, 33
Diderot, Denis, 6, 41
Dodson, Charles Lutwidge: and Lewis Carroll, 50, 62
Dream: in *Alice and Wonderland* and *Through the Looking Glass*, 53–63 *passim*
Dumas, Alexander: *Mohicans de Paris*, 159
Duras, Marguerite: *The Malady of Death (La maladie de la mort)*, xiv, 15, 170–84; "the malady of death," 155

Eagleton, Terry: on Mikhail Bakhtin, 22
*Écriture féminine:* and *Finnegans Wake*, xii, 88–98 *passim*, 190*n17;* and Luce Irigaray, 34–35
Ehrenzweig, Anton: and "chaos," 73, 80
Elias, Norbert: psychohistory and witchcraft, 108–109
Entropy: and Hans Blumenberg, Sigmund Freud, fascism, and thermodynamics, 72; in *As I Lay Dying*, 126–27
Epic: and *As I Lay Dying*, 144–49
Ernst, Max, 169
Exotopy (*vnenakhodimost*), 21–22, 186*nn12,13,* 187*n24. See also* Bakhtin, Mikhail

Fanon, Frantz: *The Wretched of the Earth*, 41–42
Faulkner, William: *As I Lay Dying*, xiii, 15, 124–49
*Finnegans Wake. See* Joyce, James
Fischer, Michael M. J.: and Hans-Georg

Gadamer's hermeneutics, 186*n10;* and ethnographies, 188*n30*

*Flânerie:* in Djuna Barnes's *Nightwood,* 156–69 *passim*

Flaubert, Gustave: *Emma Bovary,* 12–14

Forbes, Esther: *A Mirror of Witches,* 107–11 *passim*

Foucault, Michel: and agencies of power, 6; romantic identification, 12–15; and Jacques Lacan, 28; otherness within cultures, 28–34; and French feminism, 33–34, 190*n17,* and nonsense, 68

Frank, Joseph, 168

Freud, Sigmund: on love and madness, 14; *fort-da,* 44; and schizophrenic language, 60–61, 63–64; on pleasure of nonsense, 65, 66; and the unconscious, 71; and entropy, 72; and the "family romance," 104; *Über den Gegensinn der Urworte,* 165; and the economy of psychic apparatus, 192*n8;* and the totem feast, 192*n9*

Gadamer, Hans-Georg: and the dialogic hermeneutic, 17–19, 186*n10*

Gardner, Martin: nonsense and the postmodern, 70

Gauthier, Xaviere: and Julia Kristeva, 36, 89

Gleick, James: *Chaos: Making a New Science,* 75–80; and nonlinearity, 95

Goethe, Johann Wolfgang von: and the *Werther* cult, 12–14

Guattari, Félix: territorialization and deterritorialization, 191*n19;* and Djuna Barnes's *Nightwood,* 192*n1*

*Hamlet. See* Bohannan, Laura; Shakespeare, William; Tiv

Handke, Peter: and Marguerite Duras's *The Malady of Death,* 195–96*n47*

Hartman, Geoffrey: on theory and interpretation, 46

Hathorne, William and John: as persecutors of witches, 113. *See also* Hawthorne, Nathaniel

Hawthorne, Nathaniel: *The Scarlet Letter,* xiii, 15, 103–104, 113–23.

Hayles, N. Katherine: *Chaos Bound,* 78, 82–83, 95

Hegel, Georg Wilhelm Friedrich, 24, 171

Hicks, D. Emily: *Border Writing: The Multidimensional Text,* 188*n30*

Holland, Norman: and interpretation, 8

Holton, Gerald: and "themata," 190*n7*

Homer: and James Joyce's *Ulysses,* 41; and William Faulkner's *As I Lay Dying,* 144

Horkheimer, Max: *Dialektik der Aufklärung,* 39–40; and anti-Semitism, 40

Huizinga, Johan: and nonsense, 65

Humpty Dumpty, 52, 55, 74, 96; and Christopher Scholz's Humpty-Dumpty-Effect, 75. *See also* Carroll, Lewis

Hutchinson, Ann: and antinomianism, 110–11

Irigaray, Luce: and Jacques Lacan, 28, 34; *Speculum of the Other Woman* and *écriture féminine,* 34–35; and Julia Kristeva, 35; and feminization of culture, 88; and James Joyce, 91–92; and nonlinearity, 95

Iser, Wolfgang: and Hans-Georg Gadamer and the Constance School, 17; and the "implied reader," 19–20

Jameson, Fredric: and the ideology of form, 43; and "surface intensities," 69; and the "waning of affect" and nonsense, 70

Jauss, Hans Robert: aesthetics of, 17; and the *Horizontverschmelzung* (fusion of horizons), 18

*Jouissance,* 90, 98, 99; and *Nightwood,* 161, 162; in Marguerite Duras's *The Malady of Death,* 173

Joyce, James: *Finnegans Wake,* xi–xii, 15, 41, 44, 71–99; anticipated by Lewis Carroll, 49; and transnationalism, 72;

and chaos theory, 73–80; and John Cage's *Roaratorio*, 73–74, 81–88, 99; and reception by French feminism, 89

Jung, Carl: and *Finnegans Wake*, 89

Kenner, Hugh: fractal and literary criticism, 77–86 *passim*

Kingston, Maxine Hong: and cultural contact, xv, 188*n26*

Knapp, Stephen, and Walter Benn Michaels: "Against Theory," 7

Krieger, Murray: and poetic language, 44; and the object, 181

Kristeva, Julia: and modernist literature, 16; and the grotesque body, 22–23; and Jacques Lacan, 28, 35; *The Revolution of Poetic Language*, 35; and Luce Irigaray, 35; and the "subject in process," 36; and identity, 88; on Isidore Ducasse, Comte de Lautréamont, James Joyce, Antonin Artaud, and Stéphane Mallarmé, 89–90; on "differentiation" and James Joyce, 91–94; on bodily fluids and *Powers of Horror*, 98–99; and Mikhail Bakhtin and the carnivalesque, 145, 186–87*n14*, 192*n13*; and moods, 181; and poetic language, 190*n17*

Krupat, Arnold: and ethnocriticism, 38; on border crossings and literature, 41–42

Lacan, Jacques, 20–34 *passim;* and Jean Piaget, 27; and psychoanalysis and reading, 27–29, 188*n26;* and French feminism and Luce Irigaray, 33–34; and extimacy, 172–74; and "empty speech," 180; critique by D. W. Winnicott, 186*n13;* on Jean-Paul Sartre's analysis of the gaze, 187*n20;* on Mikhail Bakhtin and alienation, 187*n24*

Lachmann, Renate: and somatic semiotics, 20

Larbaud, Valéry: and *As I Lay Dying*, 144–45

Lecercle, Jean-Jacques: *Philosophy Through the Looking Glass* and Gilles Deleuze's reading of Antonin Artaud and Lewis Carroll, 61–63, 70

Lévi-Strauss, Claude, 187*n18*

Levinas, Emmanuel: and otherness, 45–46

Lloyd, David: hybridity of James Joyce's Great Britain, 41

Longfellow, Henry Wadsworth: *New England Tragedies*, 107

Lyotard, Jean-François: *différand*, 190*n8*

*The Malady of Death. See* Duras, Marguerite

Mandelbrot, Benoit B.: *Fractals: Form, Chance and Dimension*, 75; *The Fractal Geometry of Nature* and scaling, 76; and the rhetoric of monsters, 97–98; coining "fractal," 190–91*n18*

Maranda, Pierre: reading cultures, 38–39

McLean, Clara: and bodily fluids in *Finnegans Wake*, 98

Metaphor and metonymy, 57–59, 67

Miles, Bernard: reading Shakespeare, 3

Miller, Arthur: *The Crucible*, 103, 107, 112

Mimesis: and mimetic language, 49–70 *passim*

Montaigne, Michel: and otherness, 6

Neal, John: *Rachel Dyer* and the romanticization of the witch, 107, 110–11

Necrophilia: and *As I Lay Dying*, 125

Negentropy, 73

Never-Never-Land: and Orange County, xvi

Nietzsche: on Greek tragedy, 13–14

*Nightwood. See* Barnes, Djuna

Nonsense: and literature, 49–70

Papin, Liliane: on Marguerite Duras's works, 193*n2*

Perloff, Marjorie, and Charles Junkerman: and "transcendental chit chat," 87

Phantasmatic: in *As I Lay Dying*, 134–49

Piaget: and Jacques Lacan, 27

Poe, Edgar Allan: and Frantz Fanon, 41

Polyphony: in *As I Lay Dying*, 124–49 *passim*

Poulet, Georges: on reading, 25–27

Pound, Ezra: read by Hugh Kenner, 77, 80

Pratt, Mary Louise: *Imperial Eyes: Travel Writing and Transculturation*, 42

Rabelais: and Frantz Fanon, 41

Rabinow, Paul: and critical cosmopolitanism, 38

*Rachel Dyer. See* Neal, John

Rapaport, Herman, 173

Reichert, Klaus: on Lewis Carroll, 68, 70

Retallack, Joan: on John Cage, 87

Retif, Françoise: on Marguerite Duras, 193*n*2

*Roaratorio. See* Cage, John

Rochefort, Christiane: "Are Women Writers Still Monsters," 98

Rossum, Frans van: on *Roaratorio* and noise, 84–85

Rotman, Brian: on infinity, 190*n*14

Rousseau, Henri: *The Dream* and *Nightwood*, 153

Rousseau, Jean-Jacques, 6; and Jacques Derrida, 148

Ruelle, David: and strange attractors, 80

Russo, Mary: and the grotesque body, 22–23

Sade, Marquis de: in *Nightwood*, 158

Saer, José: and speculative anthropology, xiv–xv

Said, Edward: on ethnocentrism, 11; on Jacques Derrida and *Hamlet*, 32–33; and natural filiation, 162–63

Sarris, Greg: *Keeping Slug Woman Alive: A Holistic Approach to American Indian Texts*, 188*n*30

Sartre, Jean-Paul: *The Family Idiot: Gustave Flaubert 1821–1857* and *The Words*, 13; and "pseudosingularity," 20–21; and the Other's gaze, 34, 174, 187*n*20; *Anti-Semite and Jew*, 44–45; and Mikhail Bakhtin, 187*n*24

Saussure, Ferdinand de: and habitual forms of speech, 58; rules of language, 66

*The Scarlet Letter. See* Hawthorne, Nathaniel

Schizophrenia: in *Alice in Wonderland* and *Through the Looking Glass*, 54–70 *passim*; and schizophrenic *délire*, 63; and mimesis and simulacrum, 70; and the schizosphere, 75; and noise in *Roaratorio*, 83

Scholz, Christopher: and the schizosphere and "Humpty-Dumpty-Effect," 75

Schwab, Manuel: as Cleopatra's tiger, 25

Scott, Sir Walter, 108

Second Law of Thermodynamics: and entropy, 72

Serres, Michel: on *Roaratorio*, 85

The Seven Dwarfs: and gender hierarchy, x

Sewell, Elizabeth: on literary nonsense, 55, 66, 68

Sexton, Anne: "Snow White and the Seven Dwarfs," ix; and Snow White as gendered object, x

Shakespeare, William: and Laura Bohannan's "Shakespeare in the Bush," 1–33 *passim*; and Frantz Fanon, 41; and James Joyce, 41

Silko, Leslie Marmon, xv

Sollers, Philippe: and *Finnegans Wake*, 72

Somatic semiotic: and Renate Lachmann, 20; and Sigmund Freud, 71; and Mikhail Bakhtin and *As I Lay Dying*, 141–42

Somnambulism: and *Nightwood*, 153, 155

Stein, Gertrude: anticipated by Joyce and Carroll, 49; criticism of, 190*n*15

Strange attractors: and chaos, *Roaratorio*, and *Finnegans Wake*, 79–86

Strehler, Giorgio: and William Shakespeare's *King Lear*, 6

Taboo: and *As I Lay Dying*, 124–49 *passim*

Theater of Cruelty: in *As I Lay Dying*, 126; and carnivalesque, 144–49. *See also* Artaud, Antonin

Theweleit, Klaus: *Male Fantasies* (*Män-nerphantasien*), 40, 98

*Through the Looking Glass. See* Carroll, Lewis

*Timaeus:* and William Butler Yeats, 72

Tiv: and Laura Bohannan's "Shakespeare in the Bush," 1–33 *passim*

Todorov, Tzvetan: and Mikhail Bakhtin and exotopy, 20–22, 186*n*12

*Tristan and Iseult:* and James Joyce, 94

Turbulence: in *Roaratorio* and *Finnegans Wake*, 85–86

*Verfremdung:* and communication, 60

Vizenor, Gerald, xv

Vorweg, Heinrich: critique of *Roaratorio*, 86

Whitford, Margaret: on Luce Irigaray, 34–35

Whittier, John Greenleaf: *Legends of New England*, 107

Wiggins, Marianne, xv

Wild West: and Charles Baudelaire and Djuna Barnes, 159

Willis, Sharon A., 177

Wilson, Robert: and staging *The Malady of Death*, 195–96*n*47

Winnicott, D. W.: and reading and otherness, 24–26; and the heteronomy of the Other, 45; critique of Jacques Lacan, 186*n*13; and "potential space," 189*n*1

*Wirkungsaesthetik:* and Wolfgang Iser, 17

Witchcraft: 103–23 *passim*; as a cultural pattern, 103–107; as erotic spectacle, 106–107; narratives of, 107–23

Wittgenstein, Ludwig: on sense and order, 51; and language games, 57, 185–86*n*7; and "transcendental chit chat," 87

Woolf, Virginia: criticism of, 190*n*15

Yeats, William Butler: *A Vision*, 71; and the planets and *Timaeus*, 72

Zen Buddhism: and "purposeful purpose-lessness," 85

Zen koan, 83

GABRIELE SCHWAB is Professor of English and Comparative Literature at the University of California-Irvine.